Musicals at the Margins

Musicals at the Margins

Genre, Boundaries, Canons

*Edited by
Julie Lobalzo Wright and
Martha Shearer*

BLOOMSBURY ACADEMIC
NEW YORK • LONDON • OXFORD • NEW DELHI • SYDNEY

BLOOMSBURY ACADEMIC
Bloomsbury Publishing Inc
1385 Broadway, New York, NY 10018, USA
50 Bedford Square, London, WC1B 3DP, UK
29 Earlsfort Terrace, Dublin 2, Ireland

BLOOMSBURY, BLOOMSBURY ACADEMIC and the Diana logo are trademarks of
Bloomsbury Publishing Plc

First published in the United States of America 2021
This paperback edition published 2022

Volume Editor's Part of the Work © Julie Lobalzo Wright and Martha Shearer

Each chapter © of Contributors

For legal purposes the Acknowledgments on p. ix constitute an extension of
this copyright page.

Cover design: Namkwan Cho
Cover image © Collection Christophel / ArenaPAL

All rights reserved. No part of this publication may be reproduced or transmitted
in any form or by any means, electronic or mechanical, including photocopying,
recording, or any information storage or retrieval system, without prior
permission in writing from the publishers.

Bloomsbury Publishing Inc does not have any control over, or responsibility for, any
third-party websites referred to or in this book. All internet addresses given in this
book were correct at the time of going to press. The author and publisher regret any
inconvenience caused if addresses have changed or sites have ceased to exist,
but can accept no responsibility for any such changes.

Library of Congress Cataloging-in-Publication Data
Names: Wright, Julie Lobalzo, editor. | Shearer, Martha, editor.
Title: Musicals at the margins / edited by Julie Lobalzo Wright and Martha Shearer.
Description: New York: Bloomsbury Academic, 2021. | Includes
bibliographical references and index.
Identifiers: LCCN 2021000624 (print) | LCCN 2021000625 (ebook) | ISBN 9781501357114
(hardback) | ISBN 9781501357107 (ebook) | ISBN 9781501357091 (pdf)
Subjects: LCSH: Musical films–History and criticism. | Motion pictures and music. |
Liminality in motion pictures.
Classification: LCC PN1995.9.M86 M8725 2021 (print) | LCC PN1995.9.M86 (ebook) |
DDC 791.43/6578–dc23
LC record available at https://lccn.loc.gov/2021000624
LC ebook record available at https://lccn.loc.gov/2021000625

ISBN: HB: 978-1-5013-5711-4
PB: 978-1-5013-7852-2
ePDF: 978-1-5013-5709-1
eBook: 978-1-5013-5710-7

Typeset by Deanta Global Publishing Services, Chennai, India

To find out more about our authors and books visit www.bloomsbury.com and
sign up for our newsletters.

CONTENTS

List of Figures vii
Acknowledgments ix

1 Introduction: Genre Panic at the Margins *Julie Lobalzo Wright and Martha Shearer* 1

Generic Boundaries 13

2 Danceploitation, Musical Disruption, and Synergy in *Saturday Night Fever, Flashdance,* and *Breakin'* *Jenny Oyallon-Koloski* 15

3 Pitching Utopia: Popular Music, Community, and Neoliberalism in the Choir Film *Eleonora Sammartino* 28

4 E-Q-U-I-T-Y: Generic Boundaries, Gender, and Real Estate in the *Magic Mike* Films *Martha Shearer* 41

5 *Saint-Louis Blues:* From Oral Storytelling to Aural Filmmaking *Estrella Sendra* 55

Musicals of the Margins 71

6 The Marseille Film Operetta *Marie Cadalanu and Phil Powrie* 73

7 Heteroglossia in the Musical Number: Song, Music Performance, and Marginalized Identity in Tony Gatlif's *Swing* (2002) *Tamsin Graves* 86

8 Sexsationalist Feminism in *The Devil's Carnival* Project (2012, 2015) *Joana Rita Ramalho* 99

Musical Sequences 113

9 The On- and Off-Screen Politics of Sophia Loren's Musical Performances in *Houseboat* (1958) and *It Started in Naples* (1960) *Sarah Culhane* 115

10 "Just a Little Warm-Up for the Job": Harold Nicholas, the Specialty Act, and the Hollywood Song-and-Dance Man *Kate Saccone* 129

11 A Language of Its Own: Mani Ratnam's Experiments with the Song Scene *Aakshi Magazine* 144

Music 157

12 Pianos, Affect, and Memory *Paul Mazey and Sarah Street* 159

13 Everybody Wants to Be a Cat: Jazz Culture and Disney Animation in the 1960s *Landon Palmer* 172

14 Short-form Pop Music Films in 1960s Britain *Richard Farmer* 187

15 "Good Evening Pasadena!": Fantastical Performance Spaces in the Rock Documentary *Richard Wallace* 199

Musicals across Media 215

16 Live Musical Spectaculars: Eventizing Network Television in the Post-Network Age *Anthony Enns* 217

17 Camp and the Celebration of the Popular Song in *RuPaul's Drag Race* "Lip Sync for Your Life" *Julie Lobalzo Wright* 230

List of Contributors 245
Index 249

FIGURES

4.1–4.2	Mike in *Magic Mike* stripping to "Pony," seen from the audience's perspective; Brooke's reaction 46
4.3	Big Dick Richie's gas station performance to "I Want It That Way" in *Magic Mike XXL*, from the cashier's point of view 49
5.1	Film poster for *Un transport en commun*/*Saint-Louis Blues* 57
5.2	Malick and Souki when Souki tells her story aurally in *Un transport en commun*/*Saint-Louis Blues* 64
5.3	Médoune Sall, the driver, during his song in *Un transport en commun*/*Saint-Louis Blues* 66
6.1	Alibert singing "J'aime la mer comme une femme" in *Un de la Canebière* 79
6.2–6.3	The final sequences of *Un de la Canebière* and *Trois de la Canebière* 82
9.1	*Houseboat* (1957) Cinzia (Sophia Loren) leads the Winters children in a rendition of *Bing! Bang! Bong!* (1957) 124
9.2	*Houseboat* (1957) Cinzia (Sophia Loren) leads the Winters children in a second rendition of *Bing! Bang! Bong!*, while Tom (Cary Grant) pleads with them to stop singing 125
9.3	*Houseboat* (1957) Cinzia (Sophia Loren) performs *Bing! Bang! Bong!* at the country club summer party 126
10.1	A March 1945 advertisement for *Reckless Age* (1944) in the *Philadelphia Tribune* that capitalizes on Harold Nicholas's fame as part of the Nicholas Brothers 132
10.2	Harold and Fayard Nicholas utilizing the objects around them in the everyday space of the train station to create their dance in *The Great American Broadcast* (1941) 136
10.3	Harold Nicholas in *Reckless Age* (1944) 137
12.1	Piano playing prompts a memory in *Madonna of the Seven Moons* 161
12.2	Manina's playing (Joan Fontaine) lapses into "September Song" 165
12.3	The pianist casts a seductive spell in *The Housemaid* (2010) 169
13.1–13.2	A connection is drawn between a cat and a young, white jazz fan 176

13.3 Echoing recreational marijuana use, Scat Cat, under psychedelic lights, instructs Toulouse (Gary Dubin) on how to "be a cat" by blowing a horn 180
13.4 Baloo "apes" King Louie 182
15.1 Alan Wilder (left) smirks at the camera, while Dave Gahan (center) and Andy Franks (right) discuss the band's entrance 202
15.2 The audience responds to Gahan's invitation to dance and the floodlights reveal a sea of arms waving in unison 209
15.3 Gahan invites the cinema audience to participate 210
17.1 Widow Von Du LSFYL in season 12, episode 8 239
17.2 Naomi Smalls LSFYL in *All Stars* season 4, episode 8 240
17.3 Monét X Change LSFYL in *All Stars* season 4, episode 8 241

ACKNOWLEDGMENTS

This book began over a couple of drinks at a book launch at the British Film Institute and has been completed during the Covid-19 global pandemic. We look forward to the time we are able to celebrate this book in person!

The editors wish to thank all our contributors for their dedication to the project and prompt delivery of chapters. The love of musicals is evident in each and every chapter. It has been a delight to edit the collection and that is mainly due to our fantastic contributors.

Thanks to the audience at our panel on this subject at the 2017 British Association of Film, Television and Screen Studies conference in Bristol.

Thank you to the publishers, Bloomsbury, for their guidance throughout this process and the insightful peer reviews from proposal and manuscript stage.

We would also like to thank our departments, colleagues, and students at King's College London, University of Warwick, and University College Dublin for their support and interest in marginal musicals.

Julie would especially like to thank her incredible coeditor and musicals expert who has guided this project at every stage of production. Martha would also like to thank her amazing coeditor for her steadfast commitment to this project and for generally being a joy to work with.

1

Introduction

Genre Panic at the Margins

Julie Lobalzo Wright and Martha Shearer

On May 27, 2020, *Variety* posted the following provocative tweet: "To clarify, Is Bradley Cooper's *A Star Is Born* a musical?" The attached poll finished with over 7,000 votes and an overwhelming majority (61 percent) that *A Star Is Born* (2018) is categorically NOT a musical. The results of the poll are less intriguing than the multitude of comments below from critics and fans debating what constitutes a musical: Is it songs that advance the plot? Or music that is representative of character's feelings? Or even the amount of songs in one film? All of these contexts are employed by commentators to argue for or against the film's inclusion in the musical genre. While the genre's criteria are constantly debated, it is evident that a certain panic endures, based solely on genre definition, and is visible with the contemporary musical and other genres at particular moments.

There is a contemporary uncertainty about the limits of the musical as a category, as well as its precarious place in the industry. At the Golden Globes in 2019, for example, both *A Star Is Born* and *Bohemian Rhapsody* (2018) competed in the drama category, rather than musical or comedy. As is often pointed out, musical numbers are widespread in films not typically understood to be musicals—for example, in romantic comedies including *10 Things I Hate About You* (1999), *The Sweetest Thing* (2002), and *(500) Days of Summer* (2009)—while some films have pushed the use of jukebox soundtracks to the extent that they have been described as almost-musicals: *Baby Driver* (2017), for example. At the same time, a number of scholars have argued that the definition of the musical has shifted so as to be overly and ahistorically identified with the integrated musical, producing an irresolvable tension in the musical as a category between this overall definition and its retrospective application to a corpus, the classical Hollywood musical, that includes vast numbers of musicals that don't fit that definition (Donnelly and Carroll 2018; Griffin 2018). For Sean Griffin, this is a further problem as it leads to "an erroneous conclusion: that the film musical genre is dying or dead already" (Griffin 2018: 2). So while the musical has historically been what Raphaelle Moine calls a "strong" genre—"about which there is general agreement, on account of the recognition of these genres, if not their definition" (Moine 2008: 57)—the contemporary musical is significantly less so. That instability is further compounded if we look beyond the feature film to television (see Kessler 2020), web series, podcast musicals, and visual albums, and to musicals produced outside the United States, a significant thread in contemporary musical scholarship, including notable musical filmmakers such as Tsai Ming-liang and Jacques Demy, and musical traditions in other national cinemas, such as France, Greece, the UK, Egypt, the Soviet Union, China, and India (see, for example, Armbrust 2004; Brown 2016; Conrich and Tincknell 2006; Creekmur and Mokdad 2012; Fan 2014; Kaganovsky 2018: 108–37; Mundy 2007; Papadimitriou 2006).[1]

Genre anxiety is, however, not limited to the contemporary musical or to musicals produced outside the United States. Even the studio-era Hollywood musical canon is far more diverse in its generic structures and narrative/number relationships than the often very narrow definitions relied on in popular criticism and sometimes even scholarship. Jane Feuer notes, for example, that "we still disagree as to just how much music a film must contain to be called a musical, how that music must relate to the diegesis (the narrative world of the film), and what proportions of singing and dancing there must be" (Feuer 2013: 59) evidenced in the "Is *A Star is Born* a musical?" *Variety* poll.

The most sustained effort to define the genre, Rick Altman's landmark text *The American Film Musical*, devotes considerable space to policing the genre's boundaries, an effort that depends upon those boundaries not being self-evident. Altman contrasts the "inclusive" generic corpus—"an unwieldy list of texts corresponding to a simple, tautological definition of the genre"—used in "generic encyclopedias or checklists" with "exclusive" lists: "a familiar canon which has little to do with the broad, tautological definition. Here, the same films are mentioned again and again, not only because they are well known or particularly well made but because they somehow seem to represent the genre more fully and faithfully than other apparently more tangential films." Such lists occur "not in a dictionary context, but instead in connection with attempts to arrive at the overall meaning or structure of a genre" (Altman 1987: 92). While Altman argues against ideas of "overall" structures of genre in favor of his semantic/syntactic model, he still goes on to set out a fairly rigid definition of the genre, exemplified by his dictum "no couple, no musical" (Altman 1987: 103). While ours is a collection about the musical, it is also an examination of genre, more broadly.

As Lincoln Geraghty and Mark Jancovich observe, "most studies of genre still seem to operate around canonical texts": "key works that are either claimed to be the artistic high points, the markers of key shifts within historical development, or are taken to represent key features, periods or tendencies within the genre" (Geraghty and Jancovich 2008: 1). Amanda Ann Klein further notes that this approach to genre is "fundamentally ahistorical, marginalizing texts that could enrich, rather than detract from, our understanding of a genre, its context, its function, and even its aesthetics" (Klein 2011: 19). Janet Staiger observes that for any study, "selection becomes a necessity and with selection usually comes a politics of inclusion and exclusion. Some films are moved to the center of attention; others, to the margins" (Staiger 1985: 8). Those margins generate questions that have guided this collection, such as the following: How do we understand those films and media texts that don't neatly fit into a generic category but seem to have some relationship to it? How useful are our genre theories once we move away from a genre's "center"? This collection focuses not on the canon but on the musical's unstable edges: films that don't quite fit established definitions and theories, musicals produced and/or consumed by marginalized communities that have accordingly been marginalized in scholarship, and cinemas that have been marginalized by an overwhelming emphasis on US cinema, and musicals beyond the feature fiction film.

Typically, marginal musicals provoke anxiety that is resolved by determining whether that text is in or out of the genre, by answering the question, "Is it a musical?" A number of scholarly essays ask precisely that question: Jane Feuer on *Dirty Dancing* (1987), Andrew Caine on *This Is Spinal Tap* (1984), Richard Dyer on *Car Wash* (1976) (Feuer 2013; Caine 2008; Dyer 2012). Dyer's piece is a useful model for this collection for its argument that *Car Wash* is "by any sensible definition" a musical, but to understand it as such requires an understanding of its place in Black cinematic traditions with which it has more in common than the "white musical" (Dyer 2012: 154). For the most part, however, such studies entail determining whether a text falls in or out of a rigidly defined category. Altman's discussion of *Woodstock* is instructive in this regard: it is a "marginal film" that might be considered a musical due to its dual-focus structure, the core component of his definition of the genre. It is "drawn into the musical corpus . . . only to the extent that the methodology implied by (constitutive of) that corpus can illuminate the film in question" (Altman

1987: 103). While this approach is not dissimilar to our understanding of the marginal musical, for Altman binary in/out decisions are inescapable.

Scholarship on the musical has also highlighted its oscillation between different aesthetic registers, situating it as perhaps the clearest expression of Hollywood cinema's tension between narrative and spectacle, a tension that has enabled comparisons with numerous other genres—pornography (Willemen 1980: 64–5; L. Williams 1999: 120–52), melodrama (Elsaesser 1981), and the giallo (Newman 2011: 145)—and the identification of forms such as the high-concept "music movie" (Wyatt 1994: 40–1) and the rockumentary (James 2016) as outgrowths of the studio-era musical. In early studies, *The Umbrellas of Cherbourg* (1964) was a particular sticking point: both Altman and Alan Williams exclude it on the grounds that it is sung-through, a criterion that would exclude contemporary films uncontroversially included in the genre, such as *Les Misérables* (2012) and *Cats* (2019) (A. Williams 1981: 156; Altman 1987: 106–7).

What we want to suggest is that such examples indicate a problem for genre studies bigger than the contemporary state of the musical, or even the musical genre. While the musical may no longer be a "strong" genre, it is true that the musical has not traditionally provoked the level of genre panic of certain other genres such as melodrama or, especially, film noir. Film noir's construction as a critical category in postwar France, always at a remove from its subject and forever marred by uncertainty about whether it is best described as a genre, a cycle, a mood, a mode, a period, or a phenomenon, has meant that it has been a particularly useful site for the rethinking of ideas of generic definition. James Naremore suggests that the instability of film noir as a category is not singular but demonstrates a more general instability of genre:

> Perhaps the very word genre, with its etymological links to biology and birth, promotes a kind of essentialism; but even when writers about film noir claim to be speaking of something other than a genre, they keep trying to list its definitive traits. To avoid troubling anomalies, they sometimes argue that the noir form is "transgeneric." The problem here is that such an argument also applies to the ostensibly stable genres: there were western musicals (*Oklahoma!*), western melodramas (*Duel in the Sun*), western science-fiction pictures (*Westworld*), and western noirs (*Pursued*). The fact is, every movie is transgeneric or polyvalent. (Naremore 1998: 6)

Genre theory has for decades questioned essentialist approaches to generic definition, notably following Andrew Tudor's contention that "The way in which the genre term is applied can quite conceivably vary from case to case. Genre notions—except the special case of arbitrary definition—are not critics' classifications made for special purposes; they are sets of cultural conventions. Genre is what we collectively believe it to be" (Tudor 2012: 6–7).

Recent work in genre studies has proposed more flexible approaches. In a piece in which he reads *Rio Bravo* as both Western and romantic comedy, Celestino Deleyto has argued against "the more linear approach according to which genres ... work in simple, predictable ways that can be investigated, known, classified, and controlled" and in favor of "a chaotic view of genres" that "underlines their instability, the impossibility of establishing clear lines of demarcation, and the nonlinearity, unpredictability, and complexity of their evolution" (Deleyto 2012: 220).[2] In her book on film cycles, Klein argues that cycles offer "a more pragmatic, localized approach to genre history" with the "potential to disrupt or complicate the discrete categories frequently generated by genre studies" (Klein 2011: 5–6). While she contends that "the mark of an established genre is stability, longevity, and resilience" (16), she also argues for an approach to genre studies itself that steps back from "the 'center' of a genre, where many studies begin and end, and instead venture[s] out to the 'borders' of its generic corpus, where the films that do not fully comply with the rules of genre reside," suggesting that "it is more illuminating to study a genre as a series of cycles rather than as a monolithic entity broken down into discrete stages of evolutionary development" (Klein 2011: 22).

This book is an effort to bring such flexible, hybrid approaches to the musical and does so using a variety of methodologies, drawing on cultural history, formal analysis, industrial discourse, marketing, and critical reception. We are inspired by scholarship on the musical that has sought to draw attention to its edges and boundaries. Amy Herzog, for example, argues that films that "push the boundaries of the musical canon," such as Jacques Demy's musical films or Esther Williams's "water-based" musical films, "spoke most forcibly about the tension between difference and repetition" that she sees as critical to the "musical moment" (Herzog 2010: 3). Desirée Garcia's *The Migration of Musical Film* valuably demonstrates how canonical generic forms, principally the folk musical, were pioneered at the margins, in ethnic cinemas of the 1930s: Black "race" films, Yiddish and Mexican cinemas (Garcia 2014).

A number of edited collections on the musical have recognized generic marginality as an issue but danced around it, typically resolving the problem through the inclusion of texts defined as nonmusicals. For us, this skips over the central problem by assuming that boundaries are clear. Ian Conrich and Estella Tincknell's collection *Film's Musical Moments*, for example, is expansive in its scope but assumes clear distinction between musical numbers in musicals and musical moments in nonmusical films, so that while the musical moment is understood as disruptive, genre itself remains undisturbed (Conrich and Tincknell 2006). Bill Marshall and Robynn Stilwell's *Musicals: Hollywood and Beyond* similarly widens the corpus, but in arguing against the general and in favor of textual specifics, genre again remains untroubled (Marshall and Stilwell 2000). K. J. Donnelly and Beth Carroll's *Contemporary Musical Film* includes attention to "musicals by any other name" with chapters on the Coens, Tarantino, and the *Fast & Furious* films, but we would suggest that instead of asking "Where should the delineation start and stop?," (Donnelly and Carroll 2018: 5) we ask, "What do marginal texts tell us about genre?"

Our project in this collection is to move away from a notion of the musical as a static object with canonical norms. Instead, we propose the concept of the marginal musical. It is our contention that there is value in thinking about such hard-to-categorize films and media objects *as marginal generic texts*: not simply as hybrids (i.e., films that fit into more than one generic category) and not simply to expand the definition of the genre but to dwell on textual instability, on the genre's unstable edges, to leave the question "is it a musical?" unanswered and unsettled. Individual chapters instead seek to think through the usefulness of existing theories of the musical—particularly key ideas including performance space, community, utopianism, the tension between narrative and spectacle, and the musical's relationship to capitalism—for their chosen texts.

This collection is multi-voiced, collating diverse subjects, perspectives, and critical frameworks. As Joana Rita Ramalho says of her case study *The Devil's Carnival* (2012), this book too is a monstrous hybrid. Marginality is also itself contingent: a text may be marginal in some contexts, places, and times, and not in others. And as we move away from the generic core, forms of marginality proliferate. This collection accordingly encompasses a range of different forms of marginality: boundary texts (films/media that are sort of/not quite musicals), musical sequences (marginalized sequences in musicals, musical sequences in films not typically understood as musicals), music films, musicals of the margins (musicals produced from social, cultural, geographical, and geopolitical margins), and musicals across media (television and new media). It is also global in scope.

The book is divided into five sections: "Generic Boundaries," "Musicals of the Margins," "Musical Sequences," "Music," and "Musicals across Media." These sections are broadly defined and overlapping, indicating the genre's flexibility and the instabilities inherent in marginal texts. "Generic Boundaries" includes films that are playful in their genre intentions while still existing on the margins, as dance, choir, and African musical films frequently do. Jenny Oyallon-Koloski argues that "danceploitation" films from the late 1970s and 1980s retain an unclear place within the musical genre due to foundational scholarship that prioritizes singing over dance. Eleonora Sammartino indicates that the choir film is connected to the musical through its utopianism; however, the neoliberal context, text, and promotion of the films curtail that utopianism. Martha Shearer considers the neoliberal urban context through the relationship to contemporary US real estate in

Magic Mike (2012) and *Magic Mike XXL* (2015). All three chapters utilize film case studies frequently excluded in musical scholarship, arguing for the value of disruption (Koloski), shifts in genre (Sammartino), and the relationship of gender and space (Shearer) to musical films. Rounding out the first section is Estrella Sendra's chapter on the Senegalese film *Saint-Louis Blues* (2009), exploring how this one example illustrates the importance of decolonizing the Western canon and incorporating regional and non-Western approaches to filmmaking, such as aural storytelling.

The second section ("Musicals of the Boundaries") features chapters that take a more cultural approach by focusing on musicals that have been relegated to the margins either through national cinema studies (Cadalanu and Powrie; Graves) or through their connection to subcultural fandom (Ramalho). These chapters consider musicals *of* the margins, as do many others featured in this collection (such as Sendra), and are attentive to how, as Graves argues, musicals about geographically, socially, and/or culturally marginalized communities have, in turn, been marginalized in musical scholarship. Marie Cadalanu and Phil Powrie approach marginality from various angles suggesting that, as a regional musical, the Marseille film operetta has been both exoticized and marginalized due to the cycle's relationship to French national cinema. Tamsin Graves continues a focus on setting, but instead of a nostalgic paradise like Marseille, Graves places the spotlight on displaced communities and a culture where the musical number becomes a privileged heteroglossic site. Graves presents the audio dissolve as an aesthetic border crossing in Tony Gatlif's *Swing* (2002), whereas Joana Rita Ramalho utilizes border crossings in relation to the hybridity of the gothic musical. Ramalho's example, *The Devil's Carnival* Project (2012, 2015), illustrates how gender conventions of the musical are reworked in films that narrativize the marginal musical as *The Devil's Carnival* does through a reconstruction of heaven and hell.

The following section ("Musical Sequences") features chapters that pick up on many issues established in previous chapters, especially musicals at the fringe of their national cinemas, frequently due to regionality (Culhane; Magazine). These contributions, however, extend their analysis to consider questions of performance, body, and exoticism. Sarah Culhane discusses Sophia Loren's vocal labor in films not typically understood as musicals, such as *Houseboat* (1958) and *It Started in Naples* (1960), and how Loren's transnationalism helped create a linguistic hybridity to her musical performances. Kate Saccone suggests that Harold Nicholas's specialty numbers do not fit the paradigms of the musical which are built around whiteness, frequently excluding the labor and performance of the Black body. Both of these chapters reread the classical Hollywood period, adhering to Ella Shohat and Robert Stam's contention that viewing the "Hollywood classics" from the margins allows us to reconstruct "cultural voices drowned out or reduced to a whisper" and begin to "hear other voices" (1994: 221). This is especially important to Saccone's chapter and the following from Aakshi Magazine who illustrates how Mani Ratnam's films are distinct from the norms of popular Indian cinema by complicating song and narrative relations. Ratnam's films are examples of marginal texts that help transform the norms of the mainstream through experimentation and conformity. Magazine's chapter adds voices from the margins to the dominant understanding of national cinema intrinsically connected to the musical.

The "Music" section features more examples of films that are not typically understood as musicals with a focus on margins in terms of medium or mode: piano playing (Mazey and Street), short films and newsreels (Farmer), documentary (Wallace), and animation (Palmer). Paul Mazey and Sarah Street note the melodrama's affinities with musicals by mobilizing affective regimes via musical performances related to feelings, memory, longing, and emotional expression in British and Korean film examples. Landon Palmer examines the marginality of animated jazz musicals by situating them within transitional moments for animation, jazz, and the musical, opening up animation's racialized histories of jazz representation. Richard Farmer's analysis of short pop music films is specific in terms of music genre (like Palmer) and marginalized due to length, but Farmer argues for the value of these short films that were a key way pop music was circulated in the 1960s. The section ends with Richard Wallace's contribution on rock documentaries, exploring *Depeche Mode: 101* (1989) as a documentary in the musical mode that features utopian musical performances (similar to Sammartino), allowing the audience to participate in the myth of entertainment (Feuer 1993).

Following on from Wallace's chapter, the final section, "Musicals across Media," draws on the pleasures and conventions of the musical. These two chapters explore the musical and television, questioning what happens when musicals move across a range of media forms. Anthony Enns explores the neglected history of live TV musicals, examining how the contemporary practice of televised live musicals taps into a nostalgia for community and the unified TV audience. Julie Lobalzo Wright discusses lip-synching through the popularity of *RuPaul's Drag Race* and the inherent connections between the "lip sync for your life moments" and generic conventions of the musical. This section considers not only different modes of musicals (in line with the "music" section) but how television specifically creates new avenues for the musical to endure and thrive long after many declared the genre finished.

As noted, there are many overlapping contexts, issues, modes, and considerations in this collection. This is not all-inclusive and there are many other case studies we wished we were able to include. What this collection will, hopefully, illustrate is the musical genre's durability, but also the limitations of genre theory and methodologies that are inflexible by ignoring the unstable edges, alternative voices, and local and regional contexts that inject genres with specificities that ultimately allow genres to persist through inevitable changes.

Notes

1. Notable podcast musicals include *36 Questions* (2017) and *Songonauts* (2017), web series musicals, *Trapped in the Closet* (2005-2012) and *Dr. Horrible's Sing-a-long Blog* (2008), and visual albums, *Black Is King* (2020).
2. See also Deleyto's (2011) *The Secret Life of Romantic Comedy*.

References

Altman, R. (1987), *The American Film Musical*, Bloomington and Indianapolis: Indiana University Press.

Armbrust, W. (2004), "Egyptian Cinema On Stage and Off," in A. Shryock (ed.), *Off Stage/On Display: Intimacy and Ethnography in the Age of Public Culture*, 69–98, Stanford: Stanford University Press.

Brown, T. (2016), *Spectacle in "Classical" Cinemas: Musicality and Historicity in the 1930s*, New York and London: Routledge.

Caine, A. (2008), "Can Rock Movies Be Musicals? The Case of This Is Spinal Tap," in L. Geraghty and M. Jancovich (eds.), *The Shifting Definitions of Genre: Essays on Labeling Films, Television Shows and Media*, 124–41, Jefferson, NC: McFarland & Co.

Conrich, I., and E. Tincknell, eds. (2006), *Film's Musical Moments*, Edinburgh: Edinburgh University Press.

Creekmur, C. K., and L. Y. Mokdad, eds. (2012), *The International Film Musical*, Edinburgh: Edinburgh University Press.

Deleyto, C. (2011), *The Secret Life of the Romantic Comedy*, Manchester: Manchester University Press.

Deleyto, C. (2012), "Film Genres at the Crossroads: What Genres and Films Do to Each Other," in B. K. Grant (ed.), *The Film Genre Reader IV*, 218–36, Austin: University of Texas Press.

Donnelly, K.J., and B. Carroll. (2018), "Introduction: Reimagining the Contemporary Musical in the Twenty-First Century," in K.J. Donnelly and B. Carroll (eds.), *Contemporary Musical Film*, 1–9, Edinburgh: Edinburgh University Press.

Dyer, R. (2012), "Is Car Wash a Musical?" in *In the Space of a Song: The Uses of Song in Film*, 145–55, London and New York: Routledge.

Elsaesser, T. (1981), "Vincente Minnelli," in R. Altman (ed.), *Genre: The Musical*, 8–27, London, Boston and Henley: Routledge and Kegan Paul.

Fan, V. (2014), "Extraterritorial Cinema: Shanghai Jazz and Post-War Hong Kong Mandarin Musicals," *The Soundtrack*, 6 (1–2): 33–52.

Feuer, J. (1993), *The Hollywood Musical*, Second edn, Bloomington and Indianapolis: Indiana University Press.

Feuer, J. (2013), "Is Dirty Dancing a Musical, and Why Should It Matter?" in Y. Tzioumakis and S. Lincoln (eds.), *The Time of Our Lives: Dirty Dancing and Popular Culture*, 59–72, Detroit: Wayne State University Press.

Garcia, D. J. (2014), *The Migration of Musical Film: From Ethnic Margins to American Mainstream*, New Brunswick, NJ, and London: Rutgers University Press.

Geraghty, L., and M. Jancovich. (2008), "Introduction: Generic Canons," in L. Geraghty and M. Jancovich (eds.), *The Shifting Definitions of Genre: Essays on Labeling Films, Televisions Shows and Media*, 1–14, Jefferson, NC: McFarland & Co.

Griffin, S. (2018), *Free and Easy? A Defining History of the American Film Musical Genre*, Oxford: Wiley-Blackwell.

Herzog, A. (2010), *Dreams of Difference, Songs of the Same: The Musical Moment in Film*, Minneapolis: University of Minnesota Press.

James, D. E. (2016), *Rock "n" Film: Cinema's Dance with Popular Music*, New York: Oxford University Press.

Kaganovsky, L. (2018), *The Voice of Technology: Soviet Cinema's Transition to Sound, 1928–1935*, Bloomington and Indianapolis: Indiana University Press.

Kessler, K. (2020), *Broadway in the Box: Television's Lasting Love Affair with the Musical*, New York: Oxford University Press.

Klein, A. A. (2011), *American Film Cycles: Reframing Genres, Screening Social Problems, & Defining Subcultures*, Austin: University of Texas Press.

Marshall, B., and R. Stilwell. (2000), *Musicals: Hollywood and Beyond*, Exeter: Intellect.

Moine, R. (2008). *Cinema Genre*. Translated by A. Fox and H. Radner, Malden, MA, and Oxford: Blackwell.

Mundy, J. (2007), *The British Musical Film*, Manchester: Manchester University Press.

Naremore, J. (1998), *More Than Night: Film Noir in Its Contexts*, Berkeley; Los Angeles; London: University of California Press.

Newman, K. (2011), *Nightmare Movies: Horror on Screen since the 1960s*, London: Bloomsbury.

Papadimitriou, L. (2006), *The Greek Film Musical: A Critical and Cultural History*, Jefferson, NC: McFarland.

Shohat, E., and R. Stam. (1994), *Unthinking Eurocentrism: Multiculturalism and the Media*, London and New York: Routledge.

Staiger, J. (1985), "The Politics of Film Canons," *Cinema Journal*, 24 (3): 4–23.

Tudor, A. (2012), "Genre," in B. K. Grant (ed.), *The Film Genre Reader IV*, 3–11, Austin: University of Texas Press.

Variety. 2020. May 27. Available at: http://www.twitter.com/variety (accessed September 16, 2020).

Willemen, P. (1980), "Letter to John," *Screen*, 21 (2): 53–65.

Williams, A. (1981), "The Musical Film and Recorded Popular Music," in R. Altman (ed.), *Genre: The Musical*, 147–58, London, Boston and Henley: Routledge and Kegan Paul.

Williams, L. (1999), *Hard Core: Power, Pleasure, and the "Frenzy of the Visible"*, Expanded edn, Berkeley; Los Angeles; London: University of California Press.

Wyatt, J. (1994), *High Concept: Movies and Marketing in Hollywood*, Austin: University of Texas Press.

Filmography

10 Things I Hate about You (1999), [Film] Dir. Gil Junger, USA: Buena Vista.
36 Questions (2017), [Podcast] Available at: https://twoupproductions.com/36-questions/podcast (accessed September 16, 2020).
(500) Days of Summer (2009), [Film] Dir. Marc Webb, USA: Fox Searchlight.
Baby Driver (2017), [Film] Dir. Edgar Wright, UK/USA: Sony Pictures.
Black Is King (2020), [Film] Dir. Beyoncé, Jenn Nkiru, Blitz the Ambassador, Jake Nava, USA: Disney+.
Bohemian Rhapsody (2018), [Film] Dir. Bryan Singer/Dexter Fletcher, UK/USA: 20th Century Fox.
Car Wash (1976), [Film] Dir. Michael Schultz, USA: Universal Pictures.
Depeche Mode: 101 (1989), [Film] Dir. David Dawkins, Chris Hegedus, D. A. Pennebaker, UK/US: Mute Film/Pennebaker Associates.
The Devil's Carnival (2012), [Film] Dir. Darren Lynn Bousman, USA: Execution Style Entertainment.
Dirty Dancing (1987), [Film] Dir. Emile Ardolino, USA: Vestron Pictures.
Dr. Horrible's Sing-a-long Blog 2008, [Television] Dir. Joss Whedon, Available at: https://drhorrible.com/#main (accessed September 16, 2020).
Houseboat (1958), [Film] Dir. Melville Shavelson, USA: Paramount.
It Started in Naples (1960), [Film] Dir. Melville Shavelson, USA: Paramount.
Magic Mike (2012), [Film] Dir. Steven Soderbergh, USA: Warner Brothers.
Magic Mike XXL (2015), [Film] Dir. Gregory Jacobs, USA: Warner Brothers.
Songonauts (2017), [Podcast]. Available at: http://www.thetruthpodcast.com/songonauts (accessed September 16, 2020).
St. Louis Blues (2009), [Film] Dir. Dyana Gaye, France/Senegal: Andolfi Production and Nataal Production.
A Star Is Born (2018), [Film] Dir. Bradley Cooper, USA: Warner Bros.
The Sweetest Thing (2002), [Film] Dir. Roger Kumble, USA: Columbia Pictures.
Swing (2002), [Film] Dir. Tony Gatlif, France/Japan: Princes Films.
This Is Spinal Tap (1984), [Film] Dir. Rob Reiner, USA: Embassy Pictures.
Trapped in the Closet (2005–2012), [Film] Dir. R. Kelly and Jim Swatffield, USA: Jive and RCA.

Generic Boundaries

2

Danceploitation, Musical Disruption, and Synergy in *Saturday Night Fever*, *Flashdance*, and *Breakin'*

Jenny Oyallon-Koloski

Saturday Night Fever (1977) and the series of dance-heavy Hollywood films it inspired, like *Flashdance* (1983) and *Breakin'* (1984), have a curious relationship to the musical. Many scholars categorize these films just within the margin of the musical genre due to a detachment of numbers from either stylistic genre conventions or their surrounding narratives, a detachment which many also suggest occurs to the denigration of the choreography.[1] Unlike the numerous classical Hollywood musicals that incorporate both songs and dances, *Saturday Night Fever* and the films that followed its formula choose to largely exclude diegetically sung numbers. This chapter will argue that it is these films' prioritization of dancing as the driver of musical number content that calls their generic status into question. The films of this "danceploitation" cycle sought to recreate *Saturday Night Fever*'s financial windfall through the incorporation of both popular music and dance; when we give greater emphasis to the function of figure movement, in *Flashdance* and *Breakin'* in particular, we can observe how the films articulate tensions between established and emerging dance forms in the musical sequences as an integral part of their narratives. These choices parallel mainstream cultural perceptions of those dance styles and the synergistic marketing strategies that perpetuated the financial success of this cycle.

The Danceploitation Cycle

From the late 1970s to the mid-1980s, Hollywood saw the emergence of a danceploitation cycle of low-budget films seeking to imitate *Saturday Night Fever*'s financial success. Amanda Ann Klein argues that most film cycles emerge from an originary film that studios seek to capitalize on by reproducing the elements that generated its financial and/or critical success. Klein's research also demonstrates a strong relationship between cycles and exploitation cinema, given the aim of both to create and sell films as quickly as possible (2011: 4–7). In this case, the key formulaic elements producers sought to replicate were based on popular dance forms as well as popular music; the financial value of these films came from the ability to repackage and sell their visual, danced content as well as their soundtracks.

Saturday Night Fever was a huge financial success for Paramount Pictures, earning over $90 million domestically on a $3.5 million budget (Box Office Mojo n.d., Griffin 2018: 282). The film also marked an important step forward in the synergistic relationship between Hollywood and the record industry, establishing soundtrack albums not only as a means for cross-promotion and ancillary revenue streams but also as a means of mitigating financial risk (Smith 2008: 143). The film's and soundtrack's profits fed each other; the Bee Gees' album performed extraordinarily well for RSO Records with twenty-four weeks at Number One on the Billboard 200. Hype around disco dancing—as well as disco music—also played a significant role in *Saturday Night Fever*'s marketing success, with star John Travolta firing up the dance floor at various parties organized as part of the film's release in the United States and the United Kingdom ("New York" 1977: 20). Disco dance competitions around the world corresponded with the film's domestic and international releases ("Chatter" 1978: 93, "Sat. Night Fever" 1978: 62, "'Fever' Bally Dance" 1978: 2). Stage shows in Chicago and Las Vegas and a "Dancing Disco" show on PBS also used the film's dances as choreographic inspiration ("Night Club" 1978: 131, "Get Down & Boogie" 1979: 62).

Variety identified a number of attempts to capitalize on these conditions: *Sergeant Pepper's Lonely Hearts Club Band* (1978), *The Music Machine* (1979), *Staying Alive* (1983), *Flashdance* (1983), *Purple Rain* (1984), *Footloose* (1984), *Breakin'* (1984), *Breakin' 2: Electric Boogaloo* (1984), *Heavenly Bodies* (1984), *Dirty Dancing* (1987), and *Salsa* (1988).[2] Several early films in the cycle did not do as well as expected, notably Universal Pictures' *Sergeant Pepper* and *Staying Alive*, Paramount Pictures' attempt to recreate *Saturday Night Fever*'s success, featuring a return of John Travolta, another Bee Gees album, and the addition of Sylvester Stallone's directorial influence.

Flashdance is largely responsible for keeping the cycle alive; a review qualifies it as a "femme SNF" (McCarthy 1983: 12), and the trade press's discussion of the film is concisely summarized in the title "'Flashdance'

Film, LP Feeding Off Each Other; Companies Hope For Repeat Of 'SNF' Syndrome" (Gold 1983: 3). *Flashdance* didn't financially match *Saturday Night Fever*, earning a similar $90 million domestically (Box Office Mojo n.d.) on a higher $9 million budget. But the album, released by Polygram, did very well; it spent two summer weeks at Number One on the Billboard 200, not a minor feat given that it was up against Michael Jackson's *Thriller*, which was dominating the music charts. The film also "provided the initial model for film and music video cross-promotion" (Smith 2008: 147) by releasing the "Maniac" music video, as well as singles, before the film's theatrical release.

Key to this synergy was the ability to repackage visual content, including dance sequences, from the film. Given the growing interest in film-record crossovers, the New Music Seminar, an annual music conference and festival, devoted a whole panel to the topic in 1984. *Variety*'s report of the event points to the crossover potential of film and record sales as well as the importance of music videos as "pre-release promotional wedges" ("New Music Seminar" 1984: 6, 24). Kelly Kessler argues convincingly that the musical sequences' highly edited form stemmed from the producers' desire to have shots of dancing that could be reused for various promotional purposes.[3] In his review, Todd McCarthy described the film viewing experience as "looking at MTV for 96 minutes" (1983: 12). Like *Saturday Night Fever*, *Flashdance*'s narrative capitalized on popular dance trends, in addition to its figure skating numbers, having the lead character Alex embody a "flashdance" style that blended jazz, gymnastics, and aerobics, as well as more erotic content from her striptease numbers and a hint of breakdancing. The film's dance numbers also inspired live shows in Las Vegas, including one entitled "Flashdance Fever," a name that tellingly reinforces the two key films driving this cycle ("Night Club" 1984: 135).

Trade press discourse identifies Paramount's *Footloose*, described as "Flashdance Farmers" (Har. 1984: 24), and Cannon Films' *Breakin'* as successfully capitalizing on *Flashdance*'s synergistic efforts. *Breakin'*, with Orion Pictures' *Beat Street*, was one of several Hollywood attempts in 1984 to capitalize upon hip-hop, the South Bronx-based artistic movement that was gaining awareness and popularity in Los Angeles (Monteyne 2013: 43, 44).[4] *Breakin'* followed *Flashdance*'s model, this time focusing on breakdancing and broader cultural aspects of hip-hop. Publicity director Priscilla McDonald unabashedly described *Breakin'* as an exploitation project, telling *Variety* that "we wanted to beat everybody to the draw with the rash of break dance films . . . and we did" ("Break Dancing" 1984: 287). *Breakin'* pulled in a modestly lucrative $40 million domestically on a $2 million budget (Box Office Mojo n.d.), a box-office success that *Variety* predicted given the film's low cost, light tone, and entertaining breakdancing sequences (McCarthy 1984: 526). Like *Flashdance*, *Saturday Night Fever*, and *Footloose*, *Breakin*'s success also stemmed from album sales ("New Music Seminar" 1984: 6). The album was another modest hit for Polygram Records, with the soundtrack "shaping up as the diskery's biggest soundtrack LP since 'Flashdance'" and reaching eighth place on the Billboard 200 (Gold 1984: 4). Cannon Films also wasted no time putting a sequel into production, with the closing credit titles of *Breakin'* announcing the imminent arrival of *Breakin' 2: Electric Boogaloo*.

Later films, notably *Dirty Dancing* and *Salsa*, continued to replicate elements from this cycle, but direct mentions in *Variety* of the originary films peter out after 1985. *Electric Boogaloo* and *Salsa* may have contributed to the danceploitation cycle's decline with their low box-office returns, but producers of similar content also realized they could entirely avoid the loosely constructed plots associated with these films by shifting their cinematic efforts to television (Griffin 2018: 291, 292), seen in 1983's dance-heavy music videos like "Thriller," "Beat It," and "Love Is a Battlefield." However, *Saturday Night Fever* resurfaces in a 1993 article on the state of live-action Hollywood musicals. "Old-style" musicals are a hard sell, *Newsies* producer Michael Finnell tells *Variety*, because young audiences are "used to MTV, which doesn't pretend to mix reality with story, character and dialogue. Musicals are a stylized medium that is disturbing and unbelievable to them" (Brodie 1993: 75). *Saturday Night Fever* is one of several examples from the period cited as a counterpoint and as an indication of the musical's ongoing financial potential.

This categorization is striking, given that *Saturday Night Fever* features no diegetically sung performances. Instead, it and several imitators—notably *Flashdance* and *Breakin'*—largely avoid the sung musical number associated with the genre in favor of diegetically motivated dance sequences. This focus calls into question their generic status, while also encouraging us to notice the narrative roles that popular dance plays.

Generic Disruptions

Flashdance and *Breakin'* are particularly noteworthy in this film cycle given their mobilization of the synergistic potential between cinema, music, dance, and television not only in their marketing strategies but in their formal structures as well, structures that equally strain their relationship to core musical genre conventions. Two formal tensions provide a compelling way to situate films in relation to the musical genre: what relationship a musical number has to its surrounding narrative and whether that number creates the impression of diegetic plurality by introducing content that deviates from the stylistic norms of the diegesis, content described as "impossible" and "supra-diegetic" by Martin Rubin and Rick Altman, respectively (Rubin 2002: 57; Altman 1987: 62–71).[5] Accordingly, I identify films that feature musical numbers whose content both advances the plot (in a myriad of ways) and generates a rich diegetic plurality as engaging most directly with core conventions of the genre, especially those that do so through both singing and dancing. *Saturday Night Fever*, *Flashdance*, and *Breakin'* largely avoid these conventions, diegetic refraction through song, in particular. The varied ways that the soundtracks' music interacts with the films' visual content—scenes with figure movement that moves rhythmically in accordance to the music but without a clear beginning or end to mark it as a number; montages; and diegetic performances—also means that some sequences are better categorized as what Amy Herzog has theorized as musical moments, in which music—most often diegetically sourced popular songs—appears to dominate the image-sound hierarchy (Herzog 2010: 5–8). Her definition of musical moments deliberately applies to the structure of most musical numbers, but the category also encompasses sequences that include diegetic pop music, which applies to many of the musical scenes in this cycle that deviate from musical norms. In these films' dance sequences—most often practice or teaching montages and performances for audiences—we can observe the following consistencies.

First, *Saturday Night Fever*, *Flashdance*, and *Breakin'* rarely shift to supradiegetic spaces; the majority of their musical number content is motivated by the surrounding diegesis. Rick Altman's theorization of the supradiegetic emphasizes opposition: technical, thematic, and narrative (1987: 62–7). I choose to articulate musical numbers' shifts to the supradiegetic and the creation of diegetic plurality as a stylistic change in a film's intrinsic norms, stylistic norms that conflict with those of the surrounding diegesis. This correlates with Steven Cohan's conception of this formal convention as creating a "dual register, thereby breaking with the cinema's dominant codes of realism as a means of securing the unity of time and space for a film's fictive world or 'diegesis.' . . . This convention creates multiple diegeses, and it is not limited to when characters have fantasies or dreams" (2010: 3). Further dividing how numbers can engage with supradiegetic spaces allows us to observe the myriad ways numbers can activate this generic convention. Most simply, we can articulate differences between the occurrence of spatiotemporal shifts in the narrative space—lighting changes or the introduction of an implausible space, for example—and the occurrence of performative shifts—changes at the individual and collective level—through both vocalization and figure movement.

The films of this cycle predominantly motivate the performances that occur in their diegeses, avoiding stark stylistic shifts in numbers and building training and rehearsal scenes into their narratives—even in relation to the improvisatory nature of breakdancing—to downplay a sense of fantastical spontaneity. Despite this, diegetic plurality does infrequently occur. During the disco competition that occurs near the end of *Saturday Night Fever*, Tony and Stephanie's planned choreography pauses momentarily as they kiss, shifting their performance and the space to the supradiegetic. The sequence introduces slow-motion cinematography as the camera circles them, and added reverberation changes the sonic quality of the Bee Gees' "More Than a Woman" accompanying them on the soundtrack. The rest of the cycle also largely eschews supradiegetic spaces, though such shifts are associated with Turbo's character in both *Breakin'* and *Electric Boogaloo*. Turbo's broom begins to float in *Breakin'* as part of his sweeping-inspired dance and the sound quality of the music does not match the diegetic confines of the space, despite the visible boom box in the initial shot of the number. In *Electric Boogaloo*, his excitement over a love interest leads to a more dramatic, performative, and spatial shift as he dances across the walls and ceiling of his room, referencing Fred Astaire's number in *Royal Wedding* (1951).

Second, the films of this cycle largely eliminate diegetically sung numbers.[6] Both *Saturday Night Fever* and *Flashdance* feature many popular songs on their soundtracks which are frequently paired with danced sequences, but neither feature any diegetically sung content in either musical numbers or the larger narrative. In these films, for example, we frequently hear popular songs (with lyrics) accompanying montages, rehearsals, various forms of social dancing, or performances, but the songs are never performed live, a point that *Variety* emphasizes in discussion of *Saturday Night Fever*'s marketing (Everett 1977: 67). *Breakin'* and other films from this cycle also employ a similar model, with occasional diegetic vocal performances. Danced content accompanied by boom boxes is the norm in *Breakin'*'s musical sequences, but DJ-ing and MC-ing are performed live within the diegesis at community gatherings that the main characters attend.

Finally, this distinction is crucial given that diegetically sung content frequently leads a film's musical numbers to continue the narrative's momentum. Despite this, we can observe these films' dance sequences engaging with the generic convention of including narratively integrated numbers. Due to Hollywood's association with explicit, redundant narration, diegetic songs frequently fulfill a communicative function that dance does not. John Mueller's taxonomy of narratively integrated musical content articulates the various ways content can be more or less engaged in moving the plot forward and adding to narrative information. His pivotal example of numbers which "advance the plot by their content"—to him the highest level of integration—is the all-danced "Dancing in the Dark" number from *The Band Wagon* (1953). He argues compellingly that the number serves two functions. It proves to Cyd Charisse's and Fred Astaire's characters that they can successfully dance together. In addition, through the process of discovering their compatibility, they fall in love (1984: 33–5). These claims of narrative integration are not contentious, but extracting meaning from the figure movement requires additional work on the part of the viewer. We implicitly determine the couple's romantic compatibility from this sequence by decoding the dance's intimation that the two have overcome their disparate dance styles; how we determine that physical compatibility is the result of viewing practices and cultural training. In comparison, in the "Boy Next Door" number from *Meet Me in St Louis* (1944), Judy Garland's character communicates her love of neighbor John through song lyrics. Over the course of the number, we are given several specific pieces of information that require no additional interpretation for those familiar with the English language. We learn that, while she has observed him, they have never officially met. We also learn a highly granular narrative detail: their addresses. She lives at "fifty-one-thirty-five Kensington Avenue / And he lives at fifty-one-thirty-three." Astaire's and Charisse's physicality adds value to *The Band Wagon*'s narrative as Garland's singing does to *Meet Me in St. Louis*'s, but the nature of that value differs.

This should not suggest that dance can never serve as an explicit form of communication; Bharatanatyam conveys precise information through mudras (hand and finger gestures), and *ballet d'action* employs highly codified gestures to impart specific meanings. However, these approaches to dance are rare in the Hollywood musical. Because figure movement in musicals lacks the linguistic specificity of lyrics, viewers' comprehension of the movement's meaning will depend even more so on their background knowledge and familiarity with the movement tradition. While these danceploitation films lack more explicitly communicative musical numbers from the absence of diegetic songs, their dance sequences inarguably contribute information to plot and character development.

In particular, each film includes a competition or audition sequence that serves a causal narrative function. In the final dance competition in *Saturday Night Fever*, the specific moves executed by the various contestants are less important than leading the audience to perceive an inequality of performance skill between the pairs. Tony and his partner Stephanie perform a sequence that, while cleanly executed, is less impressive than that of the other contestants seen. The final couple—whom the announcer makes a point of saying are Puerto Rican—blow Tony away with their performance. Their number is more effective, but several choreographic choices significantly impact the viewer's reading of skill levels between the two: the female dancer demonstrates greater flexibility than Stephanie does, and the latter couple executes a wider range of dance steps at a much faster speed. The numbers appear choreographed to help a general audience observe the contrast, but it's most important for the narrative that Tony realize that the couple is better, as it helps him comprehend the racist motivations that lead to himself and Stephanie winning the contest. The Bee Gees' song lyrics from "More Than a Woman" that play as Tony and Stephanie perform help us notice the progression in the couple's relationship, but a categorical difference still exists between the way these films incorporate songs with dance numbers. The lyrical content from popular songs on the soundtrack contributes to the narrative clarity, but it's significant that not a single of these sung performances occurs diegetically or supradiegetically within the film.

Formal Synergy

Saturday Night Fever, *Flashdance*, and *Breakin'* engage peripherally with the musical genre's core formal relationships between narrative and number, particularly through the avoidance of diegetically sung numbers and supradiegetic spaces. Yet the crux of the later films' narrative conflict centers on dance sequences to communicate tensions related to the institutionalization and cultural perceptions of the portrayed dance forms. *Flashdance*'s main character Alex is a self-taught dancer who performs eclectic striptease to pay the bills but aspires to the world of ballet; *Breakin*'s protagonist Kelly is frustrated and uninspired by her prestigious modern jazz dance environment until she meets break-dancers Ozone and Turbo, who accept her into their community and join her in her attempts to pursue dance professionally. *Breakin'* replicates several aspects of *Flashdance*'s narrative formula as both correspondingly explore these narrative tensions.

These films emphasize that the protagonists' success results from the mobilization of elements from established and popular dance styles, in spite of the rigid structures of the concert dance world that initially exclude them. In *Flashdance*, Alex knows from the start of the film what she wants—to audition for the Pittsburgh Dance and Repertory Company—and we see her watching televised dance and imitating a *pirouette* at home before the "Maniac" workout montage begins. Her first visit to the company's space immediately others her in relation to the conservatory students; her hairstyle, clothing, and posture are placed in stark contrast to those of the classically trained dancers, and we realize she is entirely self-taught when the woman in the admissions office repeatedly tells applicants to "be sure and list all your years of dance education." In *Breakin'* Kelly is already part of the established modern jazz world in LA and has years of technique but feels uninspired and leaves her studio when its choreographer, Franko, makes a pass at her. Her introduction to the world of breakdancing and creative collaborations with Ozone and Turbo reinvigorates her passion for dance, leading her to insist to her agent James that her professional career hinges on the three of them performing together.

Alex, Kelly, Ozone, and Turbo also impress audition judges by demonstrating the expressive potential of their dancing, dancing that is repeatedly positioned by the films as deviating from concert dance norms. Unlike in *Saturday Night Fever*, where the dance competition opens Tony's eyes to the rampant corruption and discrimination around him, *Flashdance*'s and *Breakin'*s narratives exist in a diegesis where perseverance leads to personal validation and professional success.[7] In both, the protagonists must exploit the existing structures to break through bureaucracy; Alex's boss and romantic interest Nick uses his influence to get her an invitation-only audition at the conservatory and Kelly's agent gets the trio an audition slot by registering them as the "Allegro Vivace Dance Trio" and convincing Ozone and Turbo to wear tuxedos as their costumes. In both, the dancing wins over the judges. We can observe *Breakin'* repeating key elements of *Flashdance*'s formula: a row of older, white judges watch disapprovingly, dressed in bland costumes that paint them as particularly stuffy and conservative, while broad, sturdy tables separate them from the dancers. Both performances experience delays; Alex falls and must start over, and the rival choreographer Franko tries to prevent Kelly, Ozone, and Turbo from auditioning before Ozone begins to dance in spite of protestations. Alex and Ozone make a point of staring down the line of judges during their respective performances, returning their individual gazes. By the end of each number, the judges are beaming, moving to the music, and clapping in approval. The functions of cinematography and editing are more to clearly communicate the gradual process of winning over the judges than to showcase a continuous dance performance, yet we can observe the blending of ballet or jazz—the institutionalized dance forms the judges are hoping for—and the forms being introduced to the diegesis' conception of established concert dance: aerobics, gymnastics, erotic dancing, and breakdancing.

Both *Flashdance* and *Breakin'* emphasize the role of hard work and rehearsal as key to their characters' success through montages and performances leading up to the audition sequences. The underlying message is that "flashdance" and breakdancing have value and deserve recognition, but all three films also point to cultural perceptions about the people and communities performing them, with varying levels of nuance. *Breakin'* features dance innovators of color Adolfo "Shabba-Doo" Quinones (Ozone) and Michael "Boogaloo Shrimp" Chambers (Turbo) and argues for the legitimization of hip-hop at a time when mainstream media outlets like MTV were under-representing the work of African American artists (Griffin 2018: 295).

However, the overarching message of the film is that its protagonists succeed in gaining recognition for their craft by combining the formal rigor and professional discipline of jazz dance—which by the 1980s was more so associated with white performers—with the passion and energy of breakdancing. While both qualities are portrayed as positive attributes, this division associates white performers with prestige and performers of color with an "innate cultural expressiveness" that, in the musical genre especially, evokes traditions of minstrelsy (Garcia 2014: 52) and stereotypical racial representations (Monteyne 2013: 193, 194, 205–8).

The popular forms in these films like disco, breakdancing, and erotic dance are performed and consumed by ethnic minorities, members of the working class, and women, whereas ballroom, ballet, and modern jazz are the domain of predominantly white (male and female) bodies and the upper class. *Breakin'* also completely avoids race or ethnicity in its narrative, articulating conflicts in relation to class instead. *Variety*'s review draws attention to this choice; in addition to criticizing the noticeable replication of *Flashdance*'s conceit, it describes the plot as a cop-out: "filmmakers have also played it safe in focusing the action on a nice, middle class white girl, whereas breakdancing is almost exclusively the domain of blacks and Latinos," adding that the "script also shys [sic] away from the possibility of interracial romance so latent in the story" (McCarthy 1984: 526). The choice to avoid a Kelly-Ozone match makes Kelly a more independent, goal-oriented female protagonist, however, and her subsequent platonic and professional relationship with Ozone gives his character a more nuanced masculinity than the pervasively toxic portrayals of male characters in *Saturday Night Fever* and *Flashdance*.

Both films also ultimately conclude that performing dance on stage—in a commodified setting—is the marker of true achievement. Alex's professional strengths come from her blending of movement forms, but her goal is to perform within the established ballet tradition upheld by the repertory company. Ozone is resistant to Kelly's idea that they audition for commercial gigs, insisting that people can see their dancing by coming to Venice beach. To prove his point that dancing doesn't need a stage (or ticket sales) to have value, he takes Kelly to see talented break-dancers perform, pointing to their joyful faces as the true marker of success. Yet in the next scene, Kelly expresses her excitement to be "back in a real studio," and while we see Ozone's look of disappointment at her comment, that narrative thread does not return. Instead, the trio's successful audition leads to a whole show entitled "Street Jazz," a concise summation of the performative synergy driving these films.

Young, white, mainstream audiences were the target demographic for this film cycle; films like *Breakin'* featured performers of color, but that diversity did not necessarily extend to the rest of the crew, as Sean Griffin reminds us, resulting in the films' tendencies to "present a shallow and simplistic version of urban street life" (2018: 295). Collectively, these narrative decisions reinforce the films' status as exploitation projects, with popular music and dance serving as commodities that demand to be celebrated for their artistic, as well as their ancillary, potential.

Conclusions

The core films of this danceploitation cycle capitalize on the synergistic potential of popular dance in their marketing as well as their form. Established dance techniques are not inherently the problem, their narratives argue. Rather, it is the stuffy, patriarchal structures that perpetuate them—to the exclusion of newer steps, modes of expression, and bodies—that must be won over or removed from the equation. *Flashdance*'s and *Breakin*'s narratives suggest that it is the synergy between movement forms like ballet, ballroom, and jazz on the one hand and "flashdance" and breakdancing on the other that results in powerful performances worthy of celebration, so long as that celebration occurs within the traditional frame of the proscenium.

Saturday Night Fever, *Flashdance*, and *Breakin'* balance on the periphery of the musical. In doing so, they enrich our understanding of the relationship between musical content and exploitation cinema and challenge the musical's generic definitions. The inclusion of these films within the genre in both industry and scholarly categorizations, despite their avoidance of sung musical numbers, raises an important question: Do dance numbers alone make a musical? Steve Neale offers that "in varying measures and combinations, music, song and dance have been [the musical genre's] only essential ingredients" (2000: 105). Yet these elements are rarely weighted equally; scholarship on the musical genre tends to prioritize the presence of diegetically sung content over dancing in discussions of essential genre elements, even when that hierarchy is not explicitly articulated.[8] Troubling the generic status of danceploitation films can consequently help us to articulate the permeability of our chosen generic boundaries.

Notes

1. Feuer (1982), Prince (2000), Telotte (2002), Monteyne (2013), Kessler (2016), and Griffin (2018).
2. See also Griffin (2018: 279–301) and Nowell (2013).
3. Kessler (2016: 136); see also Shore (1984: 16) and Griffin (2018: 292).
4. See Monteyne (2013: 1–38) for an in-depth history of the white American entertainment industry's capitalization upon Black bodies and culture.
5. Rubin's articulation of musical diegetic shifts is based on his evaluation of plausibility, and he identifies impossible spaces, in particular, as those that deviate from the established diegetic context. Altman has coined the term "supradiegetic" to identify musical spaces that are neither diegetic or non-diegetic; for Altman this shift is predicated on the audio dissolve, in which the soundtrack shifts its priority from the (diegetically motivated) dialogue track to the (diegetically ambiguous) music track to which the characters sing.
6. See also Kessler (2016: 130), Griffin (2018: 282) and Telotte (2002: 48).
7. Monteyne sees hip-hop musicals as similarly rife with the "potential for utopian transformations" (2013: 143).
8. Rick Altman's influential articulation of the image-sound hierarchy reversing in musical numbers, in which sound dominates image, is one prominent example (1987: 71). See also Herzog (2010).

References

Altman, R. (1987), *The American Film Musical*, Bloomington: Indiana University Press.
Box Office Mojo (n.d.), "Flashdance (1983)." Available online: https://www.boxofficemojo.com/movies/?id=flashdance.htm (accessed June 21, 2019).
Box Office Mojo (n.d.), "Flashdance (1984)." Available online: https://www.boxofficemojo.com/movies/?id=breakin.htm (accessed June 21, 2019).
Box Office Mojo (n.d.), "Saturday Night Fever (1977)." Available online: https://www.boxofficemojo.com/movies/?id=saturdaynightfever.htm (accessed June 21, 2019).
"Break Dancing Goes from Harlem Streets to the Croisette in Pics" (1984), *Variety*, 9 May: 287.
Brodie, J. (1993), "Hollywood Bursting into Song," *Variety*, 27 December: 1, 75.
"Chatter: Paris" (1978), *Variety*, 5 April: 93.
Cohan, S. (2010), *The Sound of Musicals*, London: BFI.
Everett, T. (1977), "'Sat. Nite Fever' Click a Problem," *Variety*, 7 December: 67, 72.
Feuer, J. (1982), *The Hollywood Musical*, Bloomington: Indiana University Press.
"'Fever' Bally Dance Trips on Apartheid" (1978), *Variety*, 19 April: 2.
"'Flashdance' Blazes Homevid Trail for Par" (1983), *Variety*, 31 August: 8.
"Get Down & Boogie!" (1979), *Variety*, 17 January: 53, 62.
Har. (1984), "Film Reviews: Flashdance," *Variety*, 15 February: 24.
Herzog, A. (2010), *Dreams of Difference, Songs of the Same: The Musical Moment in Film*, Minneapolis: University of Minnesota Press.
Garcia, D. (2014), *The Migration of Musical Film: From Ethnic Margins to American Mainstream*, New Brunswick: Rutgers University Press.
Gold, R. (1983), "'Flashdance' Film, LP Feeding Off Each Other; Companies Hope for Repeat of 'SNF' Syndrome," *Variety*, 11 May: 3, 46.
Gold, R. (1984), "'Breakin' Still at Lotsa Screens; Album Soars, Sequel in Works," *Variety*, 13 June: 4, 35.
Griffin, S. (2018), *Free and Easy? A Defining History of the American Film Musical Genre*, Hoboken: Wiley-Blackwell.
Kessler, K. (2016), "Gone in a *Flash*(*dance*): The Estrangement of Diegetic Performance in the 1980s Teen Dance Film," in M. Evans and M. Fogarty (eds.), *Movies, Moves and Music: The Sonic World of Dance Films*, 129–49, Sheffield: Equinox.
Klein, A. (2011), *American Film Cycles: Reframing Genres, Screening Social Problems, and Defining Subcultures*, Austin: University of Texas Press.
McCarthy, T. (1983), "Film Reviews: Flashdance," *Variety*, 20 April: 12.
McCarthy, T. (1984), "Film Reviews: Breakin,'" *Variety*, 9 May: 526.
Monteyne, K. (2013), *Hip Hop On Film: Performance Culture, Urban Space, and Genre Transformation in the 1980s*, Jackson: University Press of Mississippi.
Mueller, J. (1984), "Fred Astaire and the Integrated Musical," *Cinema Journal*, 24 (1): 28–40.
Neale, S. (2000), *Genre and Hollywood*, New York: Routledge.
"New Music Seminar Examines Resurgence of Pop-Propelled Pics" (1984), *Variety*, 15 August: 6, 24.

"New York Sound Track" (1977), *Variety*, 30 November: 20.
"Night Club Reviews: Marina, Las Vegas" (1984), *Variety*, 1 February: 135.
"Night Club Reviews: Playboy Club, Chicago" (1978), *Variety*, 19 April: 131.
Nowell, R. (2013) "Hollywood Don't Skate: US Production Trends, Industry Analysis, and the Roller Disco Movie," *New Review of Film and Television Studies*, 11 (1): 73–91.
Prince, S. (2000), *New Pot of Gold: Hollywood under the Electronic Rainbow, 1980-1989*, Berkeley: University of California Press.
Rubin, M. (2002), "Busby Berkeley and the Backstage Musical," in S. Cohan (ed.), *Hollywood Musicals: The Film Reader*, 53–61, New York: Routledge.
"Sat. Night Fever Needs 200 Prints For UK Run" (1978), *Variety*, 12 April: 62.
Shore, M. (1984), *The Rolling Stone Book of Rock Video*, New York: Rolling Stone.
Smith, J. (2008), "Ancillary Markets – Recorded Music: Charting the Rise and Fall of the Soundtrack Album," in P. McDonald and J. Wasko (eds.), *The Contemporary Hollywood Film Industry*, 143–52, Oxford: Blackwell.
Telotte, J. (2002), "The New Hollywood Musical: From *Saturday Night Fever* to *Footloose*," in S. Neale (ed.), *Genre and Contemporary Hollywood*, 48–61, London: BFI.

Filmography

The Band Wagon (1953), [Film] Dir. Vincente Minnelli, USA: MGM.
Breakin' (1984), [Film] Dir. Joel Silberg, USA: Cannon Films.
Breakin' 2: Electric Boogaloo (1984), [Film] Dir. Sam Firstenberg, USA: Cannon Films.
Dirty Dancing (1987), [Film] Dir. Emile Ardolino. USA: Vestron Pictures.
Flashdance (1983), [Film] Dir. Adrian Lyne, USA: Paramount Pictures.
Footloose (1984), [Film] Dir. Herbert Ross, USA: Paramount Pictures.
Heavenly Bodies (1984), [Film] Dir. Lawrence Dane, Canada: MGM.
Meet Me in St Louis (1944), [Film] Dir. Vincente Minnelli, USA: MGM.
The Music Machine (1979), [Film] Dir. Ian Sharp, UK: Norfolk International Pictures.
Purple Rain (1984), [Film] Dir. Albert Magnoli, USA: Warner Bros.
Royal Wedding (1951), [Film] Dir. Stanley Donen, USA: MGM.
Salsa (1988), [Film] Dir. Boaz Davidson, USA: Cannon Films.
Saturday Night Fever (1977), [Film] Dir. John Badham, USA: Paramount Pictures.
Sergeant Pepper's Lonely Hearts Club Band (1978), [Film] Dir. Michael Schultz, USA: Universal Pictures.
Staying Alive (1983), [Film] Dir. Sylvester Stallone, USA: Paramount Pictures.

3

Pitching Utopia

Popular Music, Community, and Neoliberalism in the Choir Film

Eleonora Sammartino

Once one of the most successful and iconic genres of Hollywood cinema, the musical was seemingly experiencing another one of its cyclical deaths in the 1990s. Originally conceived as a musical, *I'll Do Anything* (1994) was turned into a straight comedy after unfavorable previews (Rosenbaum 2011). Yet, ten months later, *The Lion King* (1994) became Disney's most successful feature (Miller 2000: 53). This ambivalent reaction to two films belonging to the same genre speaks to debates that have characterized critical discourses on the musical in the last thirty years. As Sean Griffin notes, "the musical genre has been hampered for generations with a limited and limiting definition" coinciding with the integrated musical, which has led to ritualistic cries for the demise of the genre (2017: 2–3). Scholars have invoked different cycles to demonstrate how the musical endured in this period. Jane Feuer gestures toward the 1990s "international art musicals," a cycle of films that intertextually reference their studio antecedents through amateur performances (2010). While Miller traces new forms in the 1990s Disney animated musicals (2000), Cohan points to the 2000s youth-oriented TV productions like *High School Musical* (2006) (2010).

However, I argue that another significant yet still largely unacknowledged cycle emerged in the 1990s beginning with *Sister Act* (1992) and flourishing across media in the new millennium: the choir film.[1] Whereas choirs featured in specific numbers in the past, as in *Cabin in the Sky* (1943), in this cycle, the choir constitutes the defining semantic-syntactic element, driving narrative, and performative moments that employ popular music genres. This chapter explores the cycle of American choir films focusing on the franchises that bookend it, *Sister Act* and *Pitch Perfect*, and briefly tracing the importance of *Glee* (Fox, 2009–15) in its redefinition. Although European cinemas have produced a few choir films, such as *The Chorus/Les choristes* (2004) and *As It Is in Heaven/Så som i himmelen* (2004), these mainly use classical music and are aesthetically inconsistent. Conversely, the choir film has proliferated in American media, also comprising pictures like *The Fighting Temptations* (2003) and *Joyful Noise* (2012). The analysis of the marketing strategies of these products will highlight that an increasing transmedia synergy between film, television, and music industries has marked a closer association of the cycle with the musical, further characterized by a shift from a folk to show musical syntax. The chapter traces this relationship through the examination of the generic conventions at work in these films, such as the opposition between individual and community and that between artificiality and spontaneity. I argue that popular music plays a determinant role in the formation of utopian communities in this cycle, as also in the musical. However, the historical contextualization of the choir film within neoliberalism, from a political-economic practice to a hegemonic cultural discourse, will reveal the ambiguities that underlie this utopia, demonstrating how the communal ethos is supplanted by individualism, while reconsidering the boundaries of the genre.

From Comedy to Musical Hybrid

Despite Disney's success with animated musicals in the early 1990s, the box office failure of live-action productions such as *Newsies* (1992) prompted Hollywood to release films with musical moments, like *Sister Act*, avoiding any explicit association with the musical (Miller 2000: 51). The film was instead promoted as a comedy, as confirmed by screenwriter Paul Rudnick, who emphasizes the generic shift from an "all-out musical," with Bette Midler originally involved (2009). The poster achieves a comedic effect through the juxtaposition of Whoopi Goldberg in a habit and her bold pose, red high heels and sunglasses, playing on the plot premise that sees her as Las Vegas singer Deloris Van Cartier, hiding in a convent under witness protection. An alternative version with the strapline "A Hilariously Divine Comedy!" makes this categorization even more overt. The trailer also relies on physical gags and one-liners rather than musical moments.

Significantly, the release of the twentieth-anniversary DVD in 2012 was publicized through a series of clips that foreground musical numbers, implicitly demonstrating this generic ambiguity. This shift in marketing practices emerged from a changed media landscape, wherein the success of music(al) programs on television had created an appetite for the genre. *High School Musical* and *Glee* revived the musical by remediating its conventions through popular music (Cohan 2010), in a transmedia continuum from the 1980s PBS telecasts of Broadway shows to the popularity of amateur performers on social media (Griffin 2017). Reality TV has further contributed to a larger market of audio-visual entertainment through formats imported from the UK that highlight competition, mainstream music and dance, as in *Dancing with the Stars* (CBS, 2005–present) and *American Idol* (Fox, 2002–2016; NBC, 2018–present) (Donnelly and Carroll 2017; Griffin 2017).

The link between the musical and reality television clearly emerges in *Glee*, which debuted in 2009 in the time slot right after *American Idol* on Fox and crucially reshaped the genre. Creator Ryan Murphy has recognized the connection between the two for their use of popular songs, while reluctantly associating *Glee* with the musical by justifying the presence of the numbers as either on-stage performances or as the characters' fantasies (Schneider 2008; Wyatt 2009). Such a rationalization speaks to anxieties over the commercial viability of the genre and is linked to a narrow ahistorical definition of the musical as integrated, which has persisted in public discourses despite an emphasis on musical performances in response to industrial transformations in the 1970s–80s (Griffin 2017: 279). The "Pilot" commercial plays comedically on the tropes of the teen show, echoed by the promotional posters that classify it as a "comedy for the underdog." However, the success of the first season, built upon the soundtrack sales (Wyatt 2009), led to a shift toward the musical, as demonstrated by the promos for the season one DVDs, which prominently present musical numbers. The wealth of transmedia products generated by the series, such as an international live tour, the reality show *The Glee Project* (Oxygen, 2011–12), merchandise and music sheets are a testament to the success of *Glee* and its contribution to the redefinition of the cycle.

This realignment is evident in *Pitch Perfect*. The poster of the first film ironically interpellates contemporary teen shows through costumes and poses of the ensemble, whereas the tagline "Get Pitch Slapped" hints to the world of a cappella choirs, relying on the audience's preexisting knowledge granted by music(al) TV programs. Unlike *Sister Act*, the trailer gives space to the protagonists singing in an extended clip from the "Riff Off" competition but makes clear that the numbers are motivated in a performative context, as in *Glee*.

Noticeably, both *Sister Act* and *Pitch Perfect* successfully originated soundtrack albums ("Gold & Platinum"; Lipshutz 2015). Since the 1980s, such synergy between the film and music industries has become a predominant strategy for the cross-promotion of products, adopted by media conglomerates incorporating record labels, film studios, and TV channels. The emergence of MTV in 1981 provided another marketing platform, leading to the widespread presence of "localized" musical moments in high-concept films like *Top Gun* (1986) that could be easily retooled for music videos (Wyatt 1994). While the conversion from analogue to digital was taking place in the music industry, *Glee* benefited from the boom of iTunes to release singles at an unprecedented volume and speed, making it the most featured act in the Hot 100 Billboard chart (Unterberger 2019). The fundamental role played by popular music in *Glee* can also be traced in the choir films.

Sister Act: Folk Values and Unstable Utopias

As in the classical musical, the opposition between popular and classical music is one of the binaries that structure the cycle, self-reflexively celebrating itself by favoring the former term (Feuer 1993: 55–6). In *Sister Act*, Deloris is directly associated with popular music through the opening medley of 1960s Motown songs. However, the performance by Deloris and her backup singers in a second-rate casino is marked as unsuccessful because of their lack of spontaneity and audience engagement, illustrated through wide shots and tracking camera movements. This is paralleled by the first performance of "Hail Holy Queen" by the nuns' choir during mass. Similar camerawork shows a few drowsy parishioners, while medium close-ups of the choir amplify their discordant voices on the soundtrack. The classical religious repertoire is equally a failure.

The nuns start harmonizing only when Deloris takes over the choir. She updates "Hail Holy Queen" through pop inflections, producing a gospel version that fills the church with younger, engaged worshippers. The subsequent performances increasingly embrace pop music, with the revised "My Guy" and "I Will Follow Him," both featured in the opening medley, wherein the "guy"/"him" is God. The first performance of the reformed choir is set in contrast with both previous unsuccessful numbers. It begins as a classic rendition of "Hail Holy Queen," intercutting close shots of the choir to those of Deloris directing. Editing and camerawork display the hierarchical structure of the choir, with Deloris in control of the singers. After a brief pause, the song picks up the rhythm, with hand clapping, the use of tambourines, and some choreography. Dynamic crane and tracking shots unite the choir and Deloris, doubling the profilmic movement while creating a joyful sense of community.

The use of gospel, here, is significant. Gospel is rooted in spirituals sung by Black slaves in response to white oppression in the nineteenth century. This type of music is characterized by an active participation from the community through hand clapping, foot stomping, body movement determining the rhythm of the singing, and a call-and-response structure between the soloist and the other participants (Burnim 2006: 52–4). Following the 1930s Great Migration, gospel developed in urban centers, deeply influenced by secular music (Southern 1997: 460). In turn, gospel informed soul music like Motown during the Civil Rights movement, as in the continuous engagement of the singers with the audience based on emotional and physical intensity (Maultsby 2006: 278–9). The performative characteristics of gospel and soul foster a sisterhood between the nuns, through Deloris's mediation.

Popular music also allows the choir to reach out to the estranged inner-city San Francisco neighborhood where the convent is located, mainly populated by a Black and Latino community. Run-down adult shops, seedy bars, and disaffected youth stereotypically conform to the representation of "the hood" perpetuated by the media since the late 1970s (Rose 1994: 33). Neoliberal policies implicitly represent the cause of such socioeconomic decline. The embracement of neoliberalism as "a theory of political economic practices" that supports private property rights, the free market and trade during the Reagan administration (1981–9) meant a significant withdrawal of the state from welfare provisions while responsibility for well-being was transferred to individuals (Harvey 2005: 2; 76). Within this economic strategy, federal urban policies were halted and grants cut, leading to a decreased assistance for low-income households and community development, and the consequent increase of homelessness and urban underclass that mainly affected the Black and Latino population (Stoetz 1992). The montage during "Just a Touch of Love" shows the nuns opening the gates of their convent, bonding through singing and dancing, while cleaning up the neighborhood and providing a space for the people. Community is key to the folk musical subgenre, traditionally rooted in a mythical Americana (Altman 1987: 127).

However, as Martha Shearer demonstrates, harmonious communities also characterized city-set, postwar musicals, responding to the anxieties produced by the contemporary urban context (2016: 46). Through popular music, the community experiences "what utopia would feel like" (Dyer 2002: 20), mediating a problem like societal fragmentation, created by capitalism, by offering seemingly unproblematic and capitalist solutions (Dyer 2002: 27).

While the nuns' social solidarity would seemingly oppose neoliberalism, they are, however, also seen collecting money during the montage, relying on the community to raise the sum required to save the convent from closure. The problems caused by neoliberalism are thus temporarily resolved through an entrepreneurial action, an expression of neoliberalism in itself.

At the start of *Sister Act 2* (1993), the same community is described as "tired, worn, and despairing" by the Mother Superior, who asks Deloris to become a teacher at the local St Francis's Academy. A community space is again under threat: the school administrator explains that the land would be more profitable as a parking lot. The disaffection experienced by the community is evident from the state of disarray of the school and from a series of scenes set at the street corner, a place of socialization and performance for the teenagers. The neighborhood also functions as a sign of authenticity and legitimation (Rose 1994: 10–11), with which the school choir is associated through their use of rap music. This emerges in the final number, in which the choir directed by Deloris performs at the state competition, hoping to win the cash prize that could save the school from closure, after having again relied on the community to raise the funds for the trip.

One of the tropes of the choir film is the crosscutting between the competitors' performances and the choir backstage. The main competitor is, however, emphasized through longer screen time, raising the stakes. The St. Francis's choir is up against a militaristic, white, wealthy group, who sing their same piece, "Ode to Joy/Joyful, Joyful," in a classic and static fashion, framed en masse through long shots and identical robes. On the other hand, Deloris's choir starts with a soul solo that then becomes a collective rap mash-up with Janet Jackson's "What Have You Done for Me Lately." The performance appears spontaneous with the energetic and yet coordinated movements, masking the labor required to produce it, as in the musical (Feuer 1981: 165). The use of rap, through which the students habitually express themselves, further emphasizes their authenticity. The choir thus fosters a collective identity as a community, which extends to the diegetic audience seen clapping along, mediating the response of the film spectators (Feuer 1981: 169). Like classical musicals, the choir film employs the affective investment of the internal audience to give a sense of shared experience, as if in a live performance (Feuer 1993: 26–8). Unlike their competitors, the students are also individualized through different costumes that express their personality and the alternation of the wider and closer shots showcasing the talents of smaller groups of singers. As individuals, the students are integrated within a utopian community.

This utopia is, however, presented as a temporary solution to the problems of the narrative. A conversation between student Rita and Sister Mary Robert hints to its limitations: despite the nun's encouragement to pursue a singing career, Rita asserts that the disadvantage experienced as an inner-city Black teen would not allow for this. Tracing a connection with the early 1990s "hood films," wherein crime and rap are associated in social problem narratives, Woods considers dance in teen dance and breakdance films as "the means of social, financial and emotional escape from a life of limited, class-driven opportunity" (2016: 62).

The choir has a comparable function. However, the solutions offered by the duology are presented as ambiguous because they are based on the appropriation and commodification of Black cultural expressions in mainstream culture (Knight 2002: 32). Black forms of music such as gospel and rap are employed to convey authenticity and spontaneity, allowing for "collective, emotional expressions of musicality" while disavowing the contextual social realities, as in the tradition of all-Black folk musicals (Garcia 2014: 46). The community itself becomes commodified as a financial source.

Despite the final choir number, the credits of the first film show a montage of magazine covers celebrating Deloris as a star. Her experience with the choir is thus turned into profit in the industry, as also shown in the opening of the sequel, a big production number performed in a premiere casino that recaps the events of the first movie. While popular music allows for a temporary utopia, the films also problematize it by adopting neoliberal measures in reaction to neoliberal politics and ultimately promoting individualism. This is also at the core of *Pitch Perfect*, in which neoliberalism is mediated through contemporary popular feminism, demonstrating its pervasiveness as a dominant discourse in popular culture in the last twenty years.

Pitch Perfect: A Neoliberal Sisterhood

The tension between individual and community characterizes the *Pitch Perfect* trilogy, from the integration of Beca (Anna Kendrick) into the all-female a cappella college choir Barden Bellas in *Pitch Perfect* (2012) to the choice between a solo career and her friends in *Pitch Perfect 3* (2017). This binary ritualistically negotiates societal conflicts in the musical, providing resolutions through narratives of integration (Schatz 1981: 25). Beca's personal ambition is opposed in each film to the community represented by the Bellas within the syntax of the show musical (Altman 1987: 202), explicitly marked through the "putting on a show" narrative and the alternation between the stage and the liminality of the backstage (Altman 1987: 208). The influence of *Glee* and reality shows can be traced in this shift, especially in the structural logic of the competition. TV programs also showcase amateur or semi-professional performers, like the Bellas, another staple of the classical musical, which defined popular entertainment as folk art through communal participation (Feuer 1993: 13–14). Yet, the foregrounding of individualism, more pronounced than in *Sister Act*, gestures toward the entrenchment of neoliberal values in the contemporary context.

As in *Sister Act*, popular music shapes utopia, here predicated upon the opposition between older and newer forms of pop rather than on the classical/popular binary, negotiated in the first film through the contrast between Aubrey and Beca. The former leads the choir favoring a repertoire of 1970s–90s songs, which is revealed as worn by the passive reaction of judges and audiences when the Bellas perform. An aspiring music producer, Beca creates mash-ups on her laptop. The use of technology marks her music as artificial, connected with a sense of isolation, as demonstrated in a short scene in which she is mixing on the college lawn, sonically insulated by the earphones while the camera moves around her to show the physical distance from the others. However, when infused with the positive and communal values of the genre, her use of technology and musical eclecticism leads the Bellas to the victory, as Deloris does in *Sister Act*.

Beca displays signs of spontaneity in the "Riff Off," where she leads the acappella community to sing together. After a moment of bonding between the Bellas, in which each one recognizes their strengths, both Beca and Aubrey understand the importance of collaboration and innovation. The successful result of the hybridization of older and contemporary hits is shown in the final number, in which the Bellas harmonize as a group, with each member contributing their specific talents, such as Lilly's beatboxing or Chloe's base notes. Free movements and personalized costumes further characterize the performance as authentic, comparable to *Sister Act 2*.

Thus, Beca fosters a sisterhood (i.e., a community) with the other Bellas through music. This relationship is strengthened in *Pitch Perfect 2* (2015). The final performance establishes the group as a family when generations of former Bellas join them on stage to sing "Flashlight." The message of mutual support expressed in the lyrics is echoed in their performance, as they look at each other. The camera particularly focuses on the exchange between Beca and Emily, the newest recruit, and Emily and her mother, a former Bella, thus highlighting intergenerational continuity. Unlike classical musicals, this form of integration does not entail the withdrawal of the individual from the homosocial group to which they belong (Altman 1987). The utopian community here coincides with the sorority, also foregrounded through the secondary role played by heterosexual romance in the films, similarly to *Sister Act*.

The importance of sisterhood is connected with the adoption of a feminist stance, acknowledged by ironically addressing forms of sexism. In making gender inequality "spectacularly visible," the films represent an example of popular feminism, wherein being visible becomes an end in itself, without questioning the structures that produce inequality. Like postfeminism, popular feminism widely circulates through media, tapping into neoliberal values like empowerment, entrepreneurialism, and self-confidence. However, in embracing liberal feminism, this differs from postfeminism, which is characterized by the idea of achieved equality in a disavowal of feminist politics (Banet-Weiser 2018). This relationship with feminism can be traced in the intergenerational connection that is established in the final number, where different generations of Bellas coexist. Yet, both postfeminism and popular feminism privilege the visibility of white, middle-class, heterosexual women as representative of a universal gender identity (Banet-Weiser 2018: 14). This emerges in the franchise through the commodification of the racial, ethnic, and sexual identities of characters like Cynthia Rose and Florencia as a source of comedy.[2]

The neoliberal context is mainly addressed in *Pitch Perfect 3* through the Bellas' directionless experience in their lives. A montage reveals their unstable work lives, marked by misfiring and exhaustion, when they meet the new formation, in which Emily's presence grants continuity after their graduation. This stresses their individual failures and obsolescence, exacerbated by meeting the younger Bellas, analogously to the "time panic" that characterizes postfeminist culture, wherein women are defined through different life stages of productivity that can be fulfilled through the negotiation of paid work, heterosexual romance, and motherhood in an essentialization of femininity (Negra 2009: 47).

Responsibility for one's destiny is displaced onto individuals as self-governing subjects, a form of regulation that is particularly directed toward women, making neoliberalism *"always already gendered"* (Gill and Scharff 2013: 7; italics in the source).

This crisis is superseded by a newfound sense of self when they sing together again. Their sisterhood proves to be a source of resilience, allowing each one to bounce back from the challenges of contemporary life, typical of this post-recessionary discourse that particularly targets middle-class women (Gill and Orgad 2018: 478). When DJ Khaled offers Beca the chance of a solo career, the sisterhood gives her the strength to make a choice, bolstered by each Bella's resolution to start their own business. The Bellas are thus empowered to be better economic individuals, reinventing themselves as entrepreneurs. In offering a sense of stability, the choir is further invested with the "promise of happiness," representing something good around which the group coheres, establishing an affective relationship with it by habituating their bodies to orient themselves toward it (Ahmed 2010: 35). Visually, this emerges in the interaction of the Bellas during their performances, such as "I Don't Like It, I Love It." Wide shots highlight the Bellas turning their bodies toward each other, particularly in the Berkeley-esque overhead shots that show the singers in a circle, moving to face each other while the audience surrounds them.

However, the emphasis on Beca's individual journey throughout the franchise, not relegated only to credits and prologue as for Deloris, ultimately reinforces neoliberal individualism and shows its widespread hold in contemporary culture. In a variation of the formula, the final number is not anticipated by an interrupted group performance but by Beca playing with DJ Khaled's console during a party. The song she improvises is performed in the finale, which negotiates the tension between individual and community. Wide shots of the amphitheater where she is about to debut as a solo act, immersed in golden lights, create a magical atmosphere. As the camera stays close to her, Beca sings her cover of George Michael's "Freedom! '90." The Bellas are in the front row, looking proud and emotional. As Beca is about to sing the chorus, she brings them all on stage. Close shots show them embracing, holding hands, and harmonizing together as they sing in a final promise of happiness. Yet, while this points toward a resolution in a utopian community, nonrepresentational elements make Beca emerge as a star. Whereas the Bellas all wear black, her golden dress and foregrounded position make her stand out on stage, especially in wide shots where the others nearly disappear into the background. The song also marks her individual success since it is sung in first person, gesturing toward Beca's own "Freedom" as she leaves the Bellas behind. The final group hug is the only last bit of utopia left.

Conclusion

Responding to the early 1990s crisis of the film musical, defined as integrated, critical debates have traced various cycles that have helped the genre proliferate since, such as the Disney Renaissance films or the international art musicals. Despite its neglected position in such debates, the choir film has been, however, fundamental in the revitalization of the musical in relation to both the industrial and the socioeconomic contexts that engendered it. While *Sister Act* could not be openly marketed as a musical because it was made at the height of the crisis, its folk elements revealed its connections with it. The influence of successful music(al) TV programs, such as reality competitions and, in particular, *Glee*, has subsequently contributed to a more overt association of the cycle with the musical and the shift toward the show musical syntax, paving the way for the popularity of *Pitch Perfect*. From both an industrial and a generic perspective, popular music has emerged as a fundamental factor, allowing for the currency of the cycle across media, as demonstrated through the success of soundtrack albums, as well as for the mediation of the conventions of the musical. Qualities like authenticity and spontaneity are associated with popular music even in this cycle, enabling the formation of utopian communities as sisterhoods among women. Nevertheless, the analysis has highlighted the key relationship between the cycle and the contemporary socioeconomic context in the reconfiguration of generic conventions in favor of individual narratives, exposing the untenability of utopia. Whereas the effects of neoliberalism as a political-economic practice are revealed through the social decline of the neighborhood in *Sister Act*, the entrepreneurial answer of the community and its commodification for individual success show the embracement of neoliberal culture, which promotes self-government and self-empowerment. The pervasiveness of neoliberalism as a hegemonic cultural discourse is foregrounded in *Pitch Perfect*, where it informs popular feminism and entrepreneurial individualism, without being questioned. As the musical continues to experience a period of revitalization on film and TV, the choir cycle is still positioned at the margins of the genre but reveals itself to be a useful tool to historically rethink generic and media boundaries while also demonstrating the enduring popularity of the musical.

Notes

1 Amanda Ann Klein defines "cycle" as a group of films sharing images and themes released in a relatively brief period because of their commercial viability and public discourses surrounding them (2011: 4).
2 The treatment of Florencia is exemplary of this. Originally from Guatemala, she often deadpans about her experiences of kidnapping, drug trafficking, and hunger to highlight the Bellas' white privilege whenever they complain about their lives. Yet, this solidifies negative stereotypes associated with Latin immigrants.

References

Ahmed, S. (2010), "Happy Objects," in M. Gregg and G.J. Seigworth (eds.), *The Affect Theory Reader*, 29–51, Durham and London: Duke University Press.
Altman, R. (1987), *The American Film Musical*, London; Bloomington: Indiana University Press.
Banet-Weiser, S. (2018), *Empowered: Popular Feminism and Popular Misogyny*, Durham; London: Duke University Press.
Burnim, M. V. (2006), "Religious Music," in M.V. Burnim and P. K. Maultsby (eds.), *African American Music: An Introduction*, 51–77, New York; London: Routledge.
Cohan, S. (2010), "Introduction: How Do You Solve a Problem Like the Film Musical?" in S. Cohan (ed.), *The Sound of Musicals*, 54–65, London: BFI.
Donnelly, K.J., and B. Carroll (2017), "Introduction: Reimagining the Contemporary Musical in the Twenty-first Century," in K.J. Donnelly and B. Carroll (eds.), *Contemporary Musical Film*, 1–10, Edinburgh: Edinburgh University Press.
Dyer, R. (2002), "Entertainment and Utopia," in *Only Entertainment*, 2nd edn, 19–35, New York: Routledge.
Feuer, J. (1981), "The Self-Reflective Musical and the Myth of Entertainment," in R. Altman (ed.), *Genre: The Musical. A Reader*, 159–74, London: Routledge & Kegan Paul.
Feuer, J. (1993), *The Hollywood Musical*, 2nd edn, Basingstoke: Macmillan.
Feuer, J. (2010), "The International Art Musical: Defining and Periodizing Post-1980s Musicals," in S. Cohan (ed.), *The Sound of Musicals*, 54–65, London: BFI.
Garcia, D.J. (2014), *The Migration of Musical Film: From Ethnic Margins to American Mainstream*, New Brunswick and London: Rutgers University Press.
Gill, R., and C. Scharff (2013), "Introduction," in R. Gill and C. Scharff (eds.), *New Femininities: Postfeminism, Neoliberalism and Subjectivity*, 1–19, Basingstoke: Palgrave Macmillan.
Gill, R. and S. Orgad (2018), "The Amazing Bounce-Backable Woman: Resilience and the Psychological Turn in Neoliberalism," *Sociological Research Online*, 23 (2): 477–95.

"Gold & Platinum," Riaa.com (n.d.) Available online: https://www.riaa.com/gold-platinum/?tab_active=default-award&se=sister+act#search_section (accessed June 21, 2019).

Griffin, S. (2017), *Free and Easy? A Defining History of the American Film Musical Genre*, Chichester: Wiley-Blackwell.

Harvey, D. (2005), *A Brief History of Neoliberalism*, Oxford: Oxford University Press.

Klein, A.A. (2011), *American Film Cycles: Reframing Genres, Screening Social Problems, and Defining Subcultures*, Austin: University of Texas Press.

Knight, A. (2002), *Disintegrating the Musical: Black Performance and American Musical Film*, Durham: Duke University Press.

Lipshutz, J. (2015), "Why Are Soundtracks Suddenly Back? Because They're Better Than Ever," *Billboard.com*, 21 April. Available online: https://www.billboard.com/articles/columns/pop-shop/6538822/soundtracks-revival- furious-7-analysis (accessed June 21, 2019).

Maultsby, P.K. (2006), "Soul," in M.V. Burnim and P.K. Maultsby (eds.), *African American Music: An Introduction*, 277–98, New York; London: Routledge.

Miller, M. (2000), "Of Tunes and Toons: The Musical of the 1990s," in W.W. Dixon (ed.), *Film Genre 2000: New Critical Essays*, 45–62, Albany: State University of New York Press.

Negra, D. (2009), *What a Girl Wants? Fantasizing the Reclamation of Self in Postfeminism*, Abingdon: Routledge.

Rose, T. (1994), *Black Noise: Rap Music and Black Culture in Contemporary America*, Hanover: University Press of New England.

Rosenbaum, J. (2011), "Song and Dance I'll Do Anything: The Musical," *Film Comment*, 47 (1): 28–9. Available online: https://search.proquest.com/docview/852579184?accountid=11862 (accessed June 21, 2019).

Rudnick, P. (2009), "Fun with Nuns. Selling Hollywood on an Updated Convent Comedy," *The New Yorker*, July 20. Available online: http://www.newyorker.com/magazine/2009/07/20/fun-with-nuns (accessed June 13, 2019).

Schatz, T. (1981), *Hollywood Genres: Formulas, Filmmaking and the Studio System*, Boston: McGraw Hill.

Schneider, M. (2008), "Fox Greenlights 'Glee' Pilot," *Variety*, 23 July. Available online: https://web.archive.org/web/20091014004435/http://www.variety.com/article/VR111 7989408.html?categoryid=14&cs=1 (accessed June 30, 2019).

Shearer, M. (2016), *New York City and the Hollywood Musical: Dancing in the Streets*, London: Palgrave Macmillan.

Southern, E. (1997), *The Music of Black Americans: A History*, 3rd edn, New York and London: W.W. Norton.

Stoetz, D. (1992), "The Fall of the Industrial City: The Reagan Legacy for Urban Policy," *The Journal of Sociology and Social Welfare*, 19 (1): 149–67.

Unterberger, A. (2019), "Ten Years Ago, One of the Biggest Forces in Billboard Hot 100 History Debuted on Primetime Television," *Billboard*, 16 May. Available online: https://www.billboard.com/biz/articles/news/tv-film/8511978/ten-years-ago-one-of- the-biggest-forces-in-billboard-hot-100 (accessed June 30, 2019).

Woods, F. (2016), "Space, Authenticity and Utopia in the Hip-Hop Teen Dance Film," in M. Evans and M. Fogarty (eds.), *Movies, Moves and Music: The Sonic World of Dance Films. Genre, Music and Sound*, 61–77, Sheffield: Equinox.

Wyatt, E. (2009), "Not That High School Musical," *The New York Times*, 15 May. Available online: https://www.nytimes.com/2009/05/17/arts/television/17wyat.html (accessed June 30, 2019).

Wyatt, J. (1994), *High Concept: Movies and Marketing in Hollywood*, Austin: University of Texas Press.

Filmography

American Idol (2002–2016; 2018–), [TV Program] Fox, NBC.
As It Is in Heaven (*Så som i himmelen*) (2004), [Film] Dir. Kay Pollak, Sweden: Sonet Film.
Cabin in the Sky (1943), [Film] Dir. Vincente Minnelli, USA: Metro-Goldwyn-Mayer.
The Chorus (*Les choristes*) (2004), [Film] Dir. Christophe Barratier, France, Germany, Switzerland: Pathé Distribution.
Dancing with the Stars (2005–), [TV Program] CBS.
The Fighting Temptations (2003), [Film] Dir. Jonathan Lynn, USA: Paramount Pictures.
Glee (2009–15), [TV Program] Fox.
The Glee Project (2011–12), [TV Program] Oxygen.
I'll Do Anything (1994), [Film] Dir. James L. Brooks, USA: Columbia Pictures.
Joyful Noise (2012), [Film] Dir. Todd Graff, USA: Warner Bros.
The Lion King (1994), [Film] Dir. Roger Allers and Rob Minkoff, USA: Buena Vista Pictures.
Newsies (1992), [Film] Dir. Kenny Ortega, USA: Buena Vista Pictures.
Pitch Perfect (2012), [Film] Dir. Jason Moore, USA: Universal Pictures.
Pitch Perfect 2 (2015), [Film] Dir. Elizabeth Banks, USA: Universal Pictures.
Pitch Perfect 3 (2017), [Film] Dir. Trish Sie, USA: Universal Pictures.
Sister Act (1992), [Film] Dir. Emile Ardolino, USA: Buena Vista Pictures.
Sister Act 2: Back in the Habit (1993), [Film] Dir. Bill Duke, USA: Buena Vista Pictures.
Top Gun (1986), [Film] Dir. Tony Scott, USA: Paramount Pictures.

4

E-Q-U-I-T-Y

Generic Boundaries, Gender, and Real Estate in the *Magic Mike* Films

Martha Shearer

On their release, critics routinely compared the *Magic Mike* films to musicals. For Amy Taubin, *Magic Mike* (2015) has "the optimism of a 1930s Depression-era musical about a bunch of kids who fix up a barn and put on a show," with the crucial difference that the star "doesn't want to make it to Hollywood—or rather Miami, the stripper's paradise," but would "rather leave showbiz behind so he can devote himself to making custom furniture" (2015: 185). For Manohla Dargis, the musical can be seen "sneaking in sideways" in the *Magic Mike* films, "where the music is canned and the dancing grindingly dirty" (2016). And for Armond White, *Magic Mike XXL* (2015) is "an odd genre hybrid—a new-millennium non-musical," but where "a proper musical uses song and dance to express its characters' feelings, the *Magic Mike* franchise choreographs self-denial" (2015). For each of these critics, the *Magic Mike* films are built around musical performance and yet remain not-quite musicals; they connect the films to the genre in order to deny their place in the category, where they do not entirely fit.

Part of the problem is the films' emphasis on dance. Jane Feuer notes that "intuitively, we call a film a musical when it contains diegetic singing," and yet "we are not so concerned about diegetic dancing," such that the generic status of a film like *Dirty Dancing* (1987) is unclear (2013: 59). As Jenny Oyallon-Koloski discusses elsewhere in this volume, the cycle of dance films produced in the late 1970s held a similarly ambiguous relationship to the musical due to their lack of singing but also their reluctance to break with the realist codes of the narrative. Indeed, J. P. Telotte argues that such "musically oriented films" depict worlds in which song and dance are "clearly circumscribed," taking place "usually within a restricted arena, a limited space the boundaries of which weigh heavily on the moment of song or dance" (Telotte 2002: 48). As Telotte suggests, a key distinction between the classical musical and the dance film is spatial, with the latter's performances much more rationalized and confined to stages. The *Magic Mike* films are an especially useful outgrowth of this tradition for their self-conscious play with generic boundaries, speaking to key tensions between the musical's core, traditional aesthetic strategies and the contemporary world.

Because of the need to secure performance space, musicals are often secretly about real estate: plots about acquiring performance space or threats to performance space. Richard Dyer has discussed how the musical's key features (dance, song) enact this acquisition of space on an aesthetic level:

> Dancing is by definition about bodies in space, about how bodies relate to other bodies, how they move through space, how they make use of or submit to the environment around them. Less obviously, singing too is about space; singing carries into space in a different way from speech and different kinds of singing, from crooning to belting, impose themselves differently on the world around the singer. (2002: 39)

For Dyer, the musical has "at the heart of [its] construction of race" a "colonial structure of feeling: expansion into space, control over what's in that space, incorporation of what's there into white agendas" (2002: 41). That colonial structure of feeling is not only at the heart of the musical's construction of race, however, but also more generally how it expresses a broader (and clearly racialized) impulse toward the ownership of space, evident in both aesthetic and narrative terms. One of the ways that impulse manifested during the studio era, for example, was in neighborhood musicals in which musical numbers are used to express community ownership over spaces threatened offscreen, and very occasionally onscreen, with redevelopment (Shearer 2016).

Since the 1970s, however, musicals have been made in a transformed spatial context. In the wake of decades of disinvestment, there were concerted efforts to make the built environment a source of profit, with neoliberal urban policy being to effectively turn over cities to developers and speculative financiers. This led to a huge expansion of capital flows in real estate; in 2006, the sociologist Kevin Fox Gotham noted efforts to "deterritorialize real estate by enmeshing the financing of residential and commercial property with global capital markets," efforts by the state to increase the liquidity of what is a fixed, immobile, and risky kind of commodity (2006: 233). With the increasing volatility in the real estate sector that came with the neoliberal turn (leading, of course, to a global financial crisis), the musical's secret preoccupation with real estate has become much more explicit. A number of musicals and dance films rely on an understanding of a relationship between performance space and the profit to be made from that space: *Honey* (2003)'s subplot about the need to rent performance space, *Burlesque* (2010)'s club being threatened with redevelopment and then saved through the acquisition of air rights, *Step Up Revolution* (2012)'s use of dance to protest the bulldozing of a working-class Latino neighborhood to build a luxury hotel.

In this chapter, I argue that the musical's historically secret preoccupation with real estate is also one that structures the *Magic Mike* films and the differences between them. The two films have radically different approaches to the staging of musical performance, and the second has received a great deal of attention for how those performances cater to female audiences such that "the frame becomes a space for the cultivation and indulgence of female desire" (Klein 2020: 267). What I want to draw attention to, however, is the intersection of genre with gender and space, which the two films address in notably distinct ways. The first film is set largely in and around a strip club in Tampa, where all of that film's performance sequences take place. But it is structured around the strippers' imminent move to their very own Miami strip club. While *Magic Mike* concludes on the brink of that move, *Magic Mike XXL* reunites some of those strippers after its failure for a road trip to a stripper convention at Myrtle Beach, South Carolina. This chapter discusses the *Magic Mike* films as boundary cases, considering how the two individual films and the ways they speak to each other engage with the musical's traditional, canonical concerns—entertainment, the spectacle of the (male) body, work, space—suggesting that they turn on the question of whether the musical's core generic strategies have continued viability in a neoliberal urban context.

Magic Mike

Midway through *Magic Mike*, the leader of its central strip troupe, Dallas (Matthew McConaughey), announces that the Kings of Tampa will imminently become "the cock-rocking kings of 4,000 square feet of Miami prime-time beachfront real estate, motherfuckers!" N. D. B. Connolly notes that Miami has been associated with dreams of real estate success since its founding in the 1890s. For investors, boosters, hoteliers, and real estate developers, it was a place "where one made fast fortunes" (2014: 5). Connolly argues that Miami is central to an American identification of real estate with freedom, "the latest form of landed investment in a country built through slavery, racial exclusion, and repeated acts of land-based expropriation" (2014: 7). But it also has a pronounced history of real estate bubbles, from the Florida Land Boom of the 1920s to the more recent subprime mortgage crisis. Anette Baldauf argues that the housing boom that led to that crisis relied on a "culture of speculation" especially evident in Florida, a "Wild West mentality" that encouraged "all kinds of people to buy and sell houses fast" and left the state "dotted with deserted construction sites, ghost subdivisions, and roads that lead nowhere" (2010: 227). According to *Forbes*, in 2012 Miami had the greatest real estate bubble of any city in the United States after 2000 (Dent 2012), drawing investors from Latin America and Wall Street, as well as money laundering from drug cartels.

Dallas begins his Miami announcement by declaring, "We've been talking a lot about the markets." Indeed, the strippers are both economically marginalized and in thrall to entrepreneurialism and the culture of speculation. Mike claims that the reason he has yet to launch his furniture business is that "the market hasn't really hit the sweet spot yet." Dallas says that if he had a son, he would not send him to school, but instead sit him in front of the flashy financial talk show *Mad Money* (CNBC 2005–). Tito (Adam Rodriguez) tells a woman at a party that he has been reading the financial advice bestseller *Rich Dad Poor Dad*. Their marginalization is strikingly gendered, consistent with Diane Negra and Yvonne Tasker's contention that in recessionary culture, men have been positioned as the "primary victims" (Negra and Tasker 2014: 2). While the film's women are in stable employment and largely in traditionally feminized clerical labor— Brooke (Cody Horn), a medical assistant, "processing nurses' paperwork," Joanna (Olivia Munn) undertaking research in behavior analysis, and Betsy Brandt's bank clerk character—the film's male characters are more identified with the body, in their conventionally masculine muscularity, and are in more precarious positions (see both Mike [Channing Tatum] and Adam [Alex Pettifer]'s array of insecure jobs). In Brooke's concern when she discovers her brother Adam shaving his legs "for work," the film also incorporates anxieties about the "femininization" of the male dancer of the kind analyzed by Cohan (1993) in relation to the studio-era musical. Miami real estate, however, comes with the promise not only of freedom but also of equity: the strippers themselves will have a stake in the operation currently run by Dallas with Mike's assistance. The word "equity" is repeated by the strippers throughout the film like an incantation; Mike even tells Dallas at one stage, "I want to hear you say the word: equity," to which Dallas responds by yelling "E- Q-U-I-T-Y." No details of what equity entails are revealed, but it stands for the promise that Miami real estate represents for them—autonomy, equality, security—a fantasy of entrepreneurial masculine mastery in contrast to their recessionary precarity.

Yet the real estate that underpins the film's structure is unseen: we never leave Tampa. Instead, the performances we see each of the film's strippers give in the club are the central component of Dallas's efforts to accrue the capital to invest in real estate. When he says he needs to close some loopholes with Miami real estate attorneys, Mike asks if he can help and is told "keep this up," meaning primarily his performances. But rather than utopian musical numbers that would aesthetically support Dallas's Miami real estate dream, the film undermines that project through breaks with generic codes, producing spectatorial distance from those performances. Martin Rubin defines the musical as "a film containing a significant proportion of musical numbers that are impossible—i.e., persistently contradictory in relation to realistic discourse of the narrative" (2002: 57). *Magic Mike* incorporates musical performance by limiting the impossibility of any musical "numbers," which are presented in the same realist mode as the narrative. For example, rather than the "audio dissolve" that typically occurs on the soundtrack of a musical number—which Rick Altman argues commonly entails a "movement from diegetic sound without music through diegetic music to non-diegetic music without diegetic sound" (1987: 67)—strip sequences are accompanied by tinny diegetic music with the cheers and chatter of the audience audible throughout. Even the most extensive performances cut between frontal, dynamic camera positions (more like a "musical number") and long shots that demonstrate the smallness of the stage and the seediness of the club.

Furthermore, the film downplays its performances' status as set piece musical numbers, deferring or offsetting their autonomous pleasures. Performance sequences are truncated, seen in montages rather than as whole performances, and integrated into the narrative not because the numbers themselves further the plot but because of the film's emphasis on the gaze of diegetic spectators. Notably, those spectators are not the performances' intended audience, the enthusiastic women who frequent the strip club. Instead, numbers are effectively filtered through the perspective of a character who is skeptical of what is taking place on stage or whom we are supposed to be skeptical of (or both). Even "Pony," the most extended performance, seen in full with low angles and close camera work, repeatedly cuts to Brooke's serious face (Figures 4.1 and 4.2); Mike's later solo performance cuts to Dallas, similarly stony-faced. The performance sequences therefore resist the musical's traditional use of internal audiences, denying a production of community. Jane Feuer argues that the musical perceives "the breakdown of community designated by the very distinction between performer and audience" as "a form of cinematic original sin" and that by idealizing community, including through the use of internal audiences to cue our responses, "the genre's rhetoric" rejoins "the producing and consuming functions severed by the passage of musical entertainment from folk to popular to mass status" (1993: 3). *Magic Mike*'s editing structures

FIGURES 4.1 AND 4.2 *Mike in* Magic Mike *stripping to "Pony," seen from the audience's perspective; Brooke's reaction.*

limit both the capacity of any performance to be showstopping and our ability to engage in its pleasures.

The strip sequences are also denied a role in a romantic narrative as the strippers are explicitly restricted from situating their performances as actual seductions—Adam is reprimanded for kissing one of the women in the audience on his first time on stage—limiting the strip sequences' capacity for integration in a romantic narrative. Those sequences also deny ways in which that integration of performance and romance have evolved since the studio era. David James suggests that 1960s rock films like *A Hard Day's Night* (1964) reconfigure the classical musical's dual-focus structure around performer and audience: a mass female audience becomes "a collective ingenue parallel to the Beatles' collective boy," the union of which is delayed and impeded until the concluding concert "when it dissolves into the spectacle, consummating their union across the proscenium stage in audio-visual rock 'n' roll" (2016: 152). *Magic Mike* separates the film spectator from its internal audience, denying Feuer's unified community and James's eroticized stage performance.

The film thoroughly decouples the musical's traditionally tight connections between craft, commerce, and romance. In studio-era musicals, musical performance is often both an expression of a true self and desired work. Mike, however, wants to leave stripping behind to make custom furniture. Altman argues that the "show musical" typically equates "success in love and success on the stage" (1987: 252). Mike and his romantic interest Brooke, however, both have conflicted feelings about stripping: she is troubled when she learns that Adam is stripping, but she also tells Mike that when she sees him perform "it all makes sense." Mike's professional and romantic goals both ultimately require the same solution: leaving stripping, abandoning success on the stage. At the film's finale, Mike escapes minutes before the troupe's last performance before the move to Miami, instead going to Brooke's apartment. While the film might have presented us with a showstopping final number, it cuts away from Adam's face as the Kings of Tampa are about to go on stage and concludes instead with two characters, Mike and Brooke, simply sitting at a table. Mike's musical performances therefore represent all that he ultimately rejects rather than a generic solution to narrative problems.

Not only is the spectator distanced from the numbers' pleasures, but they are at every level presented as hollow, manipulative, and inauthentic: *performed* rather than *expressed*. Richard Dyer's argument about *Gold Diggers of 1933* (1933)—that for these Great Depression showgirls, "women's only capital is their bodies as objects" (2002: 28)—is here reversed but also rendered more literal. The performances themselves are doubly transactional: they enable a real estate venture and the audience literally throws dollar bills at them. The stripping entails performing stereotypically masculine roles—construction worker, fireman, cowboy—associated with decades of "macho drag" in gay culture (Healey 1994), rendering the insistently straight set-up (male stripper/female audience) a hollow performance. As Michelle Stewart and Jason Pine note, "phantasmatic equity seduces men to sell their bodies as screens for consumers' projected fantasies" (2014: 197). The strippers respond by wholeheartedly and ineffectually embracing the entrepreneurial. A sequence in which Mike, dressed up in a suit and spectacles (another stereotypically masculine costume), tries to apply for a loan distills much of the film's preoccupation with men at the economic margins feeding the language of neoliberalism back to its institutions only to be rebuffed. While Dyer suggests that dancing bodies express an ownership of space and the film's performances have a narrative relationship to a real estate venture, its depictions of the male body's occupation of space are instead rendered ineffectual. Rather than expressing the spatial mastery a real estate plot entails, the film's consistent refusal of generic logic and generic pleasures enables a critical attitude toward such a venture.

The strippers may be drawn to the dream of Miami and equity, but the film itself undermines that promise, foregrounding their insecurity and exposure to risk. It similarly points to the fragility of its built environment. Mike meets Adam when Adam takes a job in construction from which he is swiftly fired for his lack of professionalism. In that sequence, the film foregrounds the ways in which Tampa is being reconstructed, including a shot of Mike and Adam on the building's roof putting their own building site in urban context, a thread that is picked up later on when Mike meets Brooke's boyfriend, who works in insurance and expresses his relief that he doesn't "have to be the guy that tells 'em that they're not gonna be able to rebuild their houses." This ostensibly points to the environmental fragility of Florida's built environment—construction after hurricanes, one of which the film depicts later in the film—but in combination with the emphasis on precarity and real estate transactions, there are also clear echoes of the foreclosure crisis. *Magic Mike* toys with but ultimately distances itself from both the pleasures of the musical and the narrative satisfaction of a successful real estate venture. The film's not-quite-a-musical state enables it to express distaste for the kind of rabid capitalism that gives rise to someone like Dallas; both he and the ambivalently presented musical performances are associated with the specter of Miami: never to be seen and haunted by the subprime mortgage crisis and Miami's history of real estate bubbles.

Magic Mike XXL

Magic Mike XXL is in many respects the inverse of its predecessor, especially in its treatment of musical performance: it includes several full musical sequences, only a few of which take place on stage or for a paying audience. Whereas *Magic Mike* emphasized the smallness of both the strip club and its stage, *Magic Mike XXL* concludes with the Kings of Tampa as the main attraction on an expansive stage at a convention center. Although all musical numbers continue to refuse the audio dissolve, the off-stage performances deploy precisely the "folk art" qualities that Feuer identifies with the musical: the impression of spontaneity, environmental choreography, bricolage (1993). "I Want It That Way" even calls attention to Big Dick Richie (Joe Manganiello)'s apparently spontaneous use of props (bursting open a packet of Cheetos, opening a bottle of water, and pouring it on himself) at the end of his routine when he asks the cashier watching him "How much for the Cheetos and the water?" Yet the film remains a generic boundary case—when I've screened it in classes on the musical my students have been distinctly reluctant to categorize it as a musical—and the film minimizes any "impossibility." Each of the songs from the apparently spontaneous off-stage numbers are rationalized as songs with which the performer is highly familiar: Mike reinterprets his "Pony" performance from the first film when the song happens to play on Spotify; vehement Backstreet Boys fan Big Dick Richie improvises to "I Want It That Way" as it plays in the convenience store; Ken (Matt Bomer) sings "Heaven" a cappella when Mae (Jane McNeil) says she and her husband used to love it and later reveals that it had been his audition song.

Moreover, the film works to unify much that the first film disarticulated, particularly its production of distance between performer, spectator, and internal audience. Its numbers place great emphasis on the reactions of women watching. While the first film intercuts its performances with the skeptical or illegible reactions of diegetic spectators, the sequel even includes a sequence built around making an impassive spectator respond with pleasure to a performance. In order to prove to him that he is capable of coming up with his own routines, the Kings of Tampa challenge Big Dick Richie to make a gas station cashier who "looks like she's never smiled a day in her life" smile. She spends much of his performance to "I Want It That Way" expressionless only to smile widely at its conclusion. That sequence includes a number of shots from her point of view, indicative of how the film breaks with its original by aligning us with its performers' intended diegetic audience, who watch with pleasure (Figure 4.3). As Amanda Ann Klein notes, in this context, the dollar bills thrown at the strippers serve less as a commodity equivalent and more as "a visualization of female climax" (2020: 271).

That aesthetic unity is accompanied by the absence of the first film's real estate plot. By the start of *Magic Mike XXL*, the Miami venture has duly failed, and Dallas and Adam have been lured to Macau by a "d-bag investor," leaving the remaining Kings of Tampa to team up for "one last ride" while they plot new lives via vaguely hopeless entrepreneurial projects. Indeed, not only are the strip sequences not an expression of ownership or the means to accrue revenue for the purposes of a real estate transaction, but they also take place in spaces that are transitory and temporary. The numbers largely

FIGURE 4.3 *Big Dick Richie's gas station performance to "I Want It That Way" in* Magic Mike XXL, *from the cashier's point of view.*

occupy what Vivian Sobchack (1998), discussing film noir, calls "rented space," spaces that are temporarily occupied and financially insecure: a roadside drag club, a gas station, Rome's (Jade Pinkett Smith) subscription-based strip club, a convention center, and Nancy's (Andie McDowell) house, where it is made clear that she is on the brink of divorce and the assets are not yet settled. By using such settings, the film is working against generic tradition. Feuer argues that "folk art" qualities, such as those evident in *Magic Mike XXL*, are typically used in settings that have some sense of rooted community (1993). I have argued (2016) that 1940s musicals set in contemporary cities deploy these qualities as a way of resisting the dramatic change they faced by asserting a sense of concrete community rooted in place. While the first film also emphasized the strippers' rootlessness, here they exchange the freedom of real estate for the freedom of the road.

For if *Magic Mike XXL* is closer to our conception of a musical, it is simultaneously something the first film—with its narrative built around *not* leaving Tampa—is clearly not: a road movie. Corey Creekmur situates the 1990s road movie as itself a kind of marginal musical. The Hollywood musical, he suggests, "may now only survive with blood on its hands," as it is "mutated and inverted into the outlaw couple road film" (1997: 103). Both are structured by an oscillation between forward motion and static set pieces. The difference is their spatiality. While musical performers on tour stop at hotels and theaters to perform, outlaw couples "pull into motels, roadside diners, gas stations, and, increasingly, convenience stores, to steal and kill before resuming running for their lives" (Creekmur 1997: 95). *Magic Mike XXL*'s musical performers get off the road to sing and dance but do so at precisely the kinds of rest stops Creekmur identifies.

Timothy Corrigan's classic analysis of the road movie ties the "explicitly desperate" genre to a crisis of male identity (1991: 138). In the 1960s and 1970s, all genres needed to "adjust their anxious relation to the sociocultural fears and complexities that threaten to make their codes and formulas at best fragmented languages and at worst the meaningless debris of history" (Corrigan 1991: 148). For the road movie, the oil crisis meant that the "security of the road" could no longer be assumed (Corrigan 1991: 159).[1] *Magic Mike XXL* is a road movie made at another moment of crisis, the aftermath of the 2008 global financial crisis, producing a degree of spatial insecurity akin to the connection between the road movie and the oil crisis that Corrigan relates. But rather than abandoning genre, *Magic Mike XXL* embraces it. What it rejects, or at least transforms, is the debris of the first film's gendered codes. Conventional ideas of masculinity, in the form of costumes for old strip routines, are literally thrown out the window of a moving vehicle. In *Magic Mike*, the strippers had been instructed by Dallas to perform hollow masculine clichés as a means of enabling a real estate venture, for the promise of equity, in a space in which they had none and therefore no creative control. In the sequel, the abandonment of the real estate plot and the turn to the road movie means performance space is necessarily temporarily appropriated due to their lack of the equity they had been promised. Those conditions allow for brief moments of creative control, expressions of subjectivity, and genuine connection between performer and audience: the bridging of Feuer's gap between producer and consumer.

But just as its transformed use of space is achieved through adherence to generic codes, so its engagement with gender also depends upon another kind of aesthetic conventionality. Whereas the first film focuses on the wounds of male performers, located in work, *Magic Mike XXL* focuses on the wounds of female spectators, largely located in love. It is repeatedly emphasized that the men in their lives do not pay attention to them or provide them with the kinds of pleasure granted by the Kings of Tampa. After his performance of "Heaven"—directly in response to Mae's testimony of her husband's sexual neglect—Ken declares, "The doctor is in the house!" Andre (Donald Glover) later describes himself and the other performers at Domina as "healers." In so doing, the film falls into a tradition of culture built around what Lauren Berlant calls the "female complaint," which foregrounds "witnessing and explaining women's disappointment in the tenuous relation of romantic fantasy to lived intimacy" (2008: 1–2). Crucially, these are expressions of disappointment but not disenchantment, where a cultural commitment to the mediation of disappointment "distracts from having to confront the potential for events to induce breaks" (Berlant 2008: 12). In her discussion of this "love affair with conventionality," Berlant explicitly invokes Dyer's "Entertainment and Utopia" and its theorization, focusing on the Hollywood musical, of the pleasures of generic fulfillment (2008: 227). *Magic Mike XXL*'s musical numbers and commitment to generic pleasure counter a felt absence of community ties and spaces, fulfilling work, and the meaningful intimacy that romantic fantasy promises women.

The film generates as much pleasure as is possible within an ultimately conventional framework. If seen in dialogue with the first film, the only way for that pleasure to be possible is when space is appropriated rather than acquired. Kristen Warner characterizes the pleasures of *Magic Mike XXL* as a step toward "the watershed moment where [women's] film tastes will become normatively embedded as a profit-driving function for a successful studio slate" (2019: 231). This account is usefully suggestive of both the film's appeal and its limitations. *Magic Mike XXL* is pleasurable not because it is radical but because it is fundamentally palliative—providing a temporary escape from the pressures of patriarchy and neoliberalism, not their rejection—and it is the film's reworking of the musical genre that allows that escape to happen. *Magic Mike*'s denial of the musical's spatial mastery and its ensuing place on the genre's boundaries are both a product of the spatial volatility produced by contemporary real estate and express the film's discomfort with real estate plots. In *Magic Mike XXL*, the musical reasserts itself as a form of stabilization for men unsure of their place in the world; musical numbers produce the time and space for reworkings of masculinity that both claim space they cannot possess and rely on a normalized heterosexual dynamic. The sequel's utopianism, kept at arm's length in *Magic Mike*, is the pleasure of generic viability in the knowledge that such viability can only take place in fleeting moments and fleeting spaces. *Magic Mike XXL* is closer to the musical than its predecessor, but the film makes clear that its generic pleasures are only possible when unsustainable.

Note

1   Corrigan argues that "if the road movie traditionally subsisted on gasoline as a metaphor for restless energy, when that gasoline begins to dry up in the seventies [after the 1973 OPEC oil embargo] the vehicles it propelled become scrap by the road" (1991: 153).

References

Altman, R. (1987), *The American Film Musical*, Bloomington: Indiana University Press.
Baldauf, A. (2010), "Betting the House," *Rethinking Marxism*, 22 (2): 219–30.
Berlant, L. (2008), *The Female Complaint: The Unfinished Business of Sentimentality in American Culture*, Durham and London: Duke University Press.
Cohan, S. (1993) "'Feminizing' the Song-and-Dance Man: Fred Astaire and the Spectacle of Masculinity in the Hollywood Musical," in S. Cohan and I. R. Hark (eds.), *Screening the Male: Exploring Masculinities in Hollywood Cinema*, 46–69, London: Routledge.
Connolly, N. D. B. (2014), *A World More Concrete: Real Estate and the Remaking of Jim Crow South Florida*, Chicago and London: University of Chicago Press.
Corrigan, T. (1991), *A Cinema Without Walls: Movies and Culture after Vietnam*, London: Routledge.
Creekmur, C. K. (1997), "On the Run and On the Road: Fame and the Outlaw Couple in American Cinema," in S. Cohan and I. R. Hark (eds.), *The Road Movie Book*, 90–109, London: Routledge.
Dargis, M. (2016), "'La La Land' Makes Musicals Matter Again," *New York Times*, 23 November. Available online: https://www.nytimes.com/2016/11/23/movies/la-la-land-makes-musicals-matter-again.html?_r=0 (accessed July 11, 2019).
Dent, H. (2012), "Greatest Real Estate Bubble In Modern History Not Done Bursting," *Forbes*, 3 October. Available online: https://www.forbes.com/sites/greatspeculations/2012/10/03/greatest-real-estate-bubble-in-modern-history-has-yet-to-really-burst/ (accessed August 13, 2019).
Dyer, R. (2002), *Only Entertainment*, London: Routledge.
Feuer, J. (1993), *The Hollywood Musical*, 2nd edn, Basingstoke and London: Macmillan.

Feuer, J. (2013), "Is *Dirty Dancing* a Musical, and Why Should It Matter?" in Y. Tzioumakis and S. Lincoln (eds.), *The Time of Our Lives: Dirty Dancing and Popular Culture*, 59–72, Detroit: Wayne State University Press.

Gotham, K. F. (2006), "The Secondary Circuit of Capital Reconsidered: Globalization and the U.S. Real Estate Sector," *American Journal of Sociology*, 112 (1): 231–75.

Healey, M. (1994), "The Mark of a Man: Masculine Identities and the Art of Macho Drag," *Critical Quarterly*, 36 (1): 86–93.

James, D. E. (2016), *Rock "n" Film: Cinema's Dance with Popular Music*, New York: Oxford University Press.

Klein, A. A. (2020), "Grown Woman Shit: A Case for *Magic Mike XXL* as Cult Text," in E. Mathijs and J. Sexton (eds.), *The Routledge Companion to Cult Cinema*, 266–74, New York: Routledge.

Negra, D. and Y. Tasker (2014), "Gender and Recessionary Culture," in D. Negra and Y. Tasker (eds.), *Gendering the Recession: Media and Culture in an Age of Austerity*, 1–30, Durham and London: Duke University Press.

Rubin, M. (2002), "Busby Berkeley and the Backstage Musical," in S. Cohan (ed.), *Hollywood Musicals, The Film Reader*, 53–62, London and New York: Routledge.

Shearer, M. (2016), *New York City and the Hollywood Musical: Dancing in the Streets*, London: Palgrave Macmillan.

Sobchack, V. (1998), "Lounge Time: Postwar Crises and the Chronotope of Film Noir," in N. Browne (ed.), *Refiguring American Film Genres: History and Theory*, 129–70, Berkeley; Los Angeles; London: University of California Press.

Stewart, M. and J. Pine (2014), "Vocational Embodiments of the Precariat in *The Girlfriend Experience* and *Magic Mike*," *TOPIA: Canadian Journal of Cultural Studies*, 30–31 (April): 183–204.

Taubin, A. (2015), "Interview: Steven Soderbergh (2012)," in A. Kaufman (ed.), *Steven Soderbergh: Interviews*, 185–91, Jackson: University of Mississippi Press.

Telotte, J. P. (2002), "The New Hollywood Musical: From *Saturday Night Fever* to *Footloose*," in S. Neale (ed.), *Genre and Contemporary Hollywood*, 48–61, London: BFI.

Warner, K. J. (2019), "The Pleasure Principle of *Magic Mike XXL*: Sonic Visibility towards Female Audiences," *Communication Culture and Critique*, 12 (2): 230–46.

White, A. (2015), "How *Magic Mike XXL* and *Eden* Destroy the Movie Musical," *National Review*, 2 July. Available online: https://www.nationalreview.com/2015/07/magic-mike-xxl-destroys-movie-musical-genre/ (accessed July 11, 2019).

Filmography

Burlesque (2010), [Film] Dir. Steven Antin, USA: Screen Gems.
Dirty Dancing (1987), [Film] Dir. Emile Ardolino, USA: Vestron Pictures.
Gold Diggers of 1933 (1933), [Film] Dir. Mervyn LeRoy, USA: Warner Bros.
A Hard Day's Night (1964), [Film] Dir. Richard Lester, UK/USA: United Artists.
Honey (2003), [Film] Dir. Billie Woodruff, USA: Universal Pictures.

Mad Money (2005–), [TV program] CNBC.
Magic Mike (2012), [Film] Dir. Steven Soderbergh, USA: Warner Bros.
Magic Mike XXL (2015), [Film] Dir. Gregory Jacobs, USA: Warner Bros.
Step Up Revolution (2012), [Film] Dir. Scott Speer, USA: Summit Entertainment.

5

Saint-Louis Blues

From Oral Storytelling to Aural Filmmaking

Estrella Sendra

Musical films in Africa remain marginalized in musical film scholarship. This may be associated with the broader "narrative of exclusion" of African film (Dovey 2015: 50). It could also be due to rigid conventions defining the musical genre (Altman, 1987), unable to grasp the diversity of local specificities, such as the orality in African filmmaking. This chapter seeks to move such margins to the center, through a focused study on Dyana Gaye's multi-award-winning musical film *Un transport en commun (Saint-Louis Blues)* (2009). Despite the circulation of the film at international film festivals, following its world premiere in the Locarno Film Festival in 2009, the attention given to the film has remained limited to popular media (Barlet 2009, 2010; Goupil 2017, among others), with the exception of recent academic publications on women in African cinema (Bisschoff and Van de Peer 2020: 19, 45, 46) and Senegalese cinema (Diop 2017: 174–5). *Saint-Louis Blues*, whose original title means "a public transport," is a film featuring the passengers of a road trip from Dakar to Saint-Louis. In American road trip films, the road is perceived as a liberating space, free from oppressive hegemonic norms around movement (Cohan and Hark 1997: 1). In *Saint-Louis Blues*, the focus is not so much on this common form of human mobility, but rather on the kind of intimate interaction the limited space of shared public transport can foster. Music operates as the language which prompts the close encounter between passengers, sharing personal stories that are both individually and collectively located. While each passenger has their own lived experience, they are all shaped by the postcolonial context of the travelled roads. As the characters move from Dakar to Saint-Louis, another kind of movement is examined, from oral storytelling to aural filmmaking.

Moine (2008) and Thomas (2018) have argued that all films are to some degree generic hybrids. In this chapter I use the concept aural filmmaking as a framework for understanding *Saint-Louis Blues* as a hybrid musical film. In so doing, it seeks to offer a decolonizing and critical approach to the musical genre, largely studied and defined in relation to the narrow Hollywood canon. The focus here is not a feature-length film, which Rick Altman sees as the desired length to develop the narrative of the musical genre (1987: 103). Instead, it is a medium-length film, which does not just show a "clear affinity" with the musical genre, as Altman suggests of American musical shorts, but whose narrative relies entirely on musical dialogues. Neither is the film located in Hollywood, but in a cultural margin. The film is set in a geographical region often marginalized in film scholarship (beyond its labeling as "African cinema") and, more specifically, in the existing literature on the musical genre. *Saint-Louis Blues*, like other musicals, also reverses the hierarchy of image over sound, allowing its characters to develop, or rather, *move*, as they interact sonically, singing and dancing along fellow passengers.

Beyond the historic concern with the aesthetic conventions defining this genre, this chapter is organized and conceived in relation to an overarching theme, movement, or, as the director Dyana Gaye puts it, "circulation." This is a multifaceted and multidirectional term. From a film narrative perspective, it refers to the film characters' human mobility, as they face and overcome social obstacles and restrictions. These are largely shaped by international relationships based on colonialism. From a production perspective, it is a theme deriving from the personal experience of the film director, also directly shaped by international postcolonial dynamics of human mobility. From a genre perspective, circulation further refers to the fluid dimension of the film form, moving from one genre to another, in between multiple genres as it shapes its own conventions. Finally, from a distribution perspective, circulation further refers to the power dynamics within the global film industry, and the implicit restriction of access to certain films, filmmakers, and regions.

The film poster (Figure 5.1) already points to this polysemic understanding of circulation. On the top, there are various "points of passage" (de Valck 2007) of the film along the festival circuit, such as the international film festivals in Locarno, Toronto, and Sundance, which add critical value to the film. The image includes the public transport gathering various passengers and their suitcases. At the very center there is Souki (Anne Jeannine Barboza).

FIGURE 5.1 *Film poster for* Un transport en commun/Saint-Louis Blues.

She is opening her arms in what seems to be a musical performance. There is a *mise en abîme* recurrent in the whole film. She is not just performing to film audiences but also, and primarily, to intradiegetic characters, those within the fiction, such as Malick (Antoine Diandy), featured on the poster. While the rest of the passengers do not seem to be interacting, Souki and Malick are clearly getting closer to each other through music. The poster design itself makes this still image highly dynamic, not just through Souki and Malick's musical encounter but also because the vehicle seems to be in the middle of nowhere, in between its point of departure and arrival. The fruits in the bottom are actually representative of an obstacle along the car's circulation, a small accident they eventually have on the road, with a van transporting fruit.

Circulation is not just an eventful topic in *Saint-Louis Blues* but a revolving theme in the director's filmography. It resonates with a range of contemporary transnational films, but also African and diaspora film (Thackway 2019). Circulation also features in Senegalese filmmakers from what Mag Maguette Diop calls the "Generation 2000," that is, those directors with Senegalese heritage whose film careers started around the year 2000, such as Alain Gomis, Mati Diop, Angèle Diabang, and Moussa Touré (Diop 2017: 167–82). The theorization of circulation offered here builds on Theshome Gabriel's view of African film as "nomadic cinema" (1988) and, more specifically, Melissa Thackway's analysis of "cinema of circulation" (2019: 446). These are terms that seek to move away from conventional generic boundaries. Similarly, in this chapter I suggest the concept of "aural filmmaking" to refer to *Saint-Louis Blues*. This is an attempt to shed light on the importance of considering different contextual factors when examining and evaluating films, such as the production and cultural background of the geographical contexts where films *move* around. As Thackway argues, filmmaking is "at the intersection of, and often blends, several forms" (2019: 445). Thackway identifies the (first-person) documentary, (auto) fiction, art, and experimental film through a series of post-2000 films (2019: 445). Here, however, I focus on a kind of *moving* image where music serves as the travelling aesthetic device unifying the various spaces and times involved along the circulation.

Saint-Louis Blues features the parallel road trip of two vehicles, a *sept-place*, which is a very popular public transport in Senegal, and a taxi. As opposed to Hollywood road trip films, movement is not just spatial but also temporal, shaped by a postcolonial context.

Characters move between two key postcolonial spaces, Dakar, the current capital of Senegal, and Saint-Louis, the first capital of French West Africa. This chapter examines the way in which characters find in music an intimate space to reflect on the implications of such a postcolonial context. Movement also features in the approach to genre, as the musical is analyzed here as in continuity with oral history. That is why the suggested term is *aural* filmmaking, further emphasizing the importance of sound in film, which has also often been marginalized in film scholarship.

Filmmaking and Orality in Senegal

Saint-Louis Blues is a film set in a country with a long history of orality. Knowledge, values, and historic accounts of the past have been transmitted across generations through the spoken word (Diop 1995: 229). This was embodied in the figure of the "*griot*." This term was used to refer to praise singers and confidents to the nobility and royal kingdoms. However, depending on the ethnicities, there were multiple terms to refer to them, such as *jeli*, or *jali*, in Mandinka, or *géwël* in Wolof. Griots are the masters of the spoken word and often embellish this through rhythm. They have been defined as unique "artisans and shapers of sound (wood and music)" (Charry 2000: 90). Music, dance, praising, and the spoken word still constitute part of Senegalese cross-generational daily life.

A number of filmmakers in Senegal and West Africa, more broadly, have drawn on their own role as modern griots. For Ousmane Sembène, for example, the filmmaker was not just a storyteller, but one embedded within a long history of orality, a modern "screen griot" in stories targeted at African audiences (Fofana 2012: 7; Thackway 2003: 48). They were the result of an inward gaze, indispensable for the decolonization of the minds. While the identification with griots does not apply to every filmmaker sharing the cultural background of the region, there is a continuous reference and acknowledgment of orality in African cinema (Diawara 1996; Dima 2018, 2019; Fisher 2016; Thackway 2003).

Orality is celebrated in a large repertoire of films in Senegal that feature music, musicians, and griots. While this is not the place to offer an in-depth analysis of each of them, it is worth mentioning some examples to contextualize *Saint-Louis Blues* as an aural film, in continuity with films drawing on orality. One such title emerges from one of the mothers of African cinema, Safi Faye, who in 1979 made *Fad'jal*, set in a Serer village in Senegal. More recent films have paid tribute to specific renowned griots in the country, such as Angèle Diabang's documentary film *Yandé Codou: la griotte de Senghor (Yandé Codou: Senghor's griotte)* (2008) and Pierre-Yves Borgeaud's *Youssou Ndour: retour à Gorée (Youssou Ndour: Return to Gorée)* (2007). Diabang's film, in particular, offers an intimate portrayal of the elderly singer and griot as a witness and recipient of Senegalese history, as well as the confident adviser of the first president of independent Senegal, Léopold Sédar Senghor. As we see her performing through archival images, her own voice is complemented by that of several people who share their intimate testimonials about her, further explaining the significance of griots in Senegalese society. Yet, despite the large amount of Bollywood films imported to African screens (Chitrapu 2013: 19–20; Vander Steene 2009), with the exception of Egypt (Mokdad 2012), very few directors in the continent and diaspora have conceived and produced their films as musicals.

Saint-Louis Blues as an Aural Film

The circulation represented in *Saint-Louis Blues* and Dyana Gaye's filmography, more broadly, is shaped by the director's dynamic cultural and educational background. Gaye was born in Paris in 1975, where she was raised and graduated with a degree in Film Studies from Université Paris VIII. Her father is Senegalese, and her mother, as Gaye puts it, is from four countries, raised in France, but also, Italian, and with Senegalese and Malian heritage from her father. When reflecting about her relation to Senegal in her work, the director starts circulating across spaces: "I have been raised in Paris, indeed, but within a culture which is very plural, at the same time, French, because it was the country where we were living, Senegal, the Italian culture from my mother. . . . That is why it is a bit strange" (pers. comm. 2020). What may be described as "strange" by the director, arguably for simplification purposes, can rather be seen as one such form of "rooted cosmopolitanism" (Appiah 2005). Theorized by Kwame Appiah, the term refers to people's identification as citizens of the world with a sense of rootedness in a particular (or various) place(s) where they feel a connection to from birth, love, friendship, heritage, or further symbolic experiences (Appiah 2005: 214). Gaye often says that she is "from a country that does not exist, that is, in the boundary between France and Senegal" (pers. comm. 2020), adding: "I don't have the feeling of belonging to one more than the other, in a way, but that I am from that imaginary country which convenes those two cultures" (pers. comm. 2020). This is a shared feeling among several filmmakers from the Generation 2000 in the Senegalese diaspora, such as Mati Diop (Thackway 2019: 457–60) and Alain Gomis (Sendra 2018: 362–3), which further appears in their filmographies.

Rooted cosmopolitans also have the characteristic, according to Appiah, of feeling certain commitments with those places of connection (2005: 241). Dyana Gaye's first short film, *Une femme pour Souleymane* (*A Wife for Souleymane*) (2000), was physically set between Paris and Dakar and was about migration. From the very beginning, the director has wanted to film in Senegal because she could offer a particular gaze, "in between two" places, France and Senegal. Ever since, all her films have taken her, in one way or another, to Senegal.

Gaye's filmography includes five short films, *A Wife for Souleymane* (2000, twenty-four minutes); *J'ai deux amours* (*I Have Two Loves*), a fifteen-minute short film featured in *Paris, la Métisse* (2005); *Deweneti (Ousmane)* (2006, sixteen minutes); *Un conte de la Goutte-d'Or* (*A tale of La Goutte-d'or*) (2014, thirteen minutes); a medium-length film, *Saint-Louis Blues* (2009, forty-eight minutes); a feature-length film, *Des étoiles* (*Under the Starry Sky*) (2013, eighty-eight minutes); and two under production (at the time of writing). Featuring characters physically or psychologically emplaced across different locations, her films embrace circulation in a way that resonates with Thackway's analysis of contemporary African and diaspora films "crossing lines" (2019: 444–63). These films shift "between genres and styles, moving through places and histories—both personal and collective—. . . question and explore memories and identity" (2019:

445). *Saint-Louis Blues* constitutes a key title in the director's filmography, adhering to Thackway's line crossings through its multifaceted celebration of circulation, a recurrent theme in Gaye's career. In other words, the representation of circulation arises from a hybrid and dynamic genre, crossing local, national, and international boundaries, either physically or psychologically. Like many African and diaspora films, it is composed of lines, roads, spaces, and times that are crossed by film characters, directors, audiences, and the film itself.

The narrative in this and her other films is also rooted in personal experiences. They constitute filmic journeys in which "the filmmaker assumes some form of personal presence of filmic persona in the diegesis" (Thackway 2019: 447); or, as Vlad Dima puts it, where the filmmakers insert themselves "into the material fabric of the stories" (2019: 176). This is particularly evident in *Saint-Louis Blues*. The film is influenced by the director's travel diaries and souvenirs made in her own journeys in *sept-place* between Dakar and Saint-Louis. The opening credits take the viewer to a temporary space of encounter, of arrivals and departures, felt sonically, through the characteristic sounds of the historic *gare routière Pompier*, the main station until 2014. These credits fade into an establishing shot of the station, a dynamic space where we are introduced to the first character, the driver. In Gaye's words, "it is a project that derives from the idea of circulation, which is a recurrent theme in my films, and of travelling" (pers. comm. 2020). Journeys are both the theme and structuring device of the aforementioned contemporary African and diaspora films of circulation. They feature "actual journeys" (Thackway 2019: 449). These are not just film devices around which the narrative is built. They may imply further and more complex forms of circulation. In *Saint-Louis Blues*, Gaye positions herself in *the fabric* of the film through the characters of Josephine (Marième Diop) and Binette (Naïma Gaye), two French women with Senegalese heritage who are in Senegal on holiday. These are a projection of Dyana Gaye and her sister, Naïma Gaye, who had been going to Senegal on vacation for decades.

In the midst of strangers who, superficially at least, have little in common aside from their journey, music appears as the icebreaker. Through music, passengers become the tellers of their own stories. For instance, as I elaborate later, it is through music that we learn that Malick is going to visit his girlfriend in Saint-Louis, but that he is actually more excited about moving even further, to Italy, in search of a better life upon the return. The musical genre is conceived here as one able to embrace the director's passions, music, and dance. During the film shooting, the set would take lunch breaks and other moments to watch some of the musical films the director had grown up with, such as *Singin' in the Rain* (1952) and *West Side Story* (1961). The director assumed these would be global references but found during shooting that these films were not well known in Senegal. This necessitated a dialogue between the Western musical tradition and the long history of oral tradition in West Africa, but shaped by rooted cosmopolitanism and celebrating the borderless dimension of music.

Despite the ever presence of music and dance in Senegal, there is not a long history of musical films. "The idea," Gaye says, "was for those characters [in *Saint-Louis Blues*] to be, in a way, conceived as griots, rooted within the long history of orality in Senegal. That link seemed to me so evident. The relation with orality is very present and strong" (pers. comm. 2020). Dima argues that "the link between orality and aural cinema may prove to be perhaps too reductive," as it may imply that cinema is just "a simple remnant of an oral tradition" (2019: 178). To him, sound is also "a way to deal with an artistic form of exile" (Dima 2019: 178). Music in aural cinema like *Saint-Louis Blues* acts as the sonic thread interweaving a variety of moving people, spaces, and temporalities, favoring an intimate and cathartic encounter with oneself and others. In line with Dima, aural filmmaking here is not merely seen as a continuation of oral storytelling. Rather, it serves as a more complex and intersectional category than that of "musical film," whose conventions are largely limited to and by a Western canon.

The music in *Saint-Louis Blues* was composed by Baptiste Bouquin, with whom the director had already worked in *Ousmane* and *I Have Two Loves*. Over thirty musicians, including the Surnatural Orchestra and the Ensemble Les Cordes, perform the instrumental music. All the voices we hear are those of the characters themselves. This aural film differs from mainstream musicals in the narrative power of *imperfection*. As the director puts it, their voices and performances are "fragile" (pers. comm. 2020). The point is not the technical quality of the singer, but rather, the use of music as a means to *perform* what is painful to communicate, that is, the hostility of an everyday informed by traces of centuries of colonialism. This suggests a continuity with oral history in the country, one transferred from generation to generation in the intimacy of the family home, as opposed to the formal music education that takes place in many Western societies. It is crucial to understand the idea of aural filmmaking as a subversive and decolonizing term for the musical genre. Cinematic quality, which is as imprecise as subjective (de Valck and Soeteman 2010), is assessed beyond the musical performance of actors in the film. Instead, "fragility" and energy in the *mise en abîme*, that is, the musical performances within the fiction of the film, are seen by the director as the great assets in the film. Hollywood musical films had long sought to evoke such fragility. As Jane Feuer puts it, "musicals go to great lengths to achieve an aura of amateurism" (Feuer 1993: 14). Highly trained professional performers, such as Judy Garland, were asked to play amateur performers. This, according to Feuer, brought characters closer to audiences, fostering a more immersive experience (Feuer 1993: 15). In *Saint-Louis Blues*, however, the desired amateurism is not emulated, or even, faked; it is rather embraced. With the exception of Naïma Gaye, a professional choreographer who plays a secondary role in the film, performers are genuinely untrained, or have an amateur relationship with music, such as Anne Jeannine Barboza (Souki), who was in the choir of a church. This fosters another kind of close relationship with the audience, one based on respect and identification with the themes shared by performers, moving away from the focus on entertainment in the Hollywood film industry.

The whole music-composition process is determined by the characters' lived experiences. According to the director, "characters and their songs were designed in relation to their position in the *sept-place*. At the same time, they are also built through opposition" (pers. comm. 2020). They were conceived with an aim to represent a spectrum as wide as possible of the Senegalese society. When they sing, they are not just addressing film audiences; they are, first and foremost, addressing each other, the passengers in the *sept-place*. Along the way, music allows them to open up to fellow passengers. Through music, they cathartically share their aspirations, everyday struggles, and various situations leading to them. This resonates with Altman's theorization of the "folk musical," based on resilience and community bonds, particularly of the family (Altman 1987: 273). The passengers in the *sept-place* are not precisely a family, but represent, however, the dialogue between different generations. As they sing, a sense of community is built, through empathy and identification with the shared stories, situated within a context of multidirectional circulation, to the capital city, for Madame Barry; to Europe, for Malick; or to the place of birth of ancestors, in the case of Souki, Binette, and Josephine. Desirée García emphasizes the role of migration and belonging in the folk musical tradition (2014: 47). According to her, the early years of the folk musical, by the late 1920s, "combined a racialized romanticism with sound technology to relocate the musical film and effectively restrict the mobility of black people" (2014: 70). This was highly contested by Black audiences and performers and led to Black musical film productions such as *Georgia Rose* (1930) that rearticulated the false dichotomies promoted by the Hollywood industry (García 2014: 46–7). It reinforced the idea of Hollywood as a place and industry of migration, where ethnic origins migrated to mainstream American screens. *Saint-Louis Blues*, set still at a margin in mainstream film, but a center in the African filmmaking context, Senegal, is also a point of convergence of multiple references and temporalities. It is a hybrid musical film, whose multifaceted nature further leads to the multi-genre music composition, migrating from folk to further music genres.

Through a variable focalization, each character becomes their own storyteller, their own screen griot. Among them, there is Malick, a character on the way to exile. This is a figure "always present" in Gaye's films (pers. comm. 2020). His binary opposite is Souki, who represents the one who resists exile. Malick sings, "Amore, amore, amore . . . è bella come il sole" (love, she is as beautiful as the sun) with his song including some lyrics in Italian, showing that a part of him is already psychologically in Italy. It unveils his intention to leave in order to then return and be highly regarded by society. While the rest of passengers in the *sept-place* join him in a chorus, Souki, who he seems to be singing to, does not. Instead, at the end, she says, "You will forget Aissata [the girlfriend he is visiting in Saint-Louis]. You will lie to your family, and you will disappear. I already know your song."

Souki represents all those people in Senegal who have, in a way or other, a story of loss. Souki is a strong leading role, a young Senegalese woman who resists the conventional direction of human movement, that is, migration to Europe. She is precisely the first one to initiate the choral song in the *gare*. Her song adopts a lullaby tone, taking her to her childhood: "one step, two steps . . . I have learned to walk without a father next to me. The news have arrived. He has just left us. I am going to Saint-Louis." It is through that lullaby-inspired song that Malick learns that she is on her way to her father's funeral, a missing figure in her life who she has never met. Once more, support is not communicated through spoken words, but rather, performed, in this case, through dance steps, as Malick listens to Souki and follows her choreography, emulating her moves and then dancing along with her, as her partner (Figure 5.2).

FIGURE 5.2 *Malick and Souki when Souki tells her story aurally in* Un transport en commun/Saint-Louis Blues.

Songs do not merely prompt the intimate encounter of passengers in the *sept-place*. By the end of the road trip, the French researcher on fieldwork, Antoine (Gaspard Manesse), sings to express his concern about being late. He is not joined by fellow passengers in the *sept-place*. Instead, he is sonically and psychologically connected to the taxi where Dorine (Adja Fall), the hairdresser he had briefly met before joining the *sept-place*, is also traveling to Saint-Louis. Dorine follows him, with brief laments about the amount of work she does in the hair salon managed by her aunt, Madame Barry (Bigué Ndoye), who happens to be sharing the *sept-place* with Antoine. However, the lamenting tone changes to a celebratory one, thankful to have met one another. What starts in a kind of call-response format, resonating with oral tradition in West Africa, continues as a duet. As they sing, their desire to reunite upon arrival increases. By the time they meet again in Saint-Louis, they were already together, through music. Their parallel trajectory was inspired by *The Young Girls of Rochefort*, a musical film by Jacques Demy (1967), where there is a similar love story for one of the twin sisters. To Gaye, "the musical genre is an enchanted space, touching magic. . . . It moves people away from the monotony of their everyday lives" (pers. comm. 2020). It fosters a dream state as well as a space of empathetic reflection. *Saint-Louis Blues* moves between different registers, from spoken dialogue and silent moments to sung-through stories. It is precisely through music that such magic is established. It moves characters across spaces and temporalities, embodying dreams and aspirations and sharing social concerns about their lived experiences. Music fosters a certain kind of agency to the characters, who feel they are allowed to dream, and to be heard, as performers. This is very noticeable in the case of Médoune Sall. In the *gare* or the car, he is *just* a driver. However, when he becomes a performer, he stands up in the car and is followed by the crowd on the road. He self-transforms into a griot, mediating the past and the present, from his own positionality. He is listened to (Figure 5.3).

As a musical film set in Senegal, expectations arose in the West about the kind of music the film *should* have. Gaye states, "In Africa, it seems like we are forced to put African music, as we were restrained to that. And one could argue that there is very beautiful music in Africa, but that is not the point. I had not said it wasn't beautiful" (pers. comm. 2020).

Music to her has no boundaries, and "it is a shame to be always brought back to this idea of 'Africanness'" (pers. comm. 2020). In fact, in the film, the only song featuring sabar and mbalax, a Wolof kind of percussion and rhythm highly popular in Senegal, is the one sung by Médoune Sall, from the top of that *sept-place*. This is a coherent aesthetic choice, as he represents an elder generation, and thus its lyrics are more overtly political: "It hurts me to live in our Senegal. . . . It hurts me to hear that France is Africa's friend." There is an explicit reference to French colonialism in Senegal, which can

FIGURE 5.3 *Médoune Sall, the driver, during his song in* Un transport en commun/Saint-Louis Blues.

still be felt in present-day postcolonial Senegal. This explains his cathartic response through a rhythm both representative of Senegalese pop music and griot culture. Just as the song brings together different musical forms, the performance also brings together Sall and the other passengers, who join in, as well as professional and nonprofessional dancers from the cars and streets in the traffic jam. In the director's words, "music travels through the characters. . . . It speaks about them" (pers. comm. 2020), shaped by them and their backgrounds. At the same time, it takes the characters elsewhere, to the past (for Madame Barry and Souki), to the future, or abroad (for Malick), and with the spectators, adding further layers to the circulation. In aural filmmaking, pleasure and politics meet, moving away from fixed expectations about African films (Dovey 2010). Music coherently sews the thread interweaving the aural fabric of the film. In so doing, it fosters a safe space for characters to externalize an intimate biographic story, not exactly through an inward gaze, but rather, an inward voice.

Conclusion

What does *Saint-Louis Blues* tell us about musical film production outside of Hollywood? The analysis in this chapter has evidenced the need to decolonize the existing scholarship. I suggest "aural filmmaking" as a term encompassing films whose narrative relies on sound, in continuity with orality. It is also a term that embraces generic hybridity. This becomes particularly pertinent for films on circulation, that is, moving across times, spaces, and genre conventions, and encountering obstacles as they travel along the international film festival and commercial exhibition circuit. Aural filmmaking challenges fixed understandings of the canon established by the Hollywood musical. Music becomes that overarching borderless and dynamic aesthetic device, making possible the circulation represented in *Saint-Louis Blues* and of the film itself. It makes characters travel to their inner and intimate souls. Aural filmmaking is a reflection of those inward and outward flows in film, of the connection of the global with the local. On screen, characters become screen griots, and as such, commentators of the social issues faced by postcolonial subjects. They are artisans of their own stories, whose "imperfect" texture embodies the complexity and erosion of everyday lives in postcolonial spaces.

References

Altman, R. *The American Film Musical*, Bloomington: Indiana University Press.
Appiah, K. A. (2005), *The Ethics of Identity*. Princeton, NJ; Oxford: Princeton University Press.
Barlet, O. (2009), « Ce qui m'intéresse, c'est de travailler sur des énergies » Entretien d'Oliver Barlet avec Dyana Gaye à propos de « Un transport en commun », *Africultures*, 24 November. Available online: http://africultures.com/ce-qui-minteresse-cest-de-travailler-sur-des-energies-9013/ (accessed April 8, 2020).
Barlet, O. (2010), Critique: Un transport en commun. De Dyana Gaye. *Africultures*, 7 June 2010. Available online: http://africultures.com/un-transport-en-commun-9520/ (accessed April 8, 2020).
Bisschoff, L., and S. Van de Peer (2020), *Women in African Cinema: Beyond the Body Politic*, London; New York: Routledge.
Charry, E. S. (2000), *Mande Music: Traditional and Modern Music of the Maninka and Mandinka of Western Africa*, Chicago: University of Chicago Press.
Chirapu, S. (2013), "The Big Stick behind 'soft power?' The Case of Indian Films in International Markets," in D. J. Schaefer and K. Karan (eds.), *Bollywood and Globalization: The Global Power of Popular Hindi cinema*, 15–28, New York: Routledge.
Cohan, S., and I. R. Hark, eds. (1997), *The Road Movie Book*, London; New York: Routledge.
de Valck, M. (2007), *Film Festivals: From European Geopolitics to Global Cinephilia*, Amsterdam: Amsterdam University Press.
de Valck, M. and M. Soetman (2010), "And the Winner Is . . . What Happens behind the Scenes of Film Festivals Competitions," *International Journal of Cultural Studies*, 13 (3): 290–307.

Diawara, M. (1992), "African Cinema Today," in *African Cinema: Politics and Culture*, 140–66, Bloomington; Indianapolis: Indiana U.P.

Diawara, M. (1996), "Popular Culture and Oral Traditions in African Film," in I. Bakari and B. C. Mbye (eds.), *African Experiences of Cinema*, London: British Film Institute.

Dima, V. (2018), "From Visual Place to Aural Space: The Films of Mahamat-Saleh Haron," *Journal of the African Literature Association*, 12 (3): 269–86.

Dima, V. (2019), "The (Aural) Life of Neo-colonial Space," in K. Harrow and C. Garritano (eds.), *A Companion to African Cinema*, 176–93, Hoboken, NJ: John Wiley & Sons.

Diop, M. M. (2017), *Cinéma Sénégalais: Sembène Ousmane. Le précurseur et son legs*, Dakar: L'Harmattan-Sénégal.

Diop, S. (1995), *The Oral History of the Wolof People of Waalo, Northern Senegal: The Master of the Word (Griot) in the Wolof Tradition*, Lewiston, NY: Edwin Mellen.

Dovey, L. (2009), "Subjects of Exile: Alienation in Francophone West African Cinema," *International Journal of Francophone Studies*, 12 (1): 55–75.

Dovey, L. (2010), "Editorial: African Film and Video: Pleasure, Politics, Performance," *Journal of African Cultural Studies*, 22 (1): 1–6.

Dovey, L. (2015), "Afri-Cannes? African Film and Filmmakers at the World's Most Prestigious Film Festivals," in *Curating Africa in the Age of Film Festivals*, 45–58, New York: Palgrave Macmillan.

Feuer, J. (1993), *The Hollywood Musical*, Basingstoke: Macmillan.

Fisher, A. (2016), "Modes of *griot* Inscription in African Cinema," *Journal of African Media Studies*, 8: 5–16.

Fofana, A. T. (2012), *The Films of Ousmane Sembène: Discourse, Culture, and Politics*, Amherst, NY: Cambria Press.

Gabriel, T. (1988), "Thoughts on Nomadic Aesthetics and the Black Independent Cinema. Traces of a Journey," in B. Mbaye and C. Andrade-Watkins (eds.), *Blackframes: Critical Perspectives on Black Independent Cinema*, 62–79, Cambridge, Massachusetts: The MIT Press.

Garcia, D. J. (2014), *The Migration of Musical Film: From Ethnic Margins to American Mainstream*, New Brunswick, New Jersey: Rutgers University Press.

Goupil, Y. (2017), "Un transport en commun" de Dyana Gaye. *Bref*, 2017. Available online: https://svod.brefcinema.com/blog/cahier-critique/un-transport-en-commun-de-dyana-gaye.html (accessed April 7, 2020).

Grant, B. K. (2012), *The Hollywood Film Musical*, Chichester [England]: Wiley-Blackwell.

Harney, E. (2004), "Rhythm as the Architecture of Being: Reflections on un *Âme Nègre*," in *Senghor's Shadow: Art, Politics, and the Avant-garde in Senegal, 1960-1995*, 19–48. Durham, NC; London: Duke University Press.

Moine, R. (2008), *Cinema Genre*, Oxford: Blackwell Publishing.

Mokdad, L. Y. (2012), "Egypt," in C. K. Creekmur (ed.), *The International Film Musical*, Edinburgh: Edinburgh University Press.

Personal communication. Interview with Dyana Gaye on 15 April 2020. Whatsapp Video.

Sendra, E. (2018), "Displacement and the Quest for Identity in Alain Gomis's Cinema," *Black Camera: An International Film Journal*, 9 (2), Spring 2018: 360–90.
Thackway, M. (2003), "Chapter 3: Screen Griots: Orature and Film," in *Africa Shoots Back: Alternative Perspectives in Sub-Saharan Francophone African Film*, 49–92, Oxford: James Currey.
Thackway, M. (2019), "Crossing Lines: Frontiers, Circulations, and Identity in Contemporary African and Diaspora Film," in K. W. Harrow and C. Garritano (eds.), *A Companion to African Cinema*, 444–63, Hoboken, New Jersey: John Wiley & Sons, Inc.
Thomas, M. W. (2018), "Whether to Laugh or to Cry? Explorations of Genre in Amharic Fiction Feature Films," in M. W. Thomas, A. Jedlowski, and A. Ashagrie (eds.), *Cine- Ethiopia: The History and Politics of Film in the Horn of Africa*, 93–117, East Lansing: Michigan State University Press.
Ukadike, F. (2002), "Interview with Djibril Diop Mambéty," in *Questioning African Cinema: Conversations with Filmmakers*, 121–31, Minnesota: University of Minnesota Press.
Vander Steene, G. (2009), "Bollywood Films and African Audiences," Paper presented at the Shastri Indo-Canadian Institute sponsored International Seminar on Bollywood's Soft Power at IIT Kharagpur, India, December 14–15.

Filmography

Album (Under production), [Film] Dir. Dyana Gaye, Senegal/France: Andolfi Production.
Des étoiles/Under the Starry Sky (2013), [Film] Dir. Dyana Gaye, Senegal/France: Rouge International, Ezekiel Film Production, Cinekap.
Deweneti (Ousmane) (2006), [Film] Dir. Dyana Gaye, Senegal/France: Andolfi Production.
Fad'jal (1979), [Film] Dir. Safi Faye, Senegal: Safi Films.
J'ai deux amours/I have two loves (2005), [Film] Dir. Dyana Gaye, France: EKLA Production.
Les demoiselles de Rochefort/The Young Girls of Rochefort (1967), [Film] Dir. Jacques Demy, France: Parc Film, Madeleine Films.
Paris la Métisse (2005), [Film] Dir. Newton I. Aduaka, Léandre-Alain Baker, Dyana Gaye, Neary Hay, Hubert Koundé, Benny Malapa, Mariette Monpierre, Stefan Sao Nelet, Kevin Pareemanen, and Juliano Ribeiro Salgado, France: Ekla Production.
Singin' in the Rain (1952), [Film] Dir. Gene Kelly and Stanley Donen, USA: MGM.
Un conte de la Goutte-d'Or/A tale of La Goutte-d'or (2014), [Film] Dir. Dyana Gaye, France: Mon voisin Productions.
Un transport en commun (Saint-Louis Blues) (2009), [Film] Dir. Dyana Gaye, Senegal/France: Andolfi Production and Nataal Production.
Une femme pour Souleymane/A wife for Souleymane (2000), [Film] Dir. Dyana Gaye, France/Senegal: Quo Vadis Cinema.

West Side Story (1961), [Film] Dir. Jerome Robbins and Robert Wise, USA: The Mirisch Company.
Yandé Codou: la griotte de Senghor (2008), [Film] Dir. Angèle Diabang, Senegal: Karoninka.
Youssou Ndour: retour à Gorée (2007), [Film] Dir. Pierre-Yves Borgeaud, Senegal: CAB Productions, Dreampixies, Iris Group.

Musicals of the Margins

6

The Marseille Film Operetta

Marie Cadalanu and Phil Powrie

The Marseille operetta film, a regional variant of the better-known French film operetta, was popular during the 1930s and early 1940s, with a few remakes during the mid-1950s. Its focus on a single city provides a fascinating case study that allows us to question some of the standard taxonomies of the film musical. We place it in the context of French film operettas and their origins in stage operettas, outlining the specificities of the Marseille film operetta subgenre, particularly its marginal and exotic nature. It was the subgenre's marginal and exotic nature that paradoxically ensured its local and national success in the 1930s and led to nostalgic remakes in the 1950s.

Operetta emerged in France in the mid-nineteenth century as a light and usually saucy variant of the increasingly serious and misnamed *opéra comique*. The operetta as a stage form saw something of a lull with the turn of the century, but returned to the Paris stages in 1918, with a new generation of composers incorporating jazz rhythms from the United States.[1] A decade later, with the coming of sound, stage operettas were made into films. Although some operettas were made specifically for the screen, the majority were based on well-known stage operettas. Claude Autant-Lara adapted Reynaldo Hahn's 1923 operetta *Ciboulette* in 1936; Hervé's 1883 operetta *Mam'zelle Nitouche* was adapted by both Marc Allégret in 1931 (starring Raimu) and his brother Yves in 1954 (starring Fernandel). Film versions of operettas that had been successful on the Paris stage opened up new regional markets, challenging the increasing hegemony of Hollywood operettas, such as those pairing Maurice Chevalier and Jeanette MacDonald, followed by Jeanette MacDonald and Nelson Eddy later in the decade. Many of these early film operettas were made in several languages to ensure wide international distribution, such as the UFA production *Der Kongreß tanzt* (The Congress Dances 1931), which was also made in French and English-language versions.

The Marseille operetta is unusual in this respect: although similar to many operetta films because it tended to adapt successful stage operettas to the screen, it was significantly different because it was located in a very specific region, indeed a specific city, but was nonetheless successful nationally. It is one of the many genres of the *cinéma méridional*, which includes vaudevilles, peasant dramas, and nativity plays among others (see Peyrusse 1986 and Bretèque 1992). The best-known representative of this regional cinema is Marcel Pagnol, originally a playwright, who set up his own film studios in Marseille and adapted many of his plays for the screen. However, this regional cinema extends well beyond his work with 150 films in the period 1929–44, of which only 11 were produced by Pagnol (Peyrusse 1986: 9). Despite its popularity during the 1930s, Kelley Conway (2013) does not refer to the Marseille operetta in an otherwise excellent overview of the French film musical. The Marseille operetta is therefore doubly marginal: it is a subgenre of an undervalued popular genre (the film musical) where academics are concerned, embedded in a *cinéma méridional* seen as geographically and industrially marginal to the national cinema.[2]

This did not prevent the Marseille operetta from being successful. Part of the subgenre's success is undoubtedly due to the exoticism associated with the South of France, which is also illustrated by the film musicals of the "three tenors": Tino Rossi, Georges Guétary, and Luis Mariano (for the latter, see Powrie 2014).[3] Rossi, as we shall see, starred in one of the Marseille operettas. Another reason might be the reassuring depiction of an unchanged community, whereas other operettas during this period were interested in the new social and geographic mobility.[4] Arguably, the exoticism and regionalism associated with the Marseille operetta are what made it at one and the same time marginal and nationally popular. It is also what makes it different from the American film musical on a number of counts: it is a folk musical (rather than a fairy-tale musical); it has an ethnically and geographically marginal focus; it privileges song rather than dance; and, finally, its focus is more homosocial than heterosexual.

First, in terms of the standard taxonomy of the musical, according to which we might have cataloged the Marseille operetta as a fairy-tale musical, it is more obviously a folk musical. Whereas two of the three subgenres identified by Rick Altman for the American film musical—the backstage musical and the fairy-tale musical—were both emulated in France, the Marseille operetta corresponds less to the fairy-tale musical that Altman associates with operetta than to an authentically national version of Altman's third category, the folk musical. As Altman writes of certain types of folk musicals, they

> portray large cities, but at a time when they were still made up of coherent neighborhoods in which everyone knows the local iceman, policeman, or shopkeeper. [. . .] In the familiar context created by the folk musical, even

the world's largest city can be tamed and made to appear no more than a slightly bigger version of one's hometown. (1987: 275–7)

The Marseille operetta, like the folk musical, is microcosmic: the action takes place not just in the city but in neighborhoods, as if Marseille, which in the early 1930s had 600,000 inhabitants, were no more than a village. Moreover, despite the fact that Marseille was France's preeminent port, with considerable immigration from Corsica, Italy, Spain, and Algeria, there is no sense in these films of ethnic groups arriving, intruding or of the characters leaving. This rootedness in place is reinforced by frequent shots of iconic Marseille locations, as if to remind spectators that the changeless neighborhood is embedded in a changeless cityscape.

Second, the community of the Marseille operetta showcases a cultural tradition that is different to France's mainstream culture, similar to a certain extent to the cultural and ethnic margins in the United States (African American, Yiddish, and Mexican). Desirée Garcia examines in *The Migration of Musical Film* (2014) how margins were essential ingredients in the melting pot of the Hollywood musical. However, in the case of the Marseille operetta, the margin is "internal" to the national identity, so that the question is not that of how the immigrants have to adapt to a new cultural environment, but how a traditional regional subculture manages to survive in the face of the growing modernization of France in the 1930s and after the Second World War.

Third, although similar to the neighborhood musicals of Hollywood in its emphasis on the local (see Shearer 2016), the Marseille operetta differs by its prevalence of exteriors rather than studio locations, and, like many other French musicals, by an emphasis on singing rather than dancing.

Fourth, the plots frequently focus on a group of male friends, the homosocial marginalizing the heterosexual romances in which the friends engage. One of the signature songs of *Un de la Canebière*—"J'aime la mer comme une femme" (I love the sea like a woman)—in which Alibert sings that the sea is his "only love," exemplifies the way in which place overwrites the romance plot so as to allow the homosocial group to bond.

It is worth asking how this closed boy's world managed to be so successful on national screens, particularly in its 1950s remakes. Part of the answer, we shall argue, lies in nostalgia for vanishing communities during France's *trente glorieuses*, the period of the country's rapid industrialization and development of a consumer culture 1945–74, brought to an abrupt end by the mid-1970s oil crisis.

The Marseille Film Operetta in the 1930s

The Marseille film operetta, while largely similar in form to the other popular film operettas of the period, has specific characteristics. The most obvious of these is the prevalence of the characters' Midi accent, which as François de la Bretèque points out, is in fact a standardized accent functioning as the indispensable complement to cultural stereotypes (1992: 69–70).

This standardized accent was familiar to film audiences from the early films of Marcel Pagnol, such as *Marius* (1931) and *Fanny* (1932), which preceded the first Marseille operetta film, *Au pays du soleil* (In the land of the sun, 1934). Those stereotypes also include references to local topography, whether Marseille locations or the landscape of Provence more generally, and the use of the songs to create local color:

> The majority of the films use and abuse song or chant as elements of local color. All of the films in the corpus based in Corsica have songs, often in dialect; the Marseille operetta is composed of songs to the glory of the local: the fishermen of Marseille, La Canebière, the fisherman's cottage, the Venice of the South, chez nous in Provence, these are the motifs of the best-known songs in *Arènes joyeuses* and *Un de la Canebière*. (Peyrusse 1986: 86)[5]

An important aspect of these films is their insistence on a utopian community rooted in geographical specificities in ways that are significantly more obvious than in other operetta films, such as those of Pills and Tabet (see Powrie 2017). In the latter films, the utopian character of the films is dependent on travel away from Paris, whether to distant colonies or more prosaically touring around France. In the Marseille operetta, characters stay in the city, and more often than not in specific neighborhoods. Criminals and police sing and dance together, and the role of the chorus—frequently friends of the principal protagonist—is to cement a sense of togetherness and a somewhat clichéd "sunny" disposition; the films "breathe optimism and reject conflict in favor of agreement" (Peyrusse 1986: 124). The plots are anchored in the local form of the *galéjade* or tall story, frequently involving elaborate pranks and practical jokes; in *Les Gangsters du château d'If* (1939), for example, the fact that the gangsters of the title turn out to be friends—reinforcing the sense of a closed community immune to danger and, more importantly, immune to significant change—is part of the attraction of the subgenre.

Formally, the Marseille operetta's songs are isolated musical numbers, mainly due to the status of the singer for whom the narrative acts as a frame, partly because of the influence of other local forms such as the stage revue. The major star of the Marseille operetta, stage and screen, was Henri Alibert, known simply as Alibert (1889–1951) who formed a team with his composer father-in-law Vincent Scotto (1874–1952). He shot to fame in 1928 with one of Scotto's songs, "Mon Paris," and quickly became typecast as a *méridional*, unlike Raimu and Fernandel, who played typical meridional characters as well as characters who were not.[6] Alibert starred in a series of stage operettas in Marseille and Paris, most of whose titles reveal their regionalist focus and many of which were very quickly turned into films one or two years later, thus spreading his local fame to the national level, for example *Au pays du soleil*, *Trois de la marine* (Three from the Navy, 1934), *Arènes joyeuses* (Happy Arena, 1935), *Un de la Canebière* (1938). The Marseille stage operetta existed before Alibert's contributions, such as *Thérèse* (1920), *Roseline* (1927), and *Mon neveu de Chicago* (My Nephew from Chicago, 1929), but Alibert gave it consistency and longevity, by having a repertory company (René Sarvil and Raymond Vincy for the librettos, Scotto for the music and René Pujol as director of three of the films), and because he brought so many of his stage operettas to the screen, making it a viable film subgenre.

The films are generally faithful to the stage operettas they adapt, with occasional omissions of songs due to length. The songs are readily identifiable musical numbers, often loosely integrated in the narrative. Moreover, given preexisting stage operettas, the songs were generally hits prior to the films, and the films are clearly intended to showcase both the singer and the major hit songs of the time. The songs of *Un de la Canebière*, for example—"Le Plus Beau Tango du monde" (The most beautiful tango in the world), "Les Pescadous de la Marsiale" (The fishermen of Marseille), "J'aime la mer comme une femme" (I love the sea like a woman), "Un petit cabanon" (The fisherman's cottage), and especially "Cane . . . Cane . . . Canebière"—were widely distributed and remain to this day well known in French film and popular musical culture. The distinction between the media used for these songs was considerably less important than the songs themselves. Song sheets often assimilated the stage and film versions, which were presented as variants of the same song. In the song sheet for "L'amour est une étoile" (Love is a star) from *Trois de la marine*, for example, the song was described as the "sung tango from *Three from the Navy*, operetta-revue in two acts and twelve tableaux"/"Tango sung by Alibert and Gaby Sims, song from the film *Three from the Navy* from H. Alibert's operetta-revue."

The songs are clearly the high points of the films, as, for example, in the song that gives its title to *Un de la Canebière*, "Cane . . . Cane . . . Canebière." The song interrupts narrative continuity as we suddenly and inexplicably cut to its performance on La Canebière, Marseille's famous "high street," for no other reason than to illustrate the street the song refers to. *Titin des Martigues* (1938), one of the few films that was not adapted from a preexisting stage operetta, and indeed one of the few films in which the character leaves Marseille, exemplifies the foregrounding of musical numbers, because it is about the rise of a singer from Marseille to fame in Paris. The first song of the film has Titin singing at Paris's biggest funfair, La Foire du Trône. As he sings "I don't dare tell you, but I'm mad about you," the camera cuts from him to the audience who comment on his singing, focusing on the cashier Yvette, who looks on admiringly. The song therefore functions as the natural expression of emotion, but also as the foregrounding of the abilities of the singer within the community and as an expression of that community. In the second song, he performs the song he was rehearsing, and this time, as elsewhere in the film, the camera closes in on his face, with cut aways to an admiring audience, both those in the radio studio and Yvette who is listening to him on the radio. The song, more particularly the singer singing the song, elides two radically different spaces, transcending them in a musical moment focused on the singer's performance.

The sequences we have just referred to demonstrate what a film can do through editing beyond the stage version of an operetta. The Marseille operetta is no less spectacular than other types of operetta when the occasion demands, the spectacular reinforcing the pause in the narrative created by the musical number. For example, as was the case with a more mainstream film operetta, *Il est charmant* (He is charming, 1932), there is a shot of a miniature character superimposed on the main shot in *Les Gangsters du château d'If* as Nine sings to a photo of her lover Jean and he leaves the photo frame to sing with her. There are also occasional dance sequences that are just as spectacular as other French Hollywood-influenced musicals. In *Titin des Martigues*, for example, there is a dance sequence with Busby Berkeley style overhead shots of dancers in geometrical patterns.

The defining characteristic of the Marseille operetta is the emphasis on local topography. Many of Alibert's films are shot in exteriors, and exterior shots are intercut with shots of the singers singing love songs, accentuating and naturalizing the link between romantic love and love for the region. In the sequences "Les Pescadous de la Marsiale" and "J'aime la mer comme une femme" from *Un de la Canebière* shots of Alibert singing are intercut with shots of the sea, the rocky foreshore, and the boats (Figure 6.1). In the song "Si tu veux faire le tour de La Corniche" (If you want to stroll around La Corniche) from Les *Gangsters du Château d'If*, Jean and Nine, captives in the Château d'If, sing about escaping, shots of the château intercut with shots of them imagining themselves on La Corniche. That particular song begins "Here at home in our Marseille," and the visual and lyrical references to Marseille occur throughout the films. The opening credits of *Les Gangsters du château d'If* comprise a vast traveling shot over the port of Marseille as we hear Alibert sing "My heart has just been sunburnt" in voice-over. *Au soleil de Marseille* opens with the title song as we see shots of monuments that are generally seen as typical of the city and often used in Marseille cinema, such as the transporter bridge and the Basilica of Notre-Dame de la Garde.[7] Emphasizing the Marseille community, the song is sung in turn by market stall holders, a fisherman, and the soap factory workers' chorus. The song celebrates the sun, its ability to make the Marseillais not just happy but peace-loving, contrasted with the unfortunate peoples of the North, typified by Belgians who go to Brussels for a football match at one point: "But when we prepare a parcel for those in the North, we say with regret to ourselves that it would be so much better if we could send a bit of our sunshine to the whole world." The emphasis on local topography is twofold: first, it gives the film a documentary feel, stressed in the opening credits: "The documentary

FIGURE 6.1 *Alibert singing "J'aime la mer comme une femme" in* Un de la Canebière.

section on the Marseille soap factory was filmed by permission of Savon Le Chat who provided all necessary materials." Second, it embeds the narrative in a very specific and close-knit urban community.

That community, imagined or not, appears in terms of the films' plots to have been untouched by the seismic changes introduced by the short-lived Popular Front in 1936–8. Other operettas during this period show a keen awareness of important social change, such as paid holidays that led to increased geographical mobility (see Powrie 2017). By contrast, the Marseille operetta generally stays resolutely anchored in its local topography, and the films during and after this period are no different than those in the early 1930s, as if the community were so enclosed that it was impervious to the rapidly changing social and political landscape. It is all the more surprising then that several of the films were remade in the 1950s, by which time France was undergoing even more rapid change.

The Marseille Film Operetta in the 1950s

It seems likely that the remakes were partly made in the wake of the successful crooner musicals starring Tino Rossi, Luis Mariano, and Georges Guétary; indeed, the first two, *Au pays du soleil* (1951) and *Trois de la Canebière*

(1955), were produced by the same company, Les Films Tellus, that had produced the first version of *Au pays du soleil* in 1934. The operettas of the "three tenors" attracted over two million spectators; indeed, Mariano's operettas set in exotic locations—principally Spain, but also Mexico—were attracting many more. The allure of a major singer in what were still seen as relatively exotic locations was clearly one of the motivating factors for these 1950s films, all of which were directed by Maurice de Canonge.

Au pays du soleil, originally a 1932 stage operetta made as a film in 1934, was the first official Marseille film operetta. The 1951 remake was clearly an attempt to recall and reboot the origins of the Marseille operetta twenty years on. *Honoré de Marseille*, less an operetta than a comedy with three songs, brought together the team of Fernandel and Jean Manse from one of the 1930s operettas, *Les Bleus de la marine*; it was the most successful of these films with 3.8 million spectators. *Trois de la Canebière* (2.8 million spectators) and *Trois de la marine* (1957; 2.7 million spectators) starred Marcel Merkès, a regular performer of stage operettas, for whom these were two of a total of three feature films he made. *Arènes joyeuses* (1958; 2.5 million spectators) starred the TV comic actor Fernand Raynaud. The films' success is all the more surprising in that unlike Alibert for the 1930s films, or Rossi for the first of the remakes, neither Merkès nor Raynaud had any connections with the Midi; Merkès was born in Bordeaux and Raynaud in Clermont-Ferrand.

As René Gieure, writing in a series of articles on song in the cinema for the influential film magazine *Image et Son*, acerbically commented, these newcomers were not the "right vintage" (Gieure 1960: 23). Moreover, compared with Alibert's exuberant and perky performances, the 1950s singers lacked the charisma or the local connections that made the Marseille operetta of the 1930s so popular: Rossi was no longer the major star he had been in the 1940s, and his staid crooner style was diametrically opposed to Alibert's; Merkès was a trained opera singer, with very little stage presence in the two films of the 1950s; Raynaud was too obviously a comedian. Their success, then, is perplexing: two of their singers were not meridional, and the films appear to clone the 1930s films, with only color being the major difference. Taking *Un de la Canebière* and *Trois de la Canebière* as an example, the basic storyline as we might expect remains the same: three friends try to impress their girlfriends by pretending to be the owners of a large sardine factory, and the women play along with this hoping to reveal the pretense. There are some significant shifts in the use of the musical numbers, however.

The stage operetta had fifteen musical numbers of which only six were retained for *Un de la Canebière*. The 1950s film in contrast has ten musical numbers, their function and occasionally their origin being different from those in *Un de la Canebière*. First, five of the songs are from different operettas: "Je ne veux pas d'autre femme que vous" (I don't want any woman other than you) is from *Arènes joyeuses*, "Viens, dans mes bras dansons" (Come into my arms and dance) from *Titin des Martigues*, and several songs—"Des mots d'amour à minuit," "Les Îles d'or" (The golden islands), and "Tout autour de la Corniche"—from *Les Gangsters du château d'If*. Second, whereas in *Un de la Canebière* each of the songs was presented in extenso and separately, in *Trois de la Canebière* we often hear only sections of the songs in medleys, accompanied by shots of iconic Marseille landmarks. In the first number of *Trois de la Canebière*, the three characters in a boat sing "Les Pescadous de la Marsiale," as had Alibert in the original; this is intercut with shots of the coast, the Château d'If, and the port. The song, therefore, comes across not only as a profession of homosocial friendship but as a celebration of the community to which they belong. In the second medley which occurs when the three friends take their girlfriends on a tour of Marseille some forty minutes into the film, we are placed, like the women, in the position of tourists, touring not just the Provençal landscape and the iconic sites of Marseille but also through a soundscape composed of well-known songs from a range of operettas. Touring, in both cases, is less about discovering Marseille than celebrating the city and its denizens in a nostalgic gesture.

If the 1950s films depended in part on the popular successes of the new generation of crooners and their spectacular operettas—Fernandel, the star of *Honoré de Marseille* was as big a star as Luis Mariano and Georges Guétary—they were also clearly a nostalgic replay of the close-knit community of the 1930s films. In the 1930s, we could argue that the Marseille operetta was already a nostalgic attempt to maintain a sense of utopian community in the face of modernization, as the focus on improbable neighborhoods in the films suggests. In the 1950s, this would have been even more acutely the case as France suffered from rural exodus, when the population of Marseille changed with peasants and immigrants attracted to the city and its new factories built as part of the postwar consumer boom. The 1950s films also demonstrate a weakening of the homosocial bonds between the male characters and a strengthening of what might be seen as the more obvious focus of the film musical: the heterosexual romance.

In *Trois de la Canebière*, all the new songs but one are romances, insisting on couple relationships rather than the local community represented by the three male friends of the title. Moreover, unlike the nostalgic medleys, in which we sample the songs of the past, the romances are all sung in extenso. This begins with "Monsieur offrez des roses rouges" (Sir, offer her red roses), sung by Francine to a male client in the florist's where she works, replacing the "community" song sung by the three girlfriends in *Un de la Canebière* celebrating the cherries they are selling on the market. There are four more romances, all sung by Toinet to Francine, the last one being a new song: "Je ne veux pas d'autre femme que vous," "Des mots d'amour à minuit," "Viens, dans mes bras dansons," and "Un souvenir" (A memory). The impact of

FIGURES 6.2 AND 6.3 *The final sequences of* Un de la Canebière *and* Trois de la Canebière.

these changes to the 1930s film is to emphasize not just the individual but the couple at the expense of the community so obviously prevalent in the folk musical as exemplified by *Un de la Canebière*. What had made the Marseille operetta popular nationally during the 1930s—the unchanging (exotic) community rooted firmly in social formations of the nineteenth century—was no longer. Community was being eroded by individualism, and the exoticism associated with the Midi as the inevitable complement of integrated and close-knit community was also being eroded.

The final shots of *Un de la Canebière* and *Trois de la Canebière* are revealing in this respect (Figures 6.2 and 6.3). In the first we see Toinet and Francine's wedding, with the local community gathered around. They and the guests—family, friends, neighbors—parade past the camera saluting the spectator, integrating us in the community; the couple then enters their new home, the "petit cabanon" they sang of in the final musical number, and pull the shutters to bring the film to a close, and closing the film-space in the utopia of domestic urban bliss. In the 1950s film, by contrast, there is no assembled crowd in the final sequence; Toinet sings the same song, "Un petit cabanon," as the three friends travel on a tram that goes around Marseille in a circular route. In the 1930s film, the couple is embedded in the community both legally through marriage and geographically with their cottage as part of that community. In the 1950s film, there is no wedding, no community, and the cottage is only hinted at in the song. Twenty years after the first film, the three friends are no longer obviously part of the community going forwards—they can only circle around it. The remakes of the 1950s are palimpsests shrouded in nostalgia for a vanishing France, for an exotic regional cinema, for the homosocial bonds that were the bulwarks of a conservative community, and for the film musical subgenre associated with the unchanging past.

Notes

1 See Duteurtre (2009).

2 The only substantial work is by Georges Crescenzo, a local historian and nephew of one of the main song composers for the Marseille operetta, René Sarvil (see Crescenzo 2005 and Crescenzo and Allione 2006). Crescenzo also set up the "Association Cane Cane Canebière" in 2006, whose aim is the "protection and rehabilitation" of the Marseille stage operetta (see "Cane-Canebière").

3 All three had Mediterranean origins upon which they played both in terms of their pronounced accents and in the publicity for their songs and films: Rossi was Corsican, born Constantin Rossi in Ajaccio; Mariano was Spanish Basque, born Mariano Eusebio González y García close to the French border in the town of Irun; and Guétary was Greek, born Lámbros Vorlóou in Alexandria.

4 For a case study on the two film operettas starring Pills and Tabet, *Toi c'est moi/ You Are Me* (1936) and *Prends la route/Take to the Road* (1937), see Powrie (2017).

5 Translations from the French are ours.
6 For an analysis of these stars' malleability, see Vincendeau (2007).
7 Similar shots occur at the start of *Marius* (1931), for example.

References

Altman, R. (1987), *The American Film Musical*, Bloomington: Indiana University Press.
Bretèque F. de la (1992), "Images of Provence: Ethnotypes and Stereotypes of the South in French Cinema," in R. Dyer and G. Vincendeau (eds.), *Popular European Cinema*, 58-71, London: Routledge.
"Cane-Canebière" n.d., *Gralon*. Available online: https://www.gralon.net/mairies-france/bouches-du-rhone/association-cane-canebiere-marseille_W133027751.htm (accessed February 18, 2019).
Conway, K. (2013), "France," in C. K. Creekmur and L. Y. Mokdad (eds.), *The International Film Musical*, 29-44, Edinburgh: Edinburgh University Press.
Crescenzo, G. (2005), *La Véritable histoire de l'opérette marseillaise*, Marseille: Autres Temps.
Crescenzo, G. and M. Allione (2006), *Sarvil: l'oublié de la Canebière*, Marseille: Autres Temps.
Duteurtre, B. (2009), *L'Opérette en France*, Paris: Fayard.
Garcia, D. (2014), *The Migration of Musical Film: From Ethnic Margins to American Mainstream*, New Brunswick: Rutgers University Press.
Gieure, R. (1960), "Chanson et cinéma: IX. Opérette – comédie musicale – music-hall," *Image et Son*, 128: 23-6.
Peyrusse, C. (1986), *Le Cinéma méridional: le Midi dans le cinéma français (1929-1944)*, Toulouse: Eché.
Powrie, P. (2014), "Luis Mariano et l'exotisme ordinaire," in S. Layerle and R. Moine (eds.), *Voyez comment on chante!: films musicaux et cinéphilies populaires en France (1945-1958)*, 19-29, Paris: Presses Sorbonne Nouvelle.
Powrie, P. (2017), "Mobilising Desire: The Operetta Films of Pills and Tabet in 1930s France," *Historical Journal of Film Radio and Television*, 37 (3): 436-54.
Shearer, M. (2016), *New York City and the Hollywood Musical: Dancing in the Streets*, London: Palgrave Macmillan.
Vincendeau, G. (2007), "Les Acteurs méridionaux dans le cinéma français des années 1930," in V. Amiel, J. Nacache, G. Sellier and C. Viviani (eds.), *L'Acteur de cinéma, approches plurielles*, 217-32, Rennes: Presses Universitaires de Rennes.

Filmography

Arènes joyeuses (1935), [Film] Dir. Karl Anton, France: Metropa Films.
Arènes joyeuses (1958), [Film] Dir. Maurice de Canonge, France: Athos Films, Compagnie

Au pays du soleil (1934), [Film] Dir. Robert Péguy, France: Les Films Tellus.
Au pays du soleil (1951), [Film] Dir. Maurice de Canonge, France: Les Films Tellus.
Bleus de la marine, Les (1934), [Film] Dir. Maurice Cammage, France: Fortuna Films.
Ciboulette (1933), [Film] Dir. Claude Autant-Lara, France: Pathé Consortium Cinéma, Cipar Films.
Gangsters du château d'If, Les (1939), [Film] Dir. René Pujol, France: Vandas Production.
Honoré de Marseille (1957), [Film] Dir. Maurice Régamey, France: Cité Films Protis Films.
Il est charmant (1932), [Film] Dir. Louis Mercanton, France: Paramount.
Kongreß tanzt, Der/Le congrès s'amuse/Congress Dances (1931), [Film] Dir. Erik Charell, Germany: Universum Film.
Mam'zelle Nitouche (1931), [Film] Dir. Marc Allégret, France: Ondra-Lamac-Film, Vandor Film.
Mam'zelle Nitouche (1954), [Film] Dir. Yves Allégret, France/Italy, Panitalia, Paris Film Productions, Rizzoli Films
Marius (1931), [Film] Dir. Alexander Korda and Marcel Pagnol, France: Les Films Marcel Pagnol.
Merry Widow, The /La Veuve joyeuse (1934), [Film] Dir. Ernst Lubitsch, USA: MGM.
Prends la route (1937), [Film] Dir. Jean Boyer and Louis Chavance, France: ACE.
Titin des Martigues (1938), [Film] Dir. René Pujol, France: Productions Malesherbes/Vondas Films.
Toi c'est moi (1936), [Film] Dir. René Guissart, France: Pathé.
Trois de la Canebière (1955), [Film] Dir. Maurice de Canonge, France: Tellus-Films, Cocinex, Noël Films.
Trois de la marine (1934), [Film] Dir. Charles Barrois, France: Métropa Films.
Trois de la marine (1957), [Film] Dir. Maurice de Canonge, France: Les Productions
Un de la Canebière (1938), [Film] Dir. René Pujol, France: Vondas Films.

7

Heteroglossia in the Musical Number

Song, Music Performance, and Marginalized Identity in Tony Gatlif's *Swing* (2002)

Tamsin Graves

As a Romani-French filmmaker of Algerian origin, the characters in Gatlif's cinema often reflect his own hybrid, interstitial cultural background. His low budget, art-house, or festival release films are marginal within the film industry, and the locations within his films depict the geographical margins of society by frequently centering on the seaports, train stations, caravan sites, refugee camps, borders, and tunnels that Hamid Naficy describes as "transitional and transnational spaces and places" (2001: 5). Additionally, Gatlif's work sits at the margins of genre: *Latcho Drom* (1993), for instance, is described by a critic as being "at once musical, documentary, travelogue, [and] ethnographic essay" (Romney 2000). His emphasis on music, woven into the fabric of the films through the diegetic performance of song, music, and dance, combined with his foregrounding of Roma, refugee, and immigrant communities, strongly situates Gatlif's films as musicals of the margins.

While reading Gatlif's films as musicals, it is important to note that they remain marginal to the genre, as indeed they do to dominant cinema in general. This chapter offers a reading of *Swing* (2002) as a musical in order to draw out the meanings created through the film's heavy emphasis on music, rather than insisting that the films are produced and received within the confines of this generic category. In order to highlight the marginality of Gatlif's filmmaking, the chapter considers a musical reading alongside the Bakhtinian concept of heteroglossia, or "many-languagedness," which has previously been applied to film studies by Shohat and Stam as a way of facilitating "a more nuanced discussion of race and ethnicity in the cinema . . . to call attention to the cultural voices at play" (1994: 214). This method represents an important way of reading cinema of the margins: "Formulating the issue as one of voices and discourses helps us get past the 'lure' of the visual, to look beyond the epidermic surface of the text. The question, quite literally, is less of the color of the face in the image than of the actual or figurative social voice or discourse speaking 'through' the image." (Shohat and Stam 1994: 214). By combining a reading of Gatlif's films as musicals, while maintaining a heteroglossic perspective that focuses on the cultural voices at play, this chapter offers a new, nuanced approach to reading Tony Gatlif as well as broadening the definition of the musical to include multilingual, border-crossing, nonmainstream cinema. Building on the work of Shohat and Stam, this chapter will consider the specific role of heteroglossia in the musical, focusing on the ability of music performance to weave together cultural discourses and relay collective histories as a way of enacting and encoding the marginalized identities of the characters. This chapter will consider the use of the musical number as a privileged site for the expression of the multiple voices and discourses present among the multi-linguistic communities that feature so heavily in his work.

The performance of music and dance is integral to the communities Gatlif documents across his films. The musical number appears in spaces as varied as a building site in Spain or a beach in Greece (*Indignados* [2012]), in a disused factory (*Geronimo* [2014]) and a train station and desert (*Latcho Drom*). The mise-en-scène itself often contributes to the soundtrack, such as Betty's frantic banging on a closed door fusing with non-diegetic drumming in the closing sequence of *Indignados*, and a sequence in *Vengo* (2000) using percussion sounds created by the equipment of a car repair shop that has its own song title ("mecanique garage") listed in the credits. The frequent integration of mise-en-scène into the musical number provides a variation on bricolage as discussed by Jane Feuer, where making use of the location in order to contribute to the sound or performance functions to "create the imaginary world of the musical number" (1993: 4). The instances in which bricolage occurs for Gatlif, however, differ from the examples cited by Feuer as they do not operate as part of a complex choreography designed to showcase the technical dancing ability of performers such as Fred Astaire or Gene Kelly. Where for Feuer the use of props and mise-en-scène in dance routines establishes the film set as a fictional, transformative, and somewhat fantasy space, reminding the viewer of its artifice and encouraging the suspension of disbelief, for Gatlif the reconfiguring of spaces to function as the site of musical production also reinforces the significance of place for marginal and often displaced communities. As Rick Altman describes, "The musical blurs the borders between the real and the ideal" (1987: 63).

Identifying this feature as an "audio dissolve," which "superimposes sounds in order to pass from one soundtrack to another," he states, "This simple expedient, perhaps more characteristic of the musical than any other stylistic trait, has long been sensed as a typical- and somewhat unrealistic- musical technique" (Altman 1987: 63). As well as reinforcing the relevance of a study of Gatlif's work as musicals, the idea of permeable borders is particularly relevant to a discussion of marginality in his cinema, with movements of migration, refuge, and exile echoed in the movement of sound across and beyond the diegesis. Altman's discussion of the merging of soundtracks in the audio dissolve is also useful in considering the complex layers of identity for marginal characters, where multilingual narratives of belonging and non-belonging interact continuously.

This chapter will use *Swing* as a case study, which, as with many of Gatlif's films, features real-life musicians in several of the acting roles, including guitar players Mandino Reinhardt and Tchavolo Schmitt in the roles of Mandino and Miraldo. Although Heather Laing differentiates between the musical genre and "those narratives which feature composers and musicians as characters" (2001: 7), this chapter will consider the musical interludes of *Swing* not merely as logical moments where musician characters sing and dance but as representing a semi-fantasy space that enables the articulation of discourses and voices for characters who are often socially and politically marginalized. *Swing* centers on a Roma family living in caravans on the outskirts of Strasbourg. Depicting marginality, music, and journeying from the outset, the opening shots show Miraldo, guitar in hand, walking through an industrial wasteland on the periphery of the city. Max, a French boy, seeks out Miraldo for guitar lessons, and subsequently develops a friendship with Swing, Miraldo's niece. Music is very easily integrated into the diegetic soundtrack: the boy's lessons, family get-togethers, and a local concert all represent moments where musical performance emerges naturally within the film's diegesis. Describing the dichotomy between the real and the fantastic, Altman explains how "the use of the stage for production numbers makes this relationship particularly obvious, but it should not be allowed to obscure the similar functioning of any space which is marked off, separated from the normal world, and reserved for an idealized, artistic presentation" (1987: 61). The performance numbers in *Swing* demonstrate Altman's observation that, through song and dance, even without a dedicated stage space, "the characters break out of the normal world into a realm of performance and art, a world where stylization and rhythm provide a sense of community and beauty absent from the real world" (1987: 61). It is conditions of marginality specific to Gatlif's film-world that encourage this natural integration of music into settings such as the caravan, a riverbank, a petrol station, with the marginal spaces Gatlif depicts all becoming filled with the near-constant diegetic music.

The first key musical sequence of *Swing* sees all the performers come together in Miraldo's caravan, where an extended version of "Les Yeux Noirs" is performed by a diverse range of musicians: instruments include an oud and derbouka as well as the more familiar acoustic guitar, double bass, and violins. In Avtar Brah's discussion of the relationship between place and identity, she describes a "politics of location" which involves "a positionality of dispersal; of simultaneous situatedness within gendered spaces of class, racism, ethnicity, sexuality, age; of movement across shifting cultural, religious and linguistic boundaries; of journeys across geographical and psychic borders" (1996: 204). The heteroglossic fluidity of music itself, with the ability to move from one melody or chord progression to another and for multiple layers of sound to be produced at the same time, provides an ideal space within the soundscape for Brah's "multi-axial locationality" to operate. Rather than a polyphonic rendition of the track where multiple melodies are played simultaneously, the sequence contains a continuous form of musical border-crossing, with the dominant melody passed between musicians, starting on the guitar and then being repeated by a violin and then a clarinet. Each rendition of the melody contains different inflections and emphases: utterances relayed with different musical accents. While the physical location of this sequence in a caravan contributes to the coding of the space as diasporic, with the camera moving constantly between interior and exterior shots and musicians situated both inside and outside the vehicle, it is the music itself that allows multiple and diverse rhythms and sounds to coexist and combine in this multiaxial, heteroglossic space. Richard Dyer describes the elasticity of space afforded to white singers and dancers in contrast to the confined sites occupied by Black performers:

> Blackness is contained in the musical, ghettoized, stereotyped, and "only entertainment." Yet containment is the antithesis of the entertainment a musical offers. Bursting from the confines of life by singing your heart out and dancing when you feel like it—this is the joy of the musical. Where the musical most disturbingly constructs a vision of race is in the fact that is it whites' privilege to be able to do this, and what that tells us about the white dream of being in the world. (2000: 25)

Transposed onto the French context, the idea that North African and Roma characters should have less freedom of movement on-screen is radically challenged through the musical element of Gatlif's film. The out-of-town traveler site becomes the locus of musical production rather than peripheral to a white French center: this reappropriation of space and inversion of colonial power structures challenges dominant codes of the classical Hollywood musical. The way in which this space is used, with musicians spilling out of the caravan while continuing to play, offers a rejection of the colonial structures that police the movement of marginalized communities.

In addition to allowing diverse musical voices to be heard, the interlude in the caravan also represents an immersive experience both for the participants and for the film's wider audience. Originating in Russia, "Les Yeux Noirs" was popularized by Django Reinhardt and Bireli Lagrene and is strongly associated with Romani Manouche Jazz. This style has been used to exoticize otherness in the soundtrack of Anglophone films set in France, for example, the use of Reinhardt and Grappelli's Minor Swing in *Chocolat* (2000), and Stephane Wrembel's manouche jazz score for Woody Allen's *Midnight in Paris* (2011). There is no doubt that Gatlif aims to showcase and celebrate the sheer enjoyment of music as spectacle with extended sequences in which songs are performed in their entirety and where cinemagoers are reflected on-screen by audiences and onlookers framed around the musicians. Feuer points out that the cinemagoer's position behind an internal, "diegetic" audience means "we are encouraged to actually become part of the audience in the film" (1993: 29) and that "only a reflexive form such as the musical can lend so much intensity to our experience of a simple song and dance" (1993: 30). In Dyer's analysis of the musical in his chapter "Entertainment and Utopia," he positions the musical an example of entertainment's function as "escape" and as "wish fulfillment." He states, "Entertainment offers the image of 'something better' to escape into" but that "the utopianism is contained in the feelings it embodies. It presents, head-on as it were, what utopia would feel like rather than how it would be organized" (Dyer 1995: 222). The almost participatory experience of the film viewer that is reflected in the internal audiences Feuer describes, where "inside and outside space have merged into a community celebration" (1993: 34), allows the musical numbers to be enjoyed and celebrated, without diminishing the conditions of marginality that give rise to the performances.

Indeed, this track has a crucial role in mediating marginality: songs can communicate feeling even when the language is not understood; rhythm and syncopation can drive emotion within the listener where there may be no other obvious point of identification with the performer. Dyer states, "we also recognize qualities in non-representational signs—color, texture, movement, rhythm, melody, camerawork" (1995: 223). While harder to analyze, as he points out, than the semiotic approach to representational signs, the nonrepresentational offers a communication of feeling and emotion associated with music and dance. Shohat and Stam state, "One alternative to the mimetic 'stereotypes-and-distortions' approach, we would argue, is to speak less of 'images' than of 'voices' and 'discourses'" (1994: 214). The nonrepresentational signs are particularly useful in creating meanings associated with marginality in the context of a film where multiple languages are spoken and sung. Beyond offering a spectacle for visual (and aural) pleasure, the utopia of the musical numbers in *Swing* provides a rare space in which discourses of marginality are centered. In this sequence Romani, Arabic, and Russian voices are articulated through melodies and instrumentation: it is unlikely an individual viewer will understand all the languages and indeed the characters (and Gatlif himself) do not. There is a utopianism in the role of music to create a unified, harmonious sound from such diverse voices. However, there is also a mode of expression through nonrepresentational signs of complex cultural histories and narratives.

Although referring to a genre of music very different to manouche jazz, David Shumway's article "Rock'n'roll Soundtracks and the Production of Nostalgia" provides a useful assessment of the significance of music in films which consist of recognizable, identifiable tracks. He states that "whereas the goal of the traditional film score was to cue an emotional response in the viewer without calling attention to itself, recent soundtracks, consisting mainly of previously recorded material, are put together on the assumption that the audience will recognize the artist, the song, or at a minimum, a familiar style" (Shumway 1999: 36–7). Discussing *The Graduate* (1967) and *Easy Rider* (1969), he goes on to state that "The music in these films is meant to be not merely recognized but often to take the foreground and displace the image as the principal locus of attention. Moreover, the music in these films secures a bond between consumer and product while also arousing a feeling of generational belonging in the audience" (Shumway 1999: 37). Even while acknowledging that viewers of Gatlif's 2002 film will not have a sense of generational belonging with the Paris Jazz club scene of the 1920s and 1930s, the function of "Les Yeux Noirs" as a recognizable tune that can evoke a visceral sense of emotional connection for the audience positions *Swing* as both marginal and a film which conforms to conventions of the musical through emotional affect. By displacing the image and assuming the primary position in communicating a discourse, the song both immerses an audience already familiar with a jazz soundtrack and opens up a heteroglossic framework which allows plural voices—voices of counterculture, exile, bilingualism, and intertextual discourse—to be heard.

Naficy considers the double function of the performance space in exilic cinema, both for enjoyment and for relaying exilic discourse, in his discussion of *Tangos* (1985):

> The actors are not acting for the camera alone but also for the tango-dy performance within the film. The spectators, too, are placed in a split position. By mixing presentational and representational modes that solicit spectatorial duality, the film simultaneously thwarts and encourages audience identification. In its presentational mode, the narrative is suspended, and the audience can appreciate the tango-dy performances as spectacle, admiring the beauty of the dancers, the elegance and sensuality

of their movements, and the poignancy of the song's exilic lyrics. In its representational mode, on the other hand, the film's character-driven narrative and editing strategy encourage identification with both the characters and their exilic concerns, suturing the viewers into the diegesis. (2001: 272)

With this analysis in mind, the enjoyment and elements of nostalgia evoked by Shumway's understanding of the function of the recognizable track need not diminish the impact of dialogues of "highly fluid, exilic and diasporic identities" (Naficy 2001: 6) that are integral to the marginal film. Shohat and Stam state that "formulating the issue as one of voices and discourses helps us get past the 'lure' of the visual, to look beyond the epidermic surface of the text. . . . Less important than a film's 'accuracy' is that it relays the voices and perspectives—we emphasize the plural—of the community or communities in question" (1994: 215). The use of coded generic conventions of the musical within marginal cinema, rather than a point of contention, represents an additional voice or discourse within heteroglossia which Shohat and Stam conclude "is just another name for the socially generated contradictions that constitute the subject, like the media, as the site of conflicting discourses and competing voices" (1994: 215).

In contrast to the contained space of the caravan, with the camera constantly permeating the border by moving from interior to exterior and back again, the next musical number takes place in the open air of a petrol station forecourt. Naficy places importance on "transitional and transnational places and spaces, such as borders, tunnels, seaports, airports, and hotels and vehicles of mobility," considering these "privileged sites" in his "examination of journeys of and struggles over identity" (2001: 5) in accented cinema. The petrol station, in an isolated, rural location, functions similarly to the airport in Naficy's description of "actual physical locations in which exilic narratives are enacted." He states, "for many exiles and refugees, airports are not just rhizomatic points of linkage to other points in an abstract network of relation and commerce, as they may be for transnationals and cosmopolitans. These are nodal sites of high intensity in which their belonging and unbelonging are juxtaposed in often cruel, sometimes humorous ways" (2001: 246). The juxtaposition of belonging and unbelonging is complicated further in *Swing*, as the petrol station is revealed to be the home of Abdelatif Chaarani's character Khaled. During this sequence, a cassette tape is played through the car's speakers, and the passengers spill out of the car onto the tarmac to dance. The dance moves are coded as culturally specific, with close-ups of the dancer's feet and hands showing precise and deliberate movements in synchronicity with the music, while the incongruous nature of the location renders the act spontaneous, fluid, and free from restriction. The dance is an exilic narrative overlaid onto a site of journeying and intersection. The effect is that of a musical number: a spontaneous outpouring of emotion taking place in an unexpected location that exists to convey meaning otherwise not spoken in the dialogue. Laing describes how in the musical we find "a state of music which . . . occupies an entirely new space" (2000: 8). In *Swing* this reappropriation of space as a site for heteroglossic discourse to emerge is a direct result of marginality: the only spaces available to the characters are liminal, transient sites of "unbelonging."

Once this musical interlude has served its diegetic purpose of waking Khaled, he greets Miraldo and Dr. Leiberman by acknowledging and deriving unity from their shared status as marginal with his greeting of "Le Juif! Le Manouche!" (Jew! Gypsy!), and they continue their music session. The point at which Dr. Leiberman plucks a barbed wire fence as if it were a guitar introduces an additional layer of meaning into the heteroglossic space. By using the mise-en-scène itself as a musical instrument, Gatlif prioritizes sound in relaying discourse and interconnects the cultural history performed through song with that represented by the barbed wire. Even without Leiberman commenting "a chaque fois que je vois du fils de fer barbelé, ca me fais mal au coeur" (every time I see barbed wire, it makes me sick), the association with violent segregation is clear, and is an image Gatlif has used elsewhere to illustrate stories of persecution (*Transylvania* [2006], *Liberté* [2009]). The tune played by Leiberman on the wire is a motif taken from "Chant de la Paix" which appears later in the film, and which is a love song containing verses in Arabic, Yiddish, and Romani. In the soundscape, therefore, multiple conflicting layers of cultural identification are enacted simultaneously. Plural discourses emerge from a single character, confirming Shohat and Stam's argument around cinematic heteroglossia that "even an individual voice is itself a discursive sum, a polyphony of voices" (1994: 215).

As well as drawing out historic discourses of oppression and otherness, Gatlif's film reinforces what Naficy terms "rhizomatic group affiliations— vertical, horizontal, and transverse—across de-territorialized social formations" (2001: 7). Despite the entirety of *Swing* taking place in Strasbourg, in contrast to many of Gatlif's films which place journeying at the center of the narrative (*Transylvania, Latcho Drom, Exiles, Indignados, Djam* [2017]), it is the job of the soundtrack of *Swing* to move between Russia, Eastern Europe, and North Africa. The track "Rumania Rumania," originally by Aaron Lebedeff with the recording here performed by the Budapest Klezmer band, is a further example of the wide-ranging geography of the musical score. This sequence offers a point of difference to the other musical numbers in *Swing*, in that it involves a piece of music being played via a record, rather than being performed "live" by musicians within the diegesis. As with the concert in the caravan and the impromptu dancing at the petrol station, the riverside location of the gramophone sequence refers to the idea of journeying, without the characters traveling outside of their locality. Miraldo's motivation for taking his record player to an isolated spot by the river is due to the cacophony of voices in his home preventing him from hearing his music, a process that echoes the much more literal and extensive journey undertaken by Romain Duris's character in *Gadjo Dilo* (1997) to seek out Nora Luca after becoming obsessed with the sound of her singing. The song "Rumania, Rumania" remains elusive even away from the background noise of Miraldo's home when a passing train momentarily obscures the sound of his record and pushes the music further to the margins of the audio-scape.

There is a point in this sequence when the fast-paced, energetic track shifts from the diegetic sound of the record to non-diegetic. The moment at which it becomes non-diegetic is accompanied by a cut in the image-track to a shot of Max and Swing running through a wooded area to the river, laughing uproariously and falling over themselves as they speed downhill. The freedoms of this liminal non-place, with an absence of physical borders or constraints such as the tall oppressive gates Max's grandmother keeps locked to try and keep him at home, or the more distressing symbolism of the barbed wire, are reflected in the aural fluidity between diegetic and non-diegetic. What Stilwell terms the "fantastical gap," referring to the "destabilization and multiplicity of possibility that occurs during the transition between one diegetic state to another" (2007: 187), adds a further layer of meaning to the borderless yet marginal space occupied by the two children. Returning to Avtar Brah, this liminal site between land and water at the riverside, and between diegetic and non-diegetic in the soundscape, can be viewed as a "diaspora space" which she describes as "the intersectionality of diaspora, border, and dis/location as a point of confluence of economic, political, cultural and psychic processes" (1996: 208). That Max and Swing are children is significant, their generational difference freeing them from some of the social and often gendered discourses of their elders (even Swing's gender is questioned by Max at the start of the film, as she refuses to conform to traditionally female codes of behavior and clothing), but also placing other barriers in their way as they seek to define their identities without access to some of the anchoring cultural practices familiar to the older generations. Max and Swing continue their adventures to the sound of the Budapest Klezmer band by putting the gramophone on a boat as they float up and down the river. Heather Laing describes how "whereas it is usually diegetic events which give rise to music, the musical number overturns this situation, so that the music comes to determine the course of diegetic events for the duration of the song and dance" (2000: 8). The accelerated tempo has the effect of dictating the rhythm of their activities: their "real life" is suspended as they float along the river, temporarily occupying a space between reality and fantasy as they also hover between childhood and adolescence. Having been played diegetically, when Miraldo struggles to hear it over background noise, and non-diegetically, when the gramophone is completely absent from a shot of Swing and Max running, toward the end of the sequence the song is finally positioned in both the diegetic and non-diegetic spheres at once: physically emanating from the gramophone, but heightened in the mix so that all other atmospheric sounds are canceled. Laing suggests, "This simultaneous appearance of music at both levels is one of the defining points of the musical" (2000: 8); in marginal cinema, this "fantastical gap" provides a unique site away from complex, bordered spaces and toward a greater sense of audience immersion and character identification.

Gatlif has placed huge importance on music throughout his film career, evidenced not only by his film soundtracks but also by his crossing over from screen to stage with concerts in which images from his films are screened behind live musicians and dancers. In *Swing*, he stages a concert within the film, as Miraldo, Khaled, and Dr. Leiberman tutor a choir before putting on a performance of Russian-Jewish folk song "Tumbalalaika" and the earlier mentioned "Chant de la Paix." With both the songs featuring multiple languages, this sequence facilitates the interaction of diverse narratives of exile and diaspora. The choice of venue differentiates the concert from the open or permeable spaces such as the caravan and the roadside garage, and instead takes place inside a building with a more traditional arrangement of performers facing their audience. The dimly lit, enclosed space with lingering close-ups of singers' faces and musicians' hands fosters a sense of intensity and intimacy, while the hypnotic chorus line immerses and engages the listener in the emotion being conveyed: the songs have priority over narrative progression during the concert sequence. Having shown the performers learning the lyrics by repeating them after Khaled, and a violinist copying Miraldo's guitar riff in rehearsals, the actual concert involves a repetition of the motifs that had already been sounded out in the film. Rather than an isolated act, the concert therefore becomes part of a process, linked to other occasions in the film and connected to social and cultural discourses outside of the film text through the extra-diegetic tracks. Even though each performance is slightly different, adapted in tempo, volume, or mood according to the different audiences, locations, or number of musicians in each scenario, each time a song is performed it is reinforced as a constant. Naficy states, "At certain junctures in an exile's life, it becomes important, even mandatory, to stress the fixity, not fluidity, the weightiness, not weightlessness, of identity" (2001: 287). Through repetition, the musical number becomes anchored to all the other times and places it has been performed. Though Naficy describes exile as "a structurally open ended process" (2001: 108), similar to the process of learning and rehearsing music, the moment of performance offers a moment of fixity and point of linkage, for the duration of the track, in the historical and cultural discourses relayed by the song.

While the heteroglossic space of the musical number offers a point of cultural anchorage through semi-fantasy nostalgic tropes, this is a fixedness of identity rather than a permanence of location or time period. It is significant that the key spaces of *Swing*—the caravan, petrol station, and river—are more usually associated with the act of travel than the performance of music. Despite the entire film unfolding on the periphery of Strasbourg, the narrative constantly refers to acts of journeying—Naficy's "deterritorializing and reterritorializing journeys, which take several forms, including home-seeking journeys, journeys of homelessness, and homecoming journeys" (2001: 5–6): the Roma family are threatened with eviction, Max's mother arrives at the end of the film to take him to Greece. Music, with its ability to evoke and retell cultural and historical journeys through a combination of language, rhythm, and emotion, is critical in replacing the physical journeys that are absent from the film with the aural evocation of movement across and beyond Europe through history.

Music functions at a representative level in evoking cultural histories, but is also a physical act, with character-musicians forming the site of music production. Gatlif offers a symbolic account of the inextricable link between the physical body and the discursive musical space in the moments preceding Miraldo's sudden heart attack. Miraldo urging Max to "Reste avec la cadence, garde ta cadence, la cadence, la cadence, la cadence toujours" (Keep in time, keep to the rhythm, the rhythm, the rhythm, always the rhythm) becomes a comment on the failure of the internal rhythms of his body, and the sequence closes with Miraldo collapsing to the sound of Max out of shot still playing his jumpy, arrhythmic rendition of *les yeux noirs*. The use of music to highlight the fallibility of the body shown here contrasts heavily with the musical's usual emphasis on virtuosity, which foregrounds what the body can, rather than can't, achieve. Moments of loss and grief offer a reminder that Gatlif is a marginal director whose key themes of migration and exile are not precluded by the escapism and celebration of the musical numbers.

As Gatlif has pointed out, "music is the only authentic document the Roma have; any written records are police records" (Naficy 2001: 99), and a heteroglossic reading confirms the importance Gatlif places on music not just as spectacle to be enjoyed, but in its ability to facilitate the intersection of the multiple and marginal voices of this film. *Swing* confirms a rejection of written documentation in favor of the aural discourse of the soundscape: in the closing sequence of the film when Max sees Swing for the last time, he gives her the diary he has written documenting his experiences with the Reinhardt family over the summer, causing her to comment "Je sais pas lire" (I can't read). The final shot of the film shows the diary in close-up where she has left it on the ground, and then tilts up to track her slowly walking back into her house and closing the door. Naficy states that "the Romas' highly developed musical tradition helps them to both preserve and express their odyssey of displacement and cohesiveness. Music is perhaps their true home" (2001: 99). By describing music as "home," Naficy draws out the role of music for communicating identity in the displaced, socially marginalized characters of his film. The performance space is a key site of discourse in Gatlif's films, rather than a traditional soundtrack designed merely "to cue an emotional response in the viewer without calling attention to itself" (Shumway 1999: 36). The soundtrack of *Swing* fulfills a dual role of providing the celebratory, immersive experience of the musical, while also facilitating the multiple, sometimes conflicting discourses of heteroglossia.

References

Altman, R. (1987), *The American Film Musical*, Bloomington: Indiana University Press.
Brah, A. (1996), *Cartographies of Diaspora: Contesting Identities*, London and New York: Routledge.
Dyer, R. (1995), "Entertainment and Utopia," in B. Nichols (ed.), *Movies and Methods: Volume II*, 220–32, London: BFI.
Dyer, R. (2000), "The Colour of Entertainment," in B. Marshall and R. Stilwell (eds.), *Musicals: Hollywood and Beyond*, 21–30, Exeter: Intellect.
Feuer, J. (1993), *The Hollywood Musical*, 2nd edn, Basingstoke and London: Macmillan.
Laing, H. (2000), "Emotion by Numbers: Music Song and the Musical," in B. Marshall and R. Stilwell (eds.), *Musicals: Hollywood and Beyond*, 5–13, Exeter: Intellect.
Naficy, H. (2001), *An Accented Cinema: Exilic and Diasporic Filmmaking*, Princeton: Princeton University Press.
Romney, J. (2000), "The Incredible Journey," *The Guardian*, 3 May. Available online: https://www.theguardian.com/film/2000/may/03/artsfeatures (accessed October 8, 2019).
Shohat, E., and R. Stam (1994), *Unthinking Eurocentrism: Multiculturalism and the Media*, London and New York: Routledge.
Shumway, D. (1999), "Rock 'n' Roll Soundtracks and the Production of Nostalgia," *Cinema Journal*, 38 (2): 36–51.
Stilwell, R. J. (2007), "The Fantastical Gap between Diegetic and Nondiegetic," in D. Goldmark, L. Kramer and R. Leppert (eds.), *Beyond the Soundtrack: Representing Music in Cinema*, 184–202, Berkeley; Los Angeles; London: University of California Press.

Filmography

Chocolat (2000), [Film] Dir. Lasse Hallström, UK/USA: Miramax.
Djam (2017), [Film] Dir. Tony Gatlif, France/Greece/Turkey: Les Films du Losange.
Easy Rider (1969), [Film] Dir. Dennis Hopper, USA: Columbia Pictures.
Gadjo Dilo (1997), [Film] Dir. Tony Gatlif, Romania/France: AFMD.
Geronimo (2014), [Film] Dir. Tony Gatlif, France: Les Films du Losange.

The Graduate (1967), [Film] Dir. Mike Nichols, USA: Embassy Pictures.
Indignados (2012), [Film] Dir. Tony Gatlif, France: Les Films du Losange.
Latcho Drom (1993), [Film] Dir. Tony Gatlif, France: Acteurs Auteurs Associés.
Liberté (2009), [Film] Dir. Tony Gatlif, France: UGC.
Midnight in Paris (2011), [Film] Dir. Woody Allen, Spain/USA/France: Mars Distribution.
Swing (2002), [Film] Dir. Tony Gatlif, France/Japan: Pyramide.
Tangos, the Exile of Gardel (1985), [Film] Dir. Fernando E. Solanas, Argentina/France: Tercine, Cinesur.
Transylvania (2006), [Film] Dir. Tony Gatlif, France: Princes Films.
Vengo (2000), [Film] Dir. Tony Gatlif, Spain/France/Germany/Japan: UGC-Fox.

8

Sexsationalist Feminism in *The Devil's Carnival* Project (2012, 2015)

Joana Rita Ramalho

Genres are mobile formations whose parameters are constantly reshaped and updated, which means that establishing a coherent history of the musical genre requires a rethinking of what the musical is, has been, and how it works in its myriad subsets. One such subset is the gothic musical, which focuses on the exploration of monstrosity, excess, decadence, entrapment, and depravity. The intersections between film, musicals, and "dark" styles or genres, such as noir and Gothic, although not new (Conrich 2006; Laderman 2010; Biesen 2014; Petermann 2015; Stokes 2016) remain widely undertheorized. With its risqué musical numbers often shot in low-key lighting, the gothic musical is, by definition, a marginal product that caters mostly to a marginal audience. The soundtrack usually mixes an operatic tone with glam rock and a punk or industrial edge and each song features incisive, witty lyrics that expose the ills and vices of society.

Darren Lynn Bousman, who is known for directing the first three sequels of the slash horror franchise *Saw* (2003–17), collaborated with writer-actor-composer Terrance Zdunich on three musicals: *Repo! The Genetic Opera* (2008), *The Devil's Carnival* (2012), and *Alleluia! The Devil's Carnival* (2015). Following in the footsteps of Jim Sharman's *The Rocky Horror Picture Show* (1975), the most obvious referent for their musical ventures, these films revolve around death, transgression, revenge, and the injustices to which certain individuals, particularly women, are subjected in contemporary societies. Their in-your-face, self-reflexive approach to taboo content and tongue-in-cheek satire appeal to a niche subcultural audience that has granted a cult status to these productions. Despite amassing a devoted following, the films have nonetheless been ignored by critics and scholars.

In this chapter, I will focus on *The Devil's Carnival* and will refer to the project's second film, *Alleluia!*, when pertinent. The project constitutes a particularly interesting case study for the way it adheres to set rules and conventions of the Gothic and the musical, while giving them a luscious apocalyptic and intergeneric twist. It innovates, for instance, in its choice of location. Unlike most European, Bollywood, and Hollywood film musicals, which take place in real (mappable) locations, *The Devil's Carnival*, save for just over a minute and a half in the first installment, is set exclusively in Hell and Heaven. It also melds a series of generic categories—musicals, horror, Gothic, and fantasy—which have traditionally occupied the lower ranks of genre hierarchy. Fred Botting observes that when "generic monsters combine, their coupling delivers monstrosities of hitherto unprecedented dimensions" (2008: 21). Botting's graphic statement aptly describes the hybrid monstrosity that is *The Devil's Carnival*, which Bousman describes as "a mish-mash of insanity. Part musical, part horror film, part undefinable . . . a carnival in every sense of the word" (Cruz 2012). Analyzing such genre-bending and self-parodic works can help re/discover a marginal (and marginalized) history of film musicals.

My investigation is informed by Marie-Luise Kohlke's notion of "sexsation," which she uses to describe the excessive eroticism of neo-Victorian gothic fiction (2008a, b). The moniker, I argue, is equally relevant to examine gothic film. Barbara Creed's definition of the "monstrous-feminine" ([1993] 2007), which extends Julia Kristeva's theory of abjection to the horror film, is also central to my analysis. In particular, Creed's understanding of female monsters not as passive victims, but as boundary-crossing, active characters that contest and confront the prevalence of the male gaze ([1993] 2007: 7) can be productively employed to study the gothic musical and reassess the film musical's typical representation of the female body as "lacking and passive, put on exhibition and looked at" (Cohan [2000] 2002: 62). My aim here is twofold. On the one hand, I will examine how the project problematizes representations of femininity through a focus on suffering and sexsation; on the other, I will analyze how it uses narrative, characterization, and mise-en-scène to forge a singular self-conscious reflection on the musical form and the film industry—all to the strains of a jazzy, cabaret, and punk-rock soundtrack.

The Aestheticization of Suffering

Initially envisioned as a TV series to serve as counterprogramming to Fox's hit-show *Glee* (2009–2015) (Childers 2015), *The Devil's Carnival* and

Alleluia! are bizarre musicals set primarily in Hell and Heaven respectively. The first film focuses on three characters—John, Ms. Merrywood, and Tamara—who die and wake up in Hell, a chief locus of gothic horrors here materialized as a lively carnival. Each doomed soul earns their one-way ticket to the netherworld for a different reason: John, a grieving father, slits his wrists after losing his son; Ms. Merrywood steals some jewelry and is killed in her trailer during a shootout with the police; and Tamara, a young woman in an abusive relationship, is shot dead in her car when trying to drive away from her angry boyfriend.

The Devil's Carnival has *Aesop's Fables* at its core, with the main characters each representing a fable and a sin.[1] John's sin is grief, Ms. Merrywood's is greed, and Tamara's is gullibility. Even though Ms. Merrywood's greed figures as the only "true" sin (John's suicide is not considered so), this broader and highly contentious interpretation of what is sinful does not compromise the film's premise, to the extent that *Aesop's Fables* are invested in teaching a moral lesson by warning us about the dangers of engaging in potentially harmful behavior, such as grieving too intensely or being too trusting. As adapted by Zdunich, they succeed as cautionary tales, with the unusual definition of sin hinting from the start at an authoritarian power that, apparently rather arbitrarily, decides who should be sent to Heaven or Hell.

Throughout the film, Lucifer (played by Zdunich) and selected carnies tell the stories of John, Tamara, and Ms. Merrywood through songs based on three fables, respectively "Grief and His Due," "The Scorpion and The Frog," and "The Dog and Its Reflection." The film's musical structure is reminiscent of cabaret theater, punctuated with short stories and bawdy songs that encourage audience participation. There is one integrated song focusing on each newcomer and one summarizing their sealed fates. Zdunich and co-composer Saar Hendelman's score combines circus, punk rock, ballad, dark cabaret, and Dust Bowl folk influences (Anderson 2015), which lend the film's soundtrack a distinctively postmodern feel.

In the carnival, there are arcade games, a circus tent, and fairground attractions run and frequented by various freaks and misfits. The carnival's populace of dead bodies, "basic forms of pollution [and] waste" that represent "the utmost in abjection," illustrates Creed's theory that horror films stage a confrontation with the abject—a body with fluid borders that is easily infected by the other and—literally, in this film—by death (Creed [1993] 2007: 9–10; Kristeva [1980] 1982: 4). Painted Doll, played by Victoriandustrial artist Emilie Autumn, is a case in point. Publicized as "the belle of Lucifer's ball" ("Devil's Carnival" 2012), this antiheroine resists classification. She has pasty white skin and her countenance is disfigured by a series of scar-like cracks that run down one side of her face, giving her the appearance of a broken porcelain doll. In *Alleluia!* we learn that Painted Doll, formerly known as June, was violently cast out of Heaven. Her transgressions included dating God's right hand (The Agent), encouraging the "abnormal sexual desire" (Creed [1993] 2007: 11) of her lesbian friend Cora (there is a queer subtext to their relationship), and breaking into the Forbidden Books section of Heaven's library. She is depicted as a modern iteration of Eve, whose thirst for knowledge results in eternal damnation. Prelapsarian June inhabited the margins and the angels shunned her as utterly abject. Her face from then on bears the physical marks of her disobedience, collapsing the borders between beauty and disfigurement. "The wound," Creed explains, "is a sign of abjection in that it violates the skin which forms a border between the inside and outside of the body" ([1993] 2007: 82). Her adopted name, "Painted Doll," also signals abjection and operates on three interrelated narrative and cultural levels: "doll" is a patriarchal and derogatory term employed to refer to women (The Agent addresses June as "dollface"); the common usage of "doll" in this sense implies the convergence of subject and object, generating uncanniness; finally, the adjective "painted" may be read as relating to makeup, to the act of women "dolling up." Painted Doll attracts and repulses, her scarred-yet-sensual face and scantily clad body disclosing a troubled relationship to notions of (s) exploitation, abjection, and empowerment that at once reject and condone conventional ideals of femininity. As Creed argues, "woman is not, by her very nature, an abject being"; it is the dominant patriarchal ideology that constructs her as such ([1993] 2007: 83). June is thus constructed as abject when Heaven's patriarchal society reveals itself fundamentally intolerant toward queer identities and independent women who fight for knowledge and self-expression.

Alongside debauchery and abjection, Lucifer's carnival promotes comradery and equality. Yet, the community is changing and the neighborly rapport between the carnies no longer precludes localized outbreaks of violence. The space of the underworld, in fact, becomes structured so as to tempt its newest residents to fall, once again, prey to their earthly sins. The closely knit hellish community will not accept any of the neophytes as part of the team without them first proving their worth—and so puts them to the test. If they are tricked into replaying the actions that led to their untimely deaths, the carnival folk intervene and violently show the newcomers how to behave properly. Unsurprisingly, John, Tamara, and Ms. Merrywood soon repeat their sins and suffer the dire consequences. John is tricked into believing his dead son is lost somewhere in the carnival and is cruelly taunted by a series of demons who refuse to tell him his whereabouts, leading him once more to succumb to grief. Naive Tamara, who wakes up in the carnival wearing a child-like satin sailor dress stressing her ingenuity, is seduced by The Scorpion, a vain scoundrel, who ends up killing her on his knife-throwing wheel. Luring her to her death with dulcet tones and the complimentary words of the song "Trust Me," The Scorpion straps credulous Tamara to the wheel while assuring her she can trust him because she is his "darling dear" and he is "so sincere" that "there's no need to tear." Once the fatal knife pierces Tamara's heart, Painted Doll recounts her tribulations through song ("Prick! Goes the Scorpion's Tale") while showing off her inanimate body to the audience. Scornfully, Painted Doll incites the carnies to "drink to true love." Delighted, they yell and applaud. The song, based on Aesop's "The Scorpion and The Frog," offers a biting commentary on gullibility and warns that some people cannot refrain from hurting others even when it means self-destruction. As for Ms. Merrywood, she wakes up in Hell lying next to heaps of jewels and trinkets, which she promptly steals, disregarding the note next to them that reads: "Take only what you need." She then embarks on a mock contest to win a large diamond, which causes her to lose most of her clothes and leaves her stripped down to magenta satin gloves and lacy black and cream-colored knickers. To atone for her greed, she is publicly scourged while Hobo Clown solemnly sings "A Penny for a Tale," a grim ballad about a narcissistic puppy whose greed leads to its untimely demise. The participatory dimension of the song (whenever the word "doggy" is mentioned, the audience woofs along three times) emphasizes the vileness of shared sensationalism toward bodily harm.

As they wander around the carnival, the two women become flagrant targets of gratuitous, male-inflicted pain. In effect, although all three characters are subjected to violence, John's torture is mostly psychological, whereas the violence that befalls Tamara and Ms. Merrywood is primarily physical. Tamara suffers a "voyeuristic re-victimisation" (Kohlke 2012: 222) that is effected in a twofold manner. She experiences a double death (in Earth and in Hell) at the hands of two evil men and is doubly punished in the carnival: she is the only character who "dies" in Hell and vanishes from the narrative. It is telling of the film's marginal status that the only carny whose femininity is conventionally coded disappears—there is no room for strict gender categorizations or naive girls among Hell's denizens.

By depriving Tamara of all rights, including her right to an afterlife, Bousman opens the film up to criticism, with some viewers accusing the director of replicating what Kohlke terms "insidious patterns of victimization" (2012: 221) and fomenting discriminatory attitudes through the deployment of a victim-blaming narrative. While on the surface this interpretation may seem justified, Tamara's story begs closer inspection. Examining the film through *Aesop's Fables*, that is, reading each character's story and fate as a cautionary tale, Tamara's second death and subsequent disappearance serve as a warning: her gullibility leads her to make the same fatal mistakes over and over again. In other words, she is doomed to repeat her so-called "sin" *ad eternum*. More than blindly trusting toxic men, her transgression therefore appears to be not learning from her mistakes, as Bousman explained (2015). Punishing the victim may be understood, in the context of the project, as a drastic measure to ensure audience engagement with timely issues in the post-millennium. As noted, this strategy is highly controversial and dangerous, in that it may be read as bolstering a normative, misogynistic, and regressive ideology. However morally and ethically reprehensible, it nevertheless succeeded in getting the audience to talk about the recurring and generalized condoning of female-oriented violence in the media and in everyday life (Hall 2015; Syn-Cypher 2016).

Carnival activities such as public flogging stress the pain/pleasure dynamic that underscores the film and highlight the endurance of patriarchal rituals of domination and submission by constructing erotic moments of punishment that fetishize the female body. The sexualized showcase of Ms. Merrywood's forced striptease and subsequent thrashing celebrate libidinous fantasies through the deployment of gendered violence, nakedness, and the trope of the subjugated, victimized woman. The emphasis here is on what Kohlke has termed "sexsation" or "erotic excess" (2008a: 54). She remarks that female and marginal bodies are often sexsationalized, that is, "transfigured into fetishized erotic spectacles" (2008a: 68).

Much like the "'gratuitous' spectacle" of the showgirl's body in a backstage musical (Rubin 1993: 2) or the odd bodies monetized in Victorian freak shows, the deviant female body is constructed as spectacle, "coded for strong visual and erotic impact" (Mulvey 1975: 11).

Torture, moreover, is "an objectification, an acting out"—"a demonstration and magnification of the felt experience of pain," which converts "the vision of suffering into the wholly illusory, but . . . wholly convincing spectacle of power" (Scarry 1985: 27). The carnies' sadistic rejoicing in Ms. Merrywood's suffering and her seeming indulgence in masochism (despite the fact that there are no obvious signs of consent) appear to legitimate patriarchal eroticism, for "the prone and naked female body [is] helplessly available to the manipulations of male desire" (Kohlke 2008b: 4). The use of BDSM imagery—from whips to leather accoutrements, knives, and straps—and the spotlight on Tamara and Ms. Merrywood's bodies afford a very tactile dimension of spectacle to the scenes. Unlike the type of spectacle normally offered in musicals, where it is the untainted singing and dancing body that captures the audience's gaze, here the body—the female body, specifically—although still the center of attention, is restrained, its movements minimal or involuntary.

Spectacle therefore arises from a different form of sexsational aesthetics: one that feeds off abjection and limits the body's freedom of movement. However, while forcefully constraining female agency facilitates the audience's voyeuristic participation in illicit pleasure, it also confronts the viewers with their immoral condoning of sensationalized torture against women, "society's internally colonized subjects or subalterns" (Kohlke 2012: 222).

The number "Kiss the Girls" further exposes the connections between sexsation, objectification, abjection, and dollhood. While roaming the carnival, John catches a glimpse of what he believes to be his son and rushes into the Big Top. As the camera quickly zooms in on his disconcerted face, he looks around and calls out for his son. A point-of-view shot reveals a deserted tent but, as the camera follows him, we notice a carny damsel in the center of the ring, quiet as a mime, still as a mannequin. She has the disturbing appearance of a life-like rag doll. John circles around her, the camera moving with him. He gets closer and, just as he touches the woman's hair, she suddenly moves and speak-sings teasingly: "Missed me, missed me?" Immediately, the remaining Woe-Maidens, a group of carny women in smudged makeup and torn fishnet stockings, join the party, followed by the Hellharmonic, which marches in through the curtains of the ring doors. Singing at John while physically assaulting him, these "active monsters," to use Creed's expression ([1993] 2007: 153, 7), challenge patriarchal views that women are essentially victims. Female dominance reigns over the sequence and John falls to his feet halfway through, unable to fight off his assailants. In a way, this moment replays the earlier BDSM visual aesthetic and fetishistic gaze of Ms. Merrywood's and Tamara's torture scenes but reverses the gender dynamics. Now, it is the male character who becomes subservient to Hell's dominatrixes. Their belligerence, marred beauty, torn clothes, and controlling behavior, along with the lyrics (repeatedly telling John he "has to" kiss the girls), deliberately defy straightforward objectification and thwart the male gaze. These women destabilize normative assumptions about the "proper feminine" (Pykett 1992: 12) and reclaim their identity as independent agents through monstrosity and dollhood.

Abjection and victimization draw unjustly mistreated souls together, forming a tight bond between them. The sexsational abuse of Tamara and Ms. Merrywood acts as a call to arms that is not wholly concretized until the final number of the second film, in which Painted Doll rallies the female carnies and starts taking down the patriarchy, one despicable male after another, beginning with her former lover, The Agent. Sent on a godly mission to the carnival, The Agent is forcibly treated to a cabaret-style song-and-dance performance, "Hoof and Lap," whereby Painted Doll becomes an almighty, all-destructive figure, representative of Creed's "femme castratrice"—an avenging female castrator who "arouses a fear of castration and death while simultaneously playing on a masochistic desire for death, pleasure and oblivion" ([1993] 2007: 130). The lyrics tell of "fillies" who want to give a "pious dog" "a round of hell." This abject performance is topped off with The Agent's forced ingestion of some sort of poison before the euphoric exhilaration of the damned. In this way, the grotesque body (the human form made abject) is politicized and the seductive hero-villain is doomed to endure the shame and harassment to which he had subjected his lover. In Hell, victimhood is exorcized and empowerment settles in its place.

The pervasive—if twisted—sisterhood and solidarity underpinning Lucifer's profligate community becomes more significant when compared to God's glamorous Heaven, whose rules are far more rigid and brutal than

Hell's. To be sure, in Satan's funhouse, everyone must abide by a set of 666 rules that detail how the miscreants must behave. No one, not even Lucifer or his second-in-command, Ticket-Keeper, is above carnival law.

Heaven, in turn, is presented in *Alleluia! The Devil's Carnival* as a lavish Hollywood film studio—HPI (Heavenly Productions, Incorporated)—where the angels are organized according to a strict, seven-category caste-like system, mirroring the seven pairs of "clean animals" and "birds of the Heavens" that boarded Noah's ark (Gen. 7:2-3). In this repressive panopticon, which has its own police and media outlets, each caste is inscribed on a fascist-like armband that God's minions are forced to wear. Physiognomic perfection is controlled by a tyrant God, studio Head of HPI, who treats human beings as his personal playthings. This troubling representation of God as maliciously wicked reflects the reality of studio moguls, who puppeteered their starlets and disposed of them when they failed to meet box-office targets or, like Bousman's God, when they no longer fit their ideal of canonical beauty (Wayne 2002; Fleming 2005; Malone 2015). There are no internal mechanisms in place to ensure that those at the top will be held accountable for any wrongdoing. They can—and do—get away with anything. Bousman and Zdunich are therefore not only playing with generic tropes and articulating sociopolitical preoccupations about gender discrimination, bigotry, and religion; they are also taking a clear stance in regard to the studio system and the minute control ruthless studio executives exerted over every aspect of the lives of their starlets, treating them like nothing more than corporate assets. The fact that the soundtrack for scenes set in Heaven was inspired by 1930s–1940s show tunes seems to attest to a deliberate attempt at allegorizing the callousness of the Hollywood studio system.

With HPI standing for the studio system, Hell, by correlation, can be read as representing the musical (and the artists) at the margins. In effect, in making Heaven a more intolerant and unethical place than Hell, which accepts those that Heaven rejects as flawed and disgusting, Bousman and Zdunich seem to narrativize an idea of the marginal musical and its place in the film industry. When compared to HPI, Hell represents unbridled freedom and opportunity: the carnivalesque Hell, or the marginal musical, is not constrained by normative discourses or a commercial rationale and is therefore freer to experiment with form and tropes. On another level, this satiric and self-reflexive representation also comments on the creative team's own experiences with the Hollywood film industry: the studios repeatedly refused to distribute their musicals, which led them to self-release the films by investing in what would prove to be a series of successful road tours across North America.[2]

The adjacent underworlds, as we have seen, converge in their resort to violence—but there is hope for Hell. Tellingly, as the carnies sneer and flog Ms. Merrywood, the camera cuts away from the action three times to frame Ticket-Keeper who, dismayed at the abuse being committed, shakes his head and looks away. He does not intervene, but takes the matter to Lucifer, who confesses he is aware of how nebulous the distinction between his honest demonic hamlet and God's corrupt society has become. Hell's unwitting corruption thus reminds us of how easy it is to fall into patterns of abuse and discrimination. The surge in senseless aggression among peers and Lucifer's belief that Hell is fast becoming exceedingly violent and therefore too similar to Heaven serves as the trigger for an otherworldly battle, leading Lucifer and his children to plot Heaven's downfall. The economy of the grotesque which subtends life in the carnival should not involve the celebration and enforcement of torture—that is Heaven's signature modus operandi. At the end of *The Devil's Carnival*, Ticket-Keeper gathers Lucifer's mischievous flock and announces they are "putting Heaven out of business."

Bousman and Zdunich had initially planned a third installment, but the endeavor has since been indefinitely postponed. This attests to the creative team's struggles to self-release their musicals and finance the long road tours. Given that most of *Alleluia!* is a flashback focused on June/Painted Doll (the remainder of the film revolves around Hell's plan of attack and Heaven's failure to keep up), there is no final showdown between the afterworlds. The fact that we do not know who would win the unholy war in the denouement means that the unfinished franchise is ambiguous in terms of the extent to which the marginal triumphs over dominant power structures. Borrowing Kohlke's words, the films "eschew the restorative justice of the Radcliffean happy ending" (2012: 223) and offer a conflicted, but potentially productive, discourse for social criticism and political engagement.

Conclusion

The Devil's Carnival films combine the colorful world of Hollywood musicals with a maniacal dystopian world of gothic excess. In privileging the comically perverse over the politically correct when dealing with specific sets of binary oppositions (feminism-patriarchy, conventionality-subversion, and sexsationalism-empowerment), this modern retelling of *Aesop's Fables* pushes ethical boundaries. Beyond the arresting visuals, the tantalizing demons, and all of the delightfully distasteful sacrilege, we uncover a scathing sociopolitical critique that works on two different levels. The project's subtext, I suggest, narrativizes the struggles of the marginal musical, represented by Lucifer's Hell, by denouncing the excessive power of Hollywood executives in the studio era and today. In addition, the narrative provocatively exposes modern societies in their contempt for and willingness to harm and dispose of certain groups because of gender, sexuality, or physical appearance. Overall, the storylines of the two installments alternate between a hellish Heaven and a heavenly Hell to criticize institutional privilege, oppression, and the patriarchal subservience still demanded of women in contemporary societies.

Hell's women combine the playful anachronism of the old-time carnival universe with a modern, rebellious, and bellicose attitude; they are tenacious, malevolent, and just as prone to violence and cruelty as men. Bousman and Zdunich scrutinize and deconstruct the clichéd image of traditional femininity and represent women carnies as strong individuals whose driving force stems from grotesqueness and an unwavering refusal to conform to the status quo. Admittedly, representing empowerment through sexsation is problematic and adds "further tension to the problem of femininity as an excessively visible and materially-animated spectacle," to borrow the words of Julie Park (2003: 53). *The Devil's Carnival*, after all, literally presents the female body as a circus attraction and capitalizes on its power to draw the voyeuristic gaze. Nevertheless, perhaps in an effort to ward off fetishization, there is a blatant scarcity of close-ups in the film, so that women are not readily or stereotypically displayed for the male spectator's scopophilia as a series of disembodied parts (Mulvey 1975: 14). There are no Berkeleyesque musical moments in either film that halt narrative linearity in order to "feminize spectacle for a masculine viewer" (Cohan 2002: 87).

Focusing on bodies outside stereotyped notions of feminine beauty and sexuality helps devise a new model for thinking the structures of looking in the film musical, enabling female bodies to produce meaning outside hetero/normative male spectatorship. The abjection of the female carnies de-idealizes them as objects exhibited for male consumption and is in line with New Woman fiction and the empowered gothic heroines of the post-*Buffy* era.[3] Hell's women—the women at the margins—reclaim ownership over their own bodies. They are not frightened by mysterious or murderous husbands, evil doctors, or conspicuous ghosts; they have witnessed and experienced first-hand the injustices and restrictions placed on women in a world of male privilege and so plot to end an entire patriarchal society, represented by Heaven.

The Devil's Carnival project renegotiates the primacy of the male gaze and proposes an emancipatory agenda that relies on abjection and the aestheticization of female pain as a paradoxical way of denouncing the banalization of gendered violence and the ubiquitous sexsationalism of female bodies in our cultural milieu. Above all, this is a story about the marginalized and the power within the margins. It tells us that abjection can be empowering and that otherness should be valued, nurtured, and praised. Moreover, it tells us that those who discriminate and abuse will eventually face their day of reckoning.

Notes

1 *Aesop's Fables* is a collection of tales attributed to Greek storyteller Aesop (sixth century BCE), many of which portray animals with human-like qualities to comment on the human condition.

2 The team relied on digital platforms to divulge the films, offered live performances before each show, held contests and Q&As, and produced exclusive online content for the fans.
3 Examples of damaged yet empowered goth/ic heroines include characters as diverse as Lisbeth Salander, from Stieg Larrson's *Millennium* series (2005–2007), and the female protagonists of The CW's *Riverdale* (2017–).

References

Anderson, D. (2015), "Exclusive Interview [Part II]: Darren Lynn Bousman & Terrance Zdunich on *Alleluia! The Devil's Carnival*," September 8. Available online: https://dailydead.com/exclusive-interview-part-ii-darren-lynn-bousman-terrance-zdunich-on-alleluia-the-devils-carnival/ (accessed September 7, 2019).
Biesen, S. C. (2014), *Music in the Shadows: Noir Musical Films*, Baltimore: Johns Hopkins.
Botting, F. (2008), *Gothic Romanced: Consumption, Gender and Technology in Contemporary Fictions*, London: Routledge.
Bousman, D. L. (2015), "Gather, Sinners!," July 14. Available online: https://www.reddit.com/r/movies/comments/3db40a/gather_sinners_i_am_darren_bousman_director_of/ (accessed April 13, 2019).
Childers, C. (2015), "'Alleluia! The Devil's Carnival' Road Show Invades L.A.," September 28. Available online: http://loudwire.com/alleluia-the-devils-carnival-road-show-invades-los-angeles/?trackback=tsmclip (accessed April 9, 2019).
Cohan, S. ([2000] 2002), "Case Study: Interpreting *Singin' in the Rain*," in C. Gledhill and L. Williams (eds.), *Reinventing Film Studies*, 53–75, London: Arnold.
Cohan, S. (2002), "Gendered Spectacles: Introduction," in S. Cohan (ed.), *Hollywood Musicals, The Film Reader*, 63–64, London: Routledge.
Conrich, I. (2006), "Musical Performance and the Cult Film Experience," in I. Conrich and E. Tincknell (eds.), *Film's Musical Moments*, 115–31, Edinburgh: Edinburgh University Press.
Creed, B. ([1993] 2007), *The Monstrous-Feminine: Film, Feminism, Psychoanalysis*, London: Routledge.
Cruz, L. (2012), "How the Creators of *The Devil's Carnival* Said 'Screw You' to Hollywood and Gained a Cult Following," August 17. Available online: http://www.laweekly.com/arts/how-the-creators-of-the-devils-carnival-said-screw-you-to-hollywood-and-gained-a-cult-following-2371324 (accessed April 9, 2019).
"The Devil's Carnival: Film Premieres, Exclusive Limited Engagements" (2012), *The Asylum Emporium*. Available online: https://www.asylumemporium.com/pages/the-devils-carnival-film-showings (accessed April 13, 2019).
Fleming, E. J. (2005), *The Fixers: Eddie Mannix, Howard Strickling and the MGM Publicity Machine*, Jefferson: McFarland.
Hall, K. (2015), "The Spider and The Fly," *British Romantic Women Writers: Poetry*, 1770–1840, October 22. Available online: http://brww.umwblogs.org (accessed April 13, 2019).
Kohlke, M.-L. (2008a), "Sexsation and the Neo-Victorian Novel: Orientalising the Nineteenth Century in Contemporary Fiction," in M.-L. Kohlke and L.

Orza (eds.), *Negotiating Sexual Idioms: Image, Text, Performance*, 53–77, Amsterdam: Rodopi.

Kohlke, M.-L. (2008b), "The Neo-Victorian Sexsation: Literary Excursions into the Nineteenth Century Erotic," in M.-L. Kohlke and L. Orza (eds.), *Probing the Problematics: Sex and Sexuality*, 345–56, Oxford: Interdisciplinary Press.

Kohlke, M.-L. (2012), "Neo-Victorian Female Gothic: Fantasies of Self-Abjection," in M.-L. Kohlke and C. Gutleben (eds.), *Neo-Victorian Gothic: Horror, Violence and Degeneration in the Re-Imagined Nineteenth Century*, 221–50, Amsterdam: Rodopi.

Kristeva, J. ([1980] 1982), *Powers of Horror: An Essay on Abjection*, trans. L. S. Roudiez, New York: Columbia University Press.

Laderman, D. (2010), *Punk Slash! Musicals: Tracking Slip-Synch on Film*, Austin: University of Texas Press.

Larson, S. (2005), *The Girl with the Dragon Tattoo*, New York: Alfred A. Knopf.

Malone, A. (2015), *Hollywood's Second Sex: The Treatment of Women in the Film Industry, 1900-1999*, Jefferson: McFarland.

Mulvey, L. (1975), "Visual Pleasure and Narrative Cinema," *Screen*, 16 (3): 6–18.

Park, J. (2003), "Unheimlich Maneuvers: Enlightenment Dolls and Repetitions in Freud," *The Eighteenth Century*, 44 (1): 45–68.

Petermann, E. (2015), "Monster Mash-Ups: Features of the Horror Musical," in L. Piatti- Farnell and D. L. Brien (eds.), *New Directions in 21st-Century Gothic: The Gothic Compass*, 71–83, London: Routledge.

Pykett, L. (1992), *The "Improper" Feminine: The Women's Sensation Novel and the New Woman Writing*, London: Routledge.

Rubin, M. (1993), *Showstoppers: Busby Berkeley and the Tradition of Spectacle*, New York: Columbia University Press.

Scarry, E. (1985), *The Body in Pain: The Making and Unmaking of the World*, Oxford: Oxford University Press.

Stokes, L. O. (2016), "'A Rose by Any Other Name': Wong Tin-lam's *The Wild, Wild Rose* as Melodrama Musical Noir Hybrid," in E. C. M. Yau and T. Williams (eds.), *Hong Kong Neo-Noir*, 13–29, Edinburgh: Edinburgh University Press.

Syn-Cypher (2016), "The Devil's Carnival," *Deviant Art*, May 11. Available online: https://www.deviantart.com/syn-cypher/journal/The-Devil-s-Carnival-608518967 (accessed April 13, 2019).

Wayne, J. E. ([2002] 2004), *The Golden Girls of MGM*, New York: Carroll & Graf.

Filmography

Alleluia! The Devil's Carnival (2015), [Film] Dir. Darren Lynn Bousman, USA: The Orchard.

The Devil's Carnival (2012), [Film] Dir. Darren Lynn Bousman, USA: The Orchard.

Glee (2009–2015), [TV program] Twentieth Century Fox.

Repo! The Genetic Opera (2008), [Film] Dir. Darren Lynn Bousman, USA: Lionsgate.

Riverdale (2017–), [TV program] The CW.
The Rocky Horror Picture Show (1975), [Film] Dir. Jim Sharman, UK/USA: Twentieth Century Fox.
Saw (2003–2017), [Film] Dir. various, USA: Lionsgate.

Musical Sequences

9

The On- and Off-Screen Politics of Sophia Loren's Musical Performances in *Houseboat* (1958) and *It Started in Naples* (1960)

Sarah Culhane

Within critical and popular discourse Sophia Loren is perhaps best known and remembered as a "Mediterranean beauty," characterized by "striking looks... dark features and opulent figure" (Gundle 2004: 77); however, this tendency to read Loren's star image solely in terms of her physical appearance has overlooked the star's labor and the actress as performer. Kirsten Pullen calls attention to this critical blind spot, highlighting how the labor of female stars has been neglected as a constituent element of performance. Borrowing from Pullen's approach, which challenges the narratives surrounding "spectacular performers best known for their physical bodies rather than their bodies of work" (2014: 13), this chapter looks at how the vocal labor of Loren's performance style can be read in the light of musical moments in *Houseboat* (1958) and *It Started in Naples* (1960) (hereafter *It Started* ...). In particular, I examine how moments of musical performance in films that sit outside what is traditionally considered the musical genre provide opportunities to reconsider the way we think about Loren's craft as an actress and the construction of her star persona. Loren's musical moments are revealing of her positioning in relation to questions of regional/national identity and motherhood. By analyzing how singing, as a mode of vocal performance, operates in Loren's Hollywood films, this chapter highlights the meanings that can be attached to this form of expression both within and beyond the narrative of individual films.

In addition to offering a close analysis of Loren's musical performances, this chapter also aims to move beyond a style of criticism that has a tendency to simply put forward "a celebratory vision of Italian female beauty" (Hipkins 2008: 224), thereby reducing Italy's most internationally successful star to sex symbol status, or as one American publication put it in 1957, "Loren la Magnifica, Rome's honey-haired symbol for TNT" ("First there was Silvana" 1957: 56–8). An example of the kind of sex symbol discourse that surrounded Loren, this comment also points to the star's national and regional identity, which is a key focus of this chapter's discussion of musical moments. The journalist in question mistakenly refers to Loren as being from Rome, yet for audiences in her native Italy, there was no doubt that Loren was a proud Neapolitan.[1] Although Loren's biographical narrative also places emphasis on her provincial identity, having been born in Pozzuoli (a port town near Naples), Loren the star traded heavily on her Neapolitan identity and continues to do so. In her recent biography, the star stresses her connection with Naples, describing the city and its people as "the most beautiful . . . in Italy" (2014: 79). The importance of Loren's association with Naples and the Campania region is particularly apparent in the final installment of the *Pane, amore e . . .* trilogy. While the first two films (starring Gina Lollobrigida) were set in the fictional hill town of Sagliena in central Italy, the third film in the series (*Pane, amore e . . .*) makes a significant relocation to Sorrento and the Bay of Naples. The film's geographic location and Loren's regional identity were explicitly highlighted by the film's English-language title, which was translated as *Scandal in Sorrento* (1955). Loren's association with the provincial is also seen in *It Started . . .* , which despite the title is actually set on the island of Capri. As Pauline Small notes, "associations with the provincial or rural setting were . . . significant to [Loren's] star image throughout her career" (2009: 70).

While Loren's identity as an Italian, and a Neapolitan, is significant in any discussion of the star's on- and off-screen persona, it is particularly important in the context of discussions about Loren's musical performances. The link between Loren's Neapolitan identity and musical performance is made explicit in *Carosello napoletano* (*Neapolitan Carousel*, 1954), featuring an episode in which Loren is serenaded by a young suitor (Giacomo Rondinella). Considering the importance of location in this film—described as "the only true Italian musical" (Marlow-Mann 2012: 84)—Richard Dyer highlights the tradition of Neapolitan song and the image of Naples as a "city in which there is always singing" (2012: 35). This perception of Neapolitan life as being musically charged is particularly evident in *It Started . . .* as the film's main locations—the city of Naples and the island of Capri—are both presented as acoustically saturated environments where music can seemingly be heard at all hours of the day and night.

The second aspect of Loren's off-screen persona that will be discussed in relation to her musical performances focuses on the way that *Houseboat* and *It Started* . . . position Loren in relation to ideas about motherhood. As Réka Buckley (2006) notes, motherhood was an important part of the press discourse surrounding female stars in postwar Italy with the pregnancies and births of actresses like Gina Lollobrigida and Silvana Mangano being publicly documented. By contrast, the off-screen motherhood of Hollywood stars was "not usually highlighted for fear that desirability and mystique would be shattered" (Buckley 2006: 41). At the time of making *Houseboat* and *It Started* . . . , Loren had not yet had children of her own. During this period, however, strategic steps were taken to present the star as a more maternal figure. As Loren sought to establish herself internationally as a Hollywood star, questions of national identity and motherhood were ones that had to be negotiated both on- and off-screen. By taking Loren's musical performance as a prism through which these issues were filtered, this chapter argues that the musical moments found in *Houseboat* and *It Started* . . . are more than just objectified female spectacle.

Loren's Musical Moments On- and Off-Screen

Although not a star typically associated with the film musical, Loren has repeatedly shown her versatility as an actress whose on- and off-screen career has been marked by musical moments. Reflecting Dyer's claim for the "pervasiveness of song in Italian cinema" (2012: 35), many of Loren's early Italian films from the 1950s feature moments of singing and dancing. In *Peccato che sia una canaglia* (*Too Bad She's Bad*, 1954), Loren is repeatedly heard singing an Italian appropriation of the song "Civilization (Bongo, Bongo, Bongo)" written by Italian American songwriter Louis Prima in 1947. *La bella mugnaia* (*The Miller's Beautiful Wife*, 1955) and *Pane, amore e* . . . also feature what Ian Conrich and Estella Tincknell refer to as "musical moments," which have both an expressive and disruptive affect within the narrative, while also allowing for a "temporary crossing of genre boundaries and expectations" (Conrich and Tincknell 2006: 5). Although the aforementioned films do not adhere to the traditional conventions of the musical genre—they are typically placed within the genre categories of romance and/or comedy—they established a precedent for the inclusion of musical moments in the cycle of Hollywood films that Loren made during the period from 1957 to 1960.

Loren's first encounter with musical performance came in 1953 when she was cast as the lead role in the Italian film, *Aida* (Clemente Fracassi). Classed as a "filmed opera," *Aida* forms part of distinctive subgenre of musical films produced in Italy in the postwar period. During the period from 1945 to

1956, the Italian film industry produced some eighteen films within the filmed opera category (Marlow-Mann 2012: 81). Utilizing the practice of post-synchronized sound, the prerecorded vocal performance of established opera singers was laid over the bodily performance of stars who mimed the action of operatic singing. In the case of *Aida*, Loren's bodily performance was synched with the singing of soprano Renata Tebaldi. Recalling her performance, Loren commented that "providing Renata Tebaldi's voice with a body was a special emotion for me" (2014: 57). However, the act of miming Tebaldi's singing was by no means an easy feat, which required Loren to undertake intensive rehearsals in order to be able to "synchronize [her lines] perfectly with the singer's." These early musical moments established the importance of singing as a performative mode for Loren.

Despite being best known for her performances in front of the camera, off-screen, Loren also had a significant recording career as a singer in the 1950s and early 1960s. While the majority of records that Loren made during this period were cross-promotional soundtracks, she successfully negotiated the difficult duality of the actor-singer role. Notwithstanding the concerns of her mentor (and later husband) Carlo Ponti that "singers never succeed as actresses," Loren proved to be adept at both (Small 2009: 16). From the outset, the Italian actress was quick to position herself as an intermedial star producing recordings of "Mambo Bacan" (1954)—which featured on the soundtrack of *La donna del fiume* (1954)—and "S'Agapo," a Greek folk song performed by Loren in *Boy on a Dolphin* (1957). In 1960, Loren had a hit single with fellow actor and comedian Peter Sellars when their single "Goodness Gracious Me" reached number five in the UK charts. Overlapping with the release of their film *The Millionairess* (1960), the unlikely, but successful, pairing of Loren and Sellars for an album of comedy songs amazed even critics, with one newspaper reviewer commenting that "Miss Loren's donation to the hilarity will come as a pleasant surprise" (Murray 1960: 22). By this stage of her career, Loren had starred in some thirty films, at least ten of which featured an element of musical performance. Still, as is indicated by the reviewer's comment above, Loren was not readily seen as a musical performer.

Following her transition from Italy to Hollywood in the late 1950s, Loren's performance style was marked by what Small refers to as "diminished verbosity" (2009: 51). When comparing Loren's performances in English with those in her native tongue, it is apparent that the verve of her delivery is somewhat inhibited. Nevertheless, it is interesting to note that in many of Loren's Hollywood films from this time, the inclusion of musical moments became a more deliberate element of her performance style. This is particularly evident in the films *Houseboat* and *It Started . . .* , both of which Loren made while under contract to Paramount Pictures. Although not musicals in the conventional sense, both films feature numerous examples of ostensive musical performance, with Loren singing a series of original and well-known popular songs such as "Bing!, Bang!, Bong! (*Houseboat*)," "Tu vuò fà l'americano," and "Carina (*It Started . . .*)." Although a proficient English speaker, the inclusion of song and dance numbers in these films could be seen as a device that allowed Loren to compensate for any loss of authenticity in her performance style. For the most part in these films, Loren was required to verbally express herself through English; however, all of the songs listed above featured a hybrid of English and Italian lyrics thereby allowing Loren to revert to her native tongue. While these musical moments can be simply viewed as a form of linguistic compensation, they also prompt closer consideration of the nuances of Loren's performance style and the way musical performance informed ideas about her off-screen persona.

An Italian in America

Reflecting on the multitude of significations denoted by vocal performance, Dyer highlights the voice's capacity to "carry markers of gender, class, ethnic, regional, geographic and other socio-cultural differences" (2012: 7). As an Italian star working in Hollywood, Loren's moments of marginal song and dance call attention to questions of national and cultural identity and provide a means by which to articulate ideas about the place of Italians in 1950s America. In *Houseboat* and *It Started . . .* , the issue of national identity and cultural difference provides a thematic touchstone for cowriters Melville Shavelson and Jack Rose; however, their depiction of the contrasts between Italians and Americans invites easy criticism for its tendency to resort to well-worn clichés and stereotypes. Across both films, trivial references to differing food cultures, attitudes toward work-life balance, and sex are used to draw superficial comparisons between Loren's Italian characters and her American counterparts. Given the presence of the same writer-producer-director team on both films, it is perhaps unsurprising that many of the same themes and narrative tropes that appear in *Houseboat* are recycled in *It Started . . . .* In each film, Loren plays Italian characters and is cast opposite an older leading man. In *Houseboat*, Loren plays Cinzia a rebellious young woman who longs to escape the stifling upper-class world of high culture, which her father's profession as an orchestra conductor places her in. An opportunity to immerse herself in American life presents itself when a chance encounter with a young boy named Robert (Charles Herbert) leads to Cinzia being offered a job as a maid by the boy's father Tom (Cary Grant). Cinzia is somewhat inept in her new role as the family maid, but she exudes a certain joie de vivre, which endears her to Robert and his two older siblings. Having recently lost their mother as a result of a car accident, the three young children have a strained relationship with their father who has been largely absent from their lives since their parents' separation. *It Started . . .* follows a similar dynamic when Loren's character Lucia is left to care for her young nephew Nando (Marietto) who is orphaned after his parents are killed in a boating accident. Like Cinzia, Lucia does not have a natural flair for domestic duties, and as far as Nando's American uncle Michael (Clark Gable) is concerned, the nightclub singer has something of a cavalier attitude toward her guardianship responsibilities. Despite their different class backgrounds, Lucia and Cinzia share a desire to break free of the limitations imposed on them by their individual circumstances.

Although these unlikely love stories play out in different contexts—*Houseboat* being set in Washington, D.C., and rural Virginia, while *It Started* . . . is set on Capri, with the opening scene taking place in Naples—the motive for the foundation of the characters' relationships is provided by the presence of children who require Loren's characters to assume a maternal role. As will be illustrated later in the chapter, Loren's musical performances in both films are used in different ways to support and problematize her characters' positions in relation to the maternal. Off-screen, Loren's relationship with the film producer Carlo Ponti, who was twenty-two years older and still legally married to his first wife, was somewhat problematic when it came to the public's perception of Loren as the maternal type. As Buckley notes, the publicity machine surrounding Loren made a concerted effort to "cultivate a maternal image" that would counteract the public and press discourse (2006: 43), which framed her as a "home-breaker" and "the siren who had stolen a man from the breast of his family without regard for morality" (Gundle 2004: 87).

In addition to her maternal image, public discourse surrounding Loren also commented on the star's linguistic hybridity. In 1961, *Life* magazine journalist Dora-Jane Hamblin wrote that "ten years ago, [Loren's] Neapolitan accent was so strong that someone else's voice had to be dubbed even into films she made in Italian. Now she speaks fine Italian, fluent unaccented English [and] good enough French to make movies directly in that language" (Hamblin 1961: 52–3). While foregrounding language as a component of star performance, Hamblin's comment also indirectly reflects what Tom Whittaker and Sarah Wright refer to as the "dynamic materiality of the voice" (Whittaker and Wright 2017: 1). In describing Loren's spoken English, the materiality of the voice is linked to the star's accent or lack thereof. As Whittaker and Wright also note, "the voice can too often conceal its own material properties" if understood simply as a "bearer of language." In *Houseboat* and *It Started* . . . , Loren's musical performances are characterized by a hybridity of language (English and Italian) that calls attention to the materiality of the star's voice. While this hybridity is often justified within the narrative—a reflection of the character's status as Italian and her positioning between cultures—the use of code-switching can also be viewed as part of a broader strategy to capture the star's Italianness through the "grain" of the voice (Barthes 1977: 179–85). In her study of immigrant language among Italian Americans, Nancy Carnevale describes code-switching as "a reflection and a performance of the hybrid identities of immigrants" (2009: 24–6). While there are a myriad of potential reasons for the practice of code-switching within real-world contexts,[2] the following section considers the significance of this linguistic phenomenon when viewed as a feature of Loren's musical performances of the songs "Tu vuò fà l'americano" in *It Started . . .* and "Bing! Bang! Bong!" in *Houseboat*.

Code-Switching, National Identity, and Performing "Tu vuò fà l'americano"

In both films, the practice of code-switching is a feature of Loren's musical performances and her spoken dialogue. Her characters repeatedly revert to spoken Italian when conveying emotions such as anger, frustration, and affection. In these incidences, the Italian spoken by Loren and other characters is left untranslated. In the absence of English subtitles, meaning is inferred through nonlinguistic cues such as Loren's use of gestures, body language, and her vocal tone. The de-prioritization of the meaning of words spoken is significant in that it prompts the audience to focus on different aspects of Loren's vocal and bodily performance and consider how they work together to convey meaning. In *It Started . . .* , the practice of code-switching is particularly dominant, given the setting in Loren's native Italy. In addition to providing an outlet for the expression of anger and endearment, switching to Italian also allows Cinzia to highlight Michael's linguistic disadvantage and creates narrative tension. This tension is manifest in Michael's cynical view of Italians and Italian society, a recurring theme throughout the film, but Loren's performance of the song "Tu vuò fà l'americano" works to counterbalance some of Michael's hostility and borderline xenophobia.

Composed by songwriter Renato Carosone and lyricist Nicola Salerno (both Neapolitans), "Tu vuò fà l'americano" was first released in 1956. The lyrics, consisting of Neapolitan dialect with English loan words, satirize the conduct of Italians who embraced an American way of life as Italy entered a period of economic prosperity in the 1950s (Ginsborg 1990: 210–16). The rise of commodity culture, and the influx of American products into the Italian market at this time, is reflected in the song's references to "whiskey and soda," "rock and roll," and "Camel" cigarettes. In *It Started. . .* , the song is performed twice by Loren.

While the version of the song penned by Carosone and Salerno is written mostly in Neapolitan dialect, the version first sung by Loren in Club Capriccio, in front of an audience of tourists, is an English reworking of the original lyrics. The decision to have Loren sing in English rather than her local dialect is justified by the fact that she is performing for a largely English-speaking audience. Given that other occurrences of code-switching to Italian are left untranslated, it is interesting that the filmmakers have consciously translated the lyrics to clarify meaning in this instance. On the one hand, Loren's English-language rendition of a Neapolitan dialect song would appear to deny her the opportunity to authentically express her regional identity, yet on the other, her performance in English allows her to clearly communicate the song's satirical criticism of the influence of American cultural imperialism within Italian society:

> You dance the rock-n-roll
> You play at baseball

The politics of identity that are raised by Loren's performance of the song feed into the film's wider commentary on the cultural and social differences between Italians and Americans. As Harris M. Berger notes, the choice of language and dialect in popular music warrants attention for the way that it allows singers and songwriters to "publicly think about, enact or perform their identities" (2003: xv). Significantly, in Loren's second performance of the song toward the end of the film, she sings the original Neapolitan dialect version. Within the context of the film's narrative, this scene occurs after Lucia has won her legal battle to keep custody of Nando, despite Michael's attempts to bring the boy back to America with him. As Lucia declares "can you imagine? He wanted you to come to America with him, to be an American, like in the song," the familiar notes of "Tu vuò fà l'americano" are heard as part of the extra-diegetic soundtrack. This moment is both a joyous celebration of Lucia and Nando's victory against the American interloper and a deliberate reclaiming of their national and regional identity as Italians and Neapolitans. However, it should be noted that the jubilation of Loren's performance is somewhat undermined by the ultimate narrative outcome of the film, which sees the reestablishment of Lucia and Michael's romantic relationship following his last-minute decision not to go back to America.

It Started... marked the last film that Loren would make as part of her contract with Paramount and signaled the final stage of what Small refers to as the star's "gradual 'withdrawal' to Europe" (Small 2009: 45). Although Loren had succeeded in establishing herself as an internationally recognized name, her Hollywood films were only moderately successful, and the star's potential as an actress was limited by the roles that were on offer to her. As Lucia, Loren knowingly pokes fun at her failure to gain recognition as a serious actress when she tells Michael that "Darryl Zanuck would like me to sign a contract, but a contract is death for an artist, don't you think?" Retrospectively, this meta-cinematic self-reference takes on even more weight, given that just one year later, Loren went on to win the Best Female Performance Oscar for her role in the Italian film *La ciociara* (*Two Women*, 1960). Loren's ebullient performance of the Neapolitan dialect version of

"Tu vuò fà l'americano" can therefore be seen as a meta-cinematic allusion to her impending departure from Hollywood and return to her origins.

Code-Switching, Fostering the Maternal and Musical Performance in *Houseboat*

Throughout *Houseboat* Cinzia is heard speaking Italian words and phrases to the children she has been hired to look after. In these cases, Italian is used to express endearment, and Cinzia's recourse to her native language becomes important to the way the film positions her as maternal. Her Italianization of Robert's name, whom she refers to as *Roberto*, conveys a sense of fondness and familiarity. The freedom to switch between languages also adds to the authenticity and naturalness of her performance style, as it provided the star with opportunities to display some of the verbosity for which she was renowned. At a script level, these sporadic transitions to Italian also establish a basis for Loren's later code-switching in the films' musical numbers.

The film's signature song, "Bing! Bang! Bong!," was an original composition, penned by the song-writing duo Jay Livingston and Ray Evans who were known for hits like "Que Sera, Sera" and "Mona Lisa." In the version of "Bing! Bang! Bong!" performed by Loren for the official *Houseboat* soundtrack, the level of code-switching is minimal and other than a few Italian words (*"prego, prego," "presto, presto"*) and Italianizations ("do your very *besto*"), the lyrics are entirely in English. However, in the version sung by Loren in the film, the Italian lyrics are more extensive with a complete verse in Italian, which opens with a call to "*Zitto, zitto*" ("Shush, shush") and concludes with the song's signature refrain:

> Ma sempre con il Bing! Bang! Bong!
> But always with a Bing! Bang! Bong![3]

The association between Cinzia and this musical refrain is established in the opening scenes when she is heard singing the tune to herself in the wings of an outdoor theater, while her father conducts an orchestra on-stage. The overlaying of Loren's singing with the formal orchestral music creates an auditory dissonance and signals the tension between father and daughter. Subsequently, the return of the song and Loren's singing is used in a contrasting manner by alluding to Cinzia's ability to create unity and harmony among the fractured family that she finds herself responsible for. This second performance by Loren of the film's theme song occurs as Cinzia, Tom, and the children drive in an open-top car toward their house in the countryside. The musical accompaniment is heard as part of the non-diegetic soundtrack, and at first, Loren sings the Italian lyrics alone. As she switches to the English lyrics, her voice is also joined by the voices of the three children who sing along to the chorus. Mirroring her father's role as a conductor, Cinzia leads the children in song as she clicks her fingers in time with the rhythm. The way in which Loren shares this musical performance with her young co-stars economically foregrounds the idea that Cinzia is a positive, maternal presence who can foster a sense of togetherness. While the setup of this scene does not allow for any kind of elaborate bodily performance, Loren nevertheless adds a certain dynamism to the musical moment by including all of the children in the performance as she playfully taps each of them on the head to correspond with the *Bing! Bang! Bong!* of the refrain. This gesture of inclusion illustrates how even in these moments of understated musical performance, music has the power to "act on [the] bod[y]" and produce physical movement (Dyer 2012: 7; Figure 9.1).

At a narrative level, the reoccurrence of this song reflects Cinzia's ability to seek and find the acceptance of those around her through musical performance. While the song is generally reserved as a kind of motif that unites Cinzia with the children—to the exclusion of their father Tom who typically responds to these displays of musical unity by continuing to talk over their singing or pleads with them to stop—there is one other significant performance of the song which occurs without the children (Figure 9.2).

When Tom invites Cinzia to a summer ball at the country club, she finds herself among an upper-class crowd. Although this stuffy scene is familiar given her upbringing, Cinzia is marked as an Other by the locals. Subject to the disparaging comments of Tom's friends and sister-in-law, music appears

FIGURE 9.1 Houseboat *(1957) Cinzia (Sophia Loren) leads the Winters children in a rendition of* Bing! Bang! Bong! *(1957).*

FIGURE 9.2 Houseboat *(1957)* Cinzia *(Sophia Loren) leads the Winters children in a second rendition of* Bing! Bang! Bong!, *while Tom (Cary Grant) pleads with them to stop singing.*

to provide Cinzia with a way to break down some of the prejudicial barriers that prevent an upper-class Italian woman from integrating into the upper classes of American society. Surrounded by a group of tuxedo-wearing men, Cinzia entertains her audience with an impromptu performance of "Bing! Bang! Bong!". Although Cinzia is clearly the focus of attention in this scene, the framing and setup allows Loren to maintain a sense of autonomy. First, the performance is shot in a single take wide shot with Loren standing just left of center. This type of tableaux vivant framing, coupled with the absence of cutaways to medium or close-up shots of Loren, maintains the integrity of her bodily performance and ensures that she is not reduced to the subordinating male gaze typically associated with the film musical and classical Hollywood cinema in general (Mulvey 1975). Second, Loren's performance visually reiterates the idea that she is a conductor who has the ability to bring those around her into her performance. Armed with drumsticks to beat out the rhythm of the song (mirroring the way that she clicked her fingers to the beat in the scene discussed earlier) gives the impression that Loren is literally conducting the performances of the men around her who enthusiastically join in (Figure 9.3).

Despite the cultural and linguistic barriers which she faces, Cinzia succeeds in fully integrating herself into American family life through her marriage to Tom at the end of the film. Although Cinzia is not a paragon of domestic servitude, her suitability for motherhood is confirmed by Tom when he comments: "With that fine Italian hand that can't cook or sew,

FIGURE 9.3 Houseboat *(1957) Cinzia (Sophia Loren) performs* Bing! Bang! Bong! *at the country club summer party.*

you've managed to put a family together again." As the above discussion illustrates, Loren's musical performances help to bring Cinzia's less obvious maternal qualities into focus.

Conclusion

At a surface level, Loren's musical performances in *Houseboat* and *It Started . . .* could be categorized in terms of Amy Lawrence's concept of "audio-spectacle," in that the use of code-switching works to deprioritize the content of the lyrics thereby inviting "the auditor to bathe in a wash of sound, music and voice" (Lawrence 1991: 96). Yet, as seen in the case of "Tu vuò fà l'americano," the transposition of the song's lyrics from Neapolitan dialect to English and the alternation between both versions of the song infuses Loren's performance with additional layers of meaning. Reflecting Dyer's definition of the star image as always being "extensive, multimedial and intertextual" (1986: 3), Loren's musical performances can be viewed as more than straightforward audio-spectacle. By placing Loren's musical performances within the wider context of her off-screen persona, it is possible to identify how the star's image is simultaneously shaped by multiple media texts (Dyer 2002: 60). Viewed in isolation, the musical moments discussed here may seem marginal or inconsequential, but by uncovering these moments from Loren's filmography, it is possible to move toward a more nuanced understanding of the star as a performer.

Notes

1 In 2016, Loren's Neapolitan identity was publicly celebrated when she was declared an honorary citizen of Naples. See "Sophia Loren" (2016).
2 Carnevale refers to code-switching as a way "to assert a specific identity, to signal in-group status or to position oneself in a particular way with relation to the addressee" (2009: 25–6).
3 Author's own translation.

References

Barthes, R. (1977), *Image, Music, Text*, trans. S. Heath, London: Fontana Press.
Berger, H. M., and M. T. Carroll, eds. (2003), *Global Pop, Local Language*, Jackson: University of Mississippi Press.
Buckley, R. (2006), "Marriage, Motherhood and the Italian Film Stars of the 1950s," in P. Morris (ed.), *Women in Italy, 1945-1960: An Interdisciplinary*, 35-49, New York and Hampshire: Palgrave Macmillan.
Carnevale, N. (2009), *A New Language, A New World: Italian Immigrants in the United States 1890-1945*, Google eBook edition, Urbana and Chicago: University of Illinois Press.
Conrich, I., and E. Tincknell, (2006), *Film's Musical Moments*, Edinburgh: Edinburgh University Press.
Dyer, R. (1986), *Heavenly Bodies Film Stars and Society*, London: The Macmillan Press.
Dyer, R. (2002), *Stars*, London: BFI Publishing.
Dyer, R. (2012), *In the Space of a Song: The Uses of Song in Film*, Oxford and New York: Routledge.
"First There Was Silvana, Then Came Gina, Now It's Sophia" (1957), *Screenland Plus TV-land*, 59 (10): 56-8.
Ginsborg, P. (1990), *A History of Contemporary Italy: Society and Politics 1943-1980*, London: Penguin Books.
Gundle, S. (2004), "Sophia Loren, Italian Icon," in L. Fischer and M. Landy (eds.) *Stars: The Film Reader*, 77-96, London: Routledge.
Hamblin, D. J. (1961), "Part Goddess, Part Imp, All Woman," *Life*, 11 August: 50-64.
Hipkins, D. (2008), "Why Italian Film Studies Needs a Second Take on Gender," *Italian Studies* 63 (2): 213-34.
"Houseboat" (1958), *Film Bulletin*, 15 September: 10.
"It Started in Naples" (1960), *Harrison's Report*, 9 July: 111.
Lawrence, A. (1991), *Echo and Narcissus: Women's Voices in Classical Hollywood Cinema*, Berkeley and Los Angeles: University of California Press.
Loren, S. (2014), *Ieri, oggi, domani*, Milan: Rizzoli.
Marlow-Mann, A. (2012), "Italy," in C. K Creekmur and L. Y. Mokdad (eds.), *The International Film Musical*, 80-91, Edinburgh: Edinburgh University Press.
Mulvey, L. (1975) "Visual Pleasure and Narrative Cinema," *Screen*, 16 (3): 6-18.

Murray, P. (1960), "Peter and Sophia," *Sunday Independent*, 11 December: 22.
Pullen, K. (2014), *Like a Natural Woman, Spectacular Female Performance in Classical Hollywood*, New Brunswick, New Jersey and London: Rutgers University Press.
Small, P. (2009), *Sophia Loren: Moulding the Star*, Bristol: Intellect Books.
"Sophia Loren becomes Honorary Citizen of Naples" (2016), *Business Insider*, 9 July. Available online: https://www.businessinsider.com/ap-sophia-loren-becomes-honorary-citizen-of-naples-2016-7?r=US&IR=T (accessed January 1, 2020).
Whittaker, T. and S. Wright. (2017), *Locating the Voice in Film: Critical Approaches and Global Practices*, New York: Oxford University Press.

Filmography

Aida (1953), [Film] Dir. Clemente Fracassi, Italy: CEI Incom.
Boy on a Dolphin (1957), [Film] Dir. Jean Negulesco, USA: Twentieth Century Fox.
Carosello napolitana (1954), [Film] Dir. Ettore Giannini, Italy: Lux Film
Houseboat (1957), [Film] Dir. Melville Shavelson, USA: Paramount Pictures.
La bella mugnaia (1955), [Film] Dir. Mario Camerini, Italy: Ponti-De Laurentis Cinematografica and Titanus.
La ciociara (1960), [Film] Dir. Vittorio De Sica, Italy/France: Titanus.
La donna del fiume (1954), [Film] Dir. Mario Soldati, Italy: Lux Film.
It Started in Naples (1960), [Film] Dir. Melville Shavelson, USA: Paramount Pictures.
The Millionairess (1960), [Film] Dir. Anthony Asquith, USA: Twentieth Century Fox.
Pane, amore e... (1955), [Film] Dir. Dino Risi, Italy: Titanus and S.C.G.
Peccato che sia una canaglia (1954), [Film] Dir. Alessandro Blasetti, Italy: Documento Film.

10

"Just a Little Warm-Up for the Job"

Harold Nicholas, the Specialty Act, and the Hollywood Song-and-Dance Man

Kate Saccone[1]

In a 1976 interview, Gene Kelly told *The Baltimore Sun* that to be a Hollywood song-and-dance man, "you need to sing, you need to dance, and you need to act—and you've got to be able to convince the audience that you're the guy to get the girl in the end" (Lippman 1976: A20). Kelly thus presents a vision of the Hollywood song-and-dance man that he and Fred Astaire helped to construct: he is not only a singer and a dancer but *also* a presence that exists outside of a musical sequence as a romantic hero and a capable actor. Or, to articulate this definition in the language of the so-called integrated musical, Kelly's Hollywood song-and-dance man is a necessary part of the classical musical's broader sense of cohesion—he must seamlessly carry both the song and dance sequences and the nonmusical portions of the narrative.

Today, few would dispute that Kelly was speaking from a privileged position. His definition, apt for him and other white male dancers, is ultimately limiting, taking for granted the presence of the Hollywood song-and-dance man outside of the musical sequence. Harold Nicholas—one half of the African American dance team the Nicholas Brothers—certainly did not fit this definition. Harold, who frequently performed on stage and screen with his older brother Fayard, and appeared in substantially fewer musicals than Kelly, was often relegated to the space of the specialty act. These standalone "nonnarrative interludes" (Trenka 2014: 241) could be extracted if necessary, and often occurred in a theatrical setting for a diegetic audience (usually the film's white characters). For a young, Black performer like Harold, "nestl[ed] in the nooks and crannies of the musical" (Knight 2002: 2), there was no scene to enact, no character to be, and no girl to get.

In turn, while there is valuable scholarship on Harold and Fayard and their complex position as two of the most famous Black specialty dancers in 1940s Hollywood,[2] it is rare for the duo, often referred to as "the Nicholas Brothers," to be individually labeled Hollywood song-and-dance men. Yet Harold, with his deep, resounding singing voice, arguably bests any vocal performance by Kelly or Astaire, and his electric, gravity-defying tap dancing awed mid-century moviegoers and continues to do so today. His very skill and presence demand a rethinking of the category and the dominant discourses of musical and bodily labor that have shaped it.

This chapter consequently looks closely at a rare cinematic solo of Harold's, "Mamãe Eu Quero" (Mommy I Want) from Universal's *Reckless Age* (Felix E. Feist, 1944). Filmed while Fayard was in the army, this tour-de-force song and tap dance sequence, which has been mostly overlooked until now,[3] is an opportunity to see how Harold embodied the only properties of Kelly's definition that he had access to as a specialty dancer. At the lyrical and choreographic levels, Harold's performance engages directly with the tension between work and play, both restaging and transforming established notions of bodily and musical labor within the genre.

More specifically, it forces us to acknowledge the centrality of labor within the Black specialty act, an element within a genre that constantly aspired to musical play and freedom. Harold's solo is thus a defiant challenge to the limiting space of the specialty act, while also offering an alternative to Kelly's future definition of the Hollywood song-and-dance man, one that is tethered to the idea of a more inclusive physical presence. Coming before Kelly fully shaped his particular brand of masculine athleticism within a romance-driven narrative, Harold's performance is a vision of the Hollywood song-and-dance man that did not become dominant: a Black man, confined to a cameo, flexing his song and dance muscles.

Harold Nicholas and *Reckless Age*

At the time of *Reckless Age*'s release, Harold and Fayard were already established dancers with robust theatrical careers and a handful of film appearances under their belts, including *Pie, Pie, Blackbird* (1932),

The Great American Broadcast (1941), *Orchestra Wives* (1942), and *Stormy Weather* (1943). On stage and screen, the brothers were immensely popular with both Black and white audiences, and were two of the first African Americans to sign a long-term contract with a major Hollywood studio, joining Twentieth Century Fox after their successful appearance in the studio's *Down Argentine Way* (1940).[4] The oft-cited descriptions of Black and white audiences across the country responding to Harold and Fayard's three-minute performance in the film with cheers and requests to rewind the print is an effective indicator of their popularity (Hill 2000: 155–6). Yet this popularity came with an asterisk. As Black stars in Hollywood, Harold and Fayard were simultaneously there and not there. As Miriam J. Petty highlights in her study of Black stars like Bill Robinson and Hattie McDaniel, nonwhite performers at the time were often "rendered spectacular by the visual, cultural, and mythical significance of racial difference, and simultaneously deprived of the full benefit of their visibility, which instead accrued to the white performers they supported and the studios that employed them" (Petty 2016: 23). "This paradox," Petty continues, "suspended them in an oddly liminal position" (2016: 23).

Unsurprisingly, then, even though Harold only appears briefly in *Reckless Age*, his name and its connection to the Nicholas Brothers' fame was routinely used in ads publicizing the film (Figure 10.1), which *Showmen's Trade Review* called a "modernized version of the 'Poor Little Rich Girl' story" ("Reckless Age" 1944: 55). In the film, singer Gloria Jean plays Linda Wadsworth, a rich young woman living with her grandfather, the owner of a department store chain. She runs away to escape a life that is planned for her, and, using a fake name, gets a job at one of her grandfather's stores in another town. Comic misunderstandings ensue as Linda attempts to bolster the store's sales and the employees' work ethics, falling in love with a coworker along the way.

"Mamãe Eu Quero," which Harold choreographed (Hill 2000: 205), comes toward the end of the sixty-minute film as Linda is devising yet another plan to help the store increase sales. At the start of the scene, Harold stands with two other African American men in what looks like the store's storage room, listening to Linda as she explains her idea: she has hired them to move the music department closer to the front door, which will attract more customers inside. Getting ready to move a piano, Harold asks, "Would it be alright if we had a little musical accompaniment?" After getting the affirmative from Linda, he moves over to a record player, which, like most of the furniture in the room, is covered in a white sheet. Recognizing its contents with "Ahh Mamãe Eu Quero," and "in Portuguese," he turns it on. He moves back to the piano and begins to sing along to the music as he and the other men get to work. Within seconds, the piano gets stuck, and Harold uses this pause in the action to not only continue singing but also to move around and on top of the instrument as the others look on. The

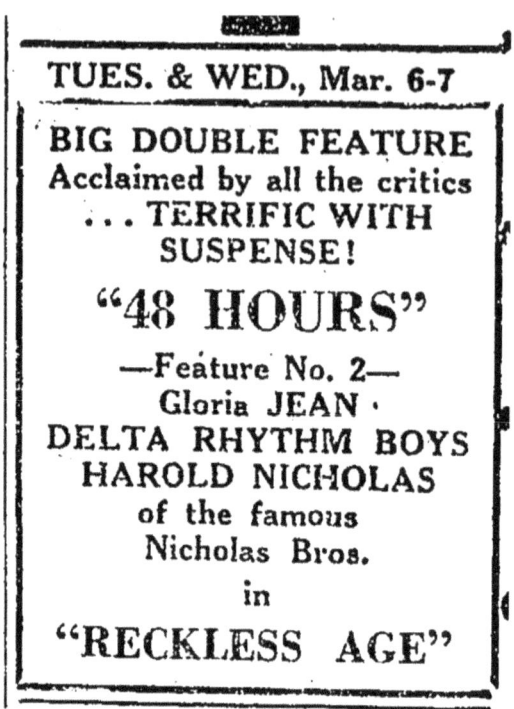

FIGURE 10.1 *A March 1945 advertisement for* Reckless Age *(1944) in the* Philadelphia Tribune *that capitalizes on Harold Nicholas's fame as part of the Nicholas Brothers.*

dance proper begins two minutes later, when Harold, who, standing on top of the piano at the song's finish, jumps off and begins to tap. Over the next few minutes, his movements dictate those of the camera as he reveals the previously unseen space of the room. Tapping on tables and leaping on and over pieces of covered furniture, Harold utilizes the objects around him as makeshift stages upon which to percussively interact.

Throughout the dance, which moves Harold toward the front of the room, he displays his hallmark expansive, fluid, and graceful corporeal style. Constance Valis Hill, one of the only scholars to describe this number in detail, highlights its fusion of opposing forces—the "hot rhythms and cool integrity of form" (2000: 207), calling it a "full-bodied rhythm dance" (2000: 206). Harold ends the sequence by tapping up a ladder at the left side of the frame and somersaulting off it. He lands and does a series of turns, goes down into a split, and rises to stand, arms outstretched, while applause is heard off-screen. Harold runs back to the others, and Linda compliments him, to which he replies, "Thank you. Just a little warm-up for the job," gesturing to the piano. After Linda clarifies that the hired men "know what needs to be done" (they respond with "yes ma'am"), she departs, and Harold's single scene in *Reckless Age* ends.

Work versus Play: The Lyrics of "Mamãe Eu Quero"

At its heart, "Mamãe Eu Quero" revolves around the idea of work, or more precisely, the disruption of work. Structured as an interruption at the narrative level, the song stems from Harold's request to play music and his spontaneous-seeming exhibition of athletic virtuosity as soon as the record starts. Even though he, as a Black "character" in a white film, must ask for permission first, his performance is still a digression that puts the job—and the white character's plan—momentarily on hold. When Harold caps the scene with his "Just a little warm-up for the job" witticism, he is reinforcing the overt difference between work and the playful demonstration that just occurred.

This tension between work and play is mirrored in the lyrics of "Mamãe Eu Quero." Composed by Brazilian musicians Vicente Paiva and Jararaca, "Mamãe Eu Quero" is a song that centralizes notions of pleasure and play. Originally recorded in 1937, it was first popularized on film by Carmen Miranda in *Down Argentine Way*, coincidentally the first Fox film in which Harold and Fayard appeared. Through its multivalent lyrics, the song foregrounds the playful fluidity of *carnaval*, a time when the tedium and grind of daily life are "reinvented [and] transformed into *brincaderia* (play, fun, amusement, joking, etc.)" (Parker [1991] 2009: 158). It is "through the notion of play," Richard G. Parker argues, that "the experience of *carnaval* is linked, simultaneously, to the innocent and carefree play of children and to the sexual play of adults" (159–60). This double meaning is evident in the first stanza of "Mamãe Eu Quero," which includes phrases that collapse the boundaries between maternal and sexual relations, such as "Mommy I want to suckle" and "Give me the pacifier/ so that the baby won't cry" (Parker 160). An example of a *carnaval* marchinha, a song intended, per José Ligiéro Coelho, for a "parade of merrymakers" (1998: 150), "Mamãe Eu Quero" is an irreverent and joyful celebration of pleasure outside of the boundaries of regular life and work.

Today, "Mamãe Eu Quero" is one of the most popular Brazilian songs of all time, its double entendres widely known. In 1944, however, the playful and sexual nature of these lyrics might not have been evident to American audiences, even though the song did have cultural currency at the time and had appeared in at least three films between *Down Argentine Way* and *Reckless Age* (Nepomuceno 1999: 254). The Portuguese language not only masks the lyrics' meaning to English-speaking audiences, but it is also what allows Harold, as a 23-year-old Black man, to get away with singing such a sexual song in the presence of a young white woman, who is visibly enjoying herself by smiling and bouncing along to the music. The fact that Harold has lighter skin—especially compared to his two companions—might have helped too, as Pamela Grenelle Krayenbuhl suggests about the Nicholas Brothers' rendition of "Argentina," which they sang in Spanish, in *Down Argentine Way*. For Krayenbuhl, the Nicholas Brothers' alignment with a Latin exoticism, which was perhaps safer than the perceived threat of (American) blackness, was how "the brothers subtly but insistently laid claim to their sexuality and maturity" (2017: 77), as they grew from nonthreatening "youngsters who had charmed and disarmed audiences with their dimpled smiles and jubilant rhythm dancing" (Hill 2000: 212–13) into dazzling Black men. In fact, their visibly increasing maturity was, Hill argues, one of the reasons why Fox did not renew the brothers' contract in the mid-1940s after Fayard's return from the army (2000: 211–13).

In "Mamãe Eu Quero," Harold seems to be less concerned with insisting upon an overt sexuality than he does with signaling a cultured maturity. He is aware of the song's playful disruptive nature. As the dialogue before indicates, he knows the material and can speak Portuguese. During the dance, his bodily movements reinforce the song's double meaning—a roll of his hips, like the lyrics, can be read both innocently and sexually—thereby suggesting that he might be in on the joke. It is even likely that Harold picked the song himself, and that he was familiar with its popularity as well as its double meanings and oral symbolism. As Sean Griffin has highlighted, minority performers, especially at studios like Fox where Harold was coming from, possessed a "greater-than-usual degree of artistic freedom" within their freestanding specialty numbers, typically handling their own choreography, which often drew heavily from earlier stage routines, and choosing collaborators (2002: 35). In 1938, Harold and Fayard also spent two months performing in Rio de Janeiro, becoming familiar with Brazilian culture, and learning a variety of songs in Portuguese and local dances like the samba (Hill 2000: 140). The brothers later performed with Carmen Miranda, who continued to regularly sing "Mamãe Eu Quero," onstage in New York in the mid-1940s, after they became friends while making *Down Argentine Way* (Hill 2000: 173–4). Within the scene from *Reckless Age*, then, Harold is subversively in on the joke, playing the eager laborer who pauses the task of transporting the piano to musically explore the space around him, while Harold-the-star likely chose a song that celebrates the exhilarating act of disrupting work and life in favor of irreverent play.

Work *and* Play: The Choreography of "Mamãe Eu Quero"

At the choreographic level, "Mamãe Eu Quero" expands upon and complicates this tension between labor and joyous freedom. In many ways, it conforms to Jane Feuer's articulation of "bricolage," or a dancer's "tinkering" with the surrounding environment and nearby objects to produce a spontaneous-seeming dance in an everyday space (1993: 4). In her seminal book *The Hollywood Musical*, Feuer describes how the movie musical—a mass art that is highly engineered and mediated—attempted to pass as folk art, a more communal, spontaneous, and unmediated form of expression. Noting the explicit tinkering as part of the choreography in many of Kelly and Astaire's numbers, Feuer also highlights the use of movements not codified as dance (non-choreography), an erasure of the inherent professionalism of the number (the skilled dancer plays a non-entertainer), or a heightened sense of naturalness (the sequence happens in an everyday place like the street, where crowds spontaneously gather) (Feuer 1993: 3–15). These different elements not only lend the musical sequence an aura of spontaneity and naturalness, but they also emphatically deny the extensive labor inherent in their own creation and performance.

Likewise, "Mamãe Eu Quero" is staged away from the proscenium in a department store, as a hired laborer uses the covered furniture, a piano, and a ladder as elements of his dance while a small audience watches. Harold's playful exploration of the space and its features is carefully choreographed, but it comes across as effortlessly improvised and natural. Yet Feuer's articulation of the different ways that the film musical could masquerade as folk art does not consider the racially marked specialty number or the nonwhite performers who existed within that space, although she does later briefly highlight jazz's "(Afro-American) ethnic folk origin" (Feuer 1993: 54). Her primary interest is in white performers and iconic MGM musicals—many coming later than *Reckless Age*—which she uses as evidence of the musical genre's propensity for engineering spontaneity and canceling out all signs of choreographic, cinematic, and narrative labor.

Consequently, "Mamãe Eu Quero" may instead best be described as an example of what Krayenbuhl calls "segregated integration" when she discusses the Nicholas Brothers' number "Alabama Bound" in *The Great American Broadcast*. In that film, they perform for two of the film's white characters and some extras in a train station. Dressed as Pullman Porters, Harold and Fayard interact with ordinary objects around them, such as suitcases and a lamppost, thereby creating a performance space out of the everyday world (Figure 10.2). Although the sequence is still a specialty act segregated from the broader narrative, it feels more like the integrated numbers by Kelly, Astaire, and others that Feuer describes. Even so, Krayenbuhl is quick to note,

> there is a crucial difference between the Astaire-Kelly brand of bricolage and what the Nicholases do here: whereas Astaire and Kelly were white mega-stars with remarkable creative control and access to vast production departments willing to engineer whatever they and their

choreographic collaborators could dream up, the Nicholases as black specialty performers (even on long-term contract) were allotted no such privilege. (Krayenbuhl 2017: 61)

Indeed, even if Harold and Fayard had choreographic control over their cameos, it was nothing compared to Kelly and Astaire's creative control over an entire production. For example, in *Cover Girl* (1944), which came out the same year as *Reckless Age*, Kelly reportedly oversaw the staging of all his numbers ("Cover Girl" 1944: 14), and also conceived of and directed the production of his now iconic technologically enhanced "alter ego" sequence, which took two weeks to shoot and reportedly cost over $100,000 (Chaplin 1994: 60). So, Krayenbuhl is right to argue that Harold and Fayard's use of bricolage is something slightly different from that of Kelly and Astaire. In using this "presumed-white form" (2017: 61), she suggests, the brothers, dressed as "dehumanized Pullman Porters" (2017: 62), perform a type of "resistive bricolage" (2017: 72) that enables them to subversively "claim a masculinity defined by innovation" (2017: 62) within the marginalized space of the specialty act.

In "Mamãe Eu Quero," Harold executes an analogous form of resistive bricolage, using his surroundings to create the aforementioned moment of

FIGURE 10.2 *Harold and Fayard Nicholas utilizing the objects around them in the everyday space of the train station to create their dance in* The Great American Broadcast *(1941).*

interruption while simultaneously proclaiming that Black bodies can also be spontaneous and inventive. It is also a number that signals how the notion of resistive bricolage itself might be extended. As a dance scholar, Hill does not use the filmic term "resistive bricolage," which Krayenbuhl coined later, but her discussion of the number demonstrates how it could additionally be understood as a form of artistic creation. For Hill, "Mamãe Eu Quero" visually and aurally embodies jazz tap dance as a "distinctly modern expression, with its emphasis on speed, attack, and force, the employment of angular and asymmetrical formations, the succession, repetition, and juxtaposition of movement rhythms, and the playing with weight as formal modes of expression" (2000: 205). For example, at one point, Harold taps atop a small table before jumping off this unintended stage to continue to move around the space (Figure 10.3). As he leaps from the table—arms flung upward—the formation of his legs resembles an isosceles triangle. This moment of stillness, weightlessness, and abstract positioning juxtaposes Harold's erect body and the rapid close-to-the-surface heel digs and shuffle steps he just performed on the table (Hill 2000: 205–6). It is one instance among many where Harold's carefully-designed-yet-seemingly-spontaneous movements function as a form of specific cultural production, making visible (and audible) the modernist impulses of jazz tap dance. With his tinkering body, Harold thus subversively creates something extratextual; his performance is a complex, multi-rhythmic sequence that powerfully claims itself to be its own artistic end goal.[5]

FIGURE 10.3 *Harold Nicholas in* Reckless Age *(1944).*

The Black Specialty Act as a Site of Double Labor

As an instance of resistive bricolage, "Mamãe Eu Quero" is a useful lens through which to see that Black specialty acts have a different relationship to musical freedom and bodily labor than the numbers that Feuer discusses. More specifically, it is a sequence where ideas and images of work are highlighted, thereby challenging Feuer's argument that notions of labor are routinely denied in the musical film. While Harold's comment that his dance was "Just a little warm-up for the job" masks the labor of constructing and performing such a sequence, it also points to the work lying ahead for his servile "character." This number occurs at his place of work, and the objects around him, like the piano he is hired to move, form part of the dance. His tucked-in shirt and trousers do not immediately read as work clothes, but, when seen together with the matching outfits of the two other hired men, they become a uniform for physical labor. And Harold's other film cameos, particularly in the studio musicals of the 1940s, are no different. In addition to performing as Pullman Porters in the aforementioned train station scene, Harold and Fayard frequently appeared onstage or in a rehearsal space, professionally clad in matching tuxedos or suits. In these instances, they are still at their "characters'" place of work, cast as paid theatrical entertainment. Even in *The Pirate* (1948), where the brothers appear alongside Kelly at his character's public hanging and outside of a context of paid entertainment, they remain tied to notions of work, since their costumes link them to the traveling theater troupe with which they belong. Looking beyond Harold, work is likewise inescapable in the few film appearances of the Berry Brothers (Ananias, James, and Warren), another popular Black specialty dance group from the period. Although less central within film scholarship today than the Nicholas Brothers, they were a successful stage act, performing their self-described "acrobatic Soft Shoe dancing" routine (Frank 1990: 159–60) in films like *Panama Hattie* (1942) and *Lady Be Good* (1941).

Often appearing onstage as themselves, with matching outfits, canes, and top hats, the Berry Brothers were continually presented as professional entertainers within their films. In *You're My Everything* (1949), Ananias and Warren do double duty, appearing onstage dressed as Pullman Porters alongside white star Dan Dailey. A similar proximity between labor and the Black specialty is evident in the "Shine on Your Shoes" sequence in *The Band Wagon* (1953), which takes place in an arcade where Leroy Daniels appears as a shoeshine man. While this is an integrated Astaire number that briefly contains a Black performer rather than a traditional specialty sequence, it is the aural and visual beats generated from Daniels's brushing of Astaire's shoes that form the foundation of this spontaneous number. Daniels, an actual shoeshine man in Los Angeles, often incorporated a similar musical routine into his real-life work. When he was reportedly spotted by a member of the film's crew during production, he was brought to Astaire, who was struggling with the development of the sequence (Knowles 2013: 82–3). Thus, Daniels's labor produces the content and context for the sequence, where Black servility and work are impossible to separate from the dancing itself.[6]

There are instances when Kelly and Astaire's dances take place at their work or revolve around musical labor (often when they are playing performers or rehearsing). However, typically musical expression for them is about romance and desire and not about presenting themselves as workers. And while there are examples of white specialty dance acts—Kelly and his brother, Fred, onstage in *Deep in My Heart* (1954) or Eleanor Powell's impromptu nightclub performance in *Duchess of Idaho* (1950)—that could similarly be connected to a place of work, they still seem part of MGM's larger tradition of celebrating glorious entertainment and white musical freedom. These are fragmentary numbers performed by white stars who *also* had the opportunity to exist as fully formed characters in other films. Harold, Fayard, Ananias, James, and Warren, among others, were always contained to this fragmentary space, presented as servile workers and objects of consumption.

The Black specialty act, as exemplified by "Mamãe Eu Quero," should then be understood as a site of *double labor*: first, the labor of the servile Black "characters" within the narrative and, second, the musical labor of the professional dancers hired (and exploited) by the white studios to perform these popular, fragmentary cameos. Put another way, it is the labor—the specialty—of these skilled Black performers that is required (to entertain the white characters, to provide a break in the narrative flow, to entertain audiences in the theater, etc.), but only insofar that it remains fragmentary, ghettoized, and stereotyped. While white musicals and stars were consistently denying the labor inherent in their end products and presenting musical freedom as disconnected from work and the daily grind, the Black specialty act was where this labor became central, echoing Richard Dyer's observation that the Black body is "the most vivid reminder of the human body as labor in a society busily denying it" (1986: 139). Thus, while Harold's performance in "Mamãe Eu Quero" exhilaratingly soars beyond the surrounding narrative, it also serves as a reminder of the types of bodies laboring in that space.

The Hollywood Song-and-Dance Man Reconsidered

This notion of double labor not only reframes our way of thinking about the specialty act in relation to existing scholarship on the musical, but it also brings focus back to the site of the musical performance itself and the body within that space. This has strong implications for reconsidering the Hollywood song-and-dance man as a category. While, for Kelly, acting within the romance-driven narrative was crucial, Harold offers an alternative definition that centralizes his bodily presence. With his closing comment, he presents his disruptive and dazzling showcase as a warm-up—a limbering of body and voice—which effectively emphasizes his physicality. In other words, his skilled voice and athletic body, here enacting the complex tension between work and play, is what defines his presence onscreen. This echoes Peter N. Chumo's discussion of the required "physical energy" of the song-and-dance man, which "must explode" into musical performance throughout the film, a defining element of the genre and a performer's skillset (1996: 46).

Yet Chumo is still operating within the integrated musical tradition. What does it mean to be an explosive physical presence in the space of the extractable specialty act? Harold's brief appearance in *Reckless Age*, divorced from the narrative trappings of Kelly's definition, presents the Hollywood song-and-dance man as first and foremost an *action* performer, defined not by his narrative location, appearance, or status as a character, but, instead, by his very presence in motion. The job of the male singer and dancer, Harold illustrates, is to create something affective and experiential with one's body and voice. It is about gestures and movements, or having "kinetic fun," to borrow a phrase from hip-hop scholar Thomas F. DeFrantz (2004: 79). This is a productive framework for thinking about the category of the Hollywood song-and-dance man today—as something active and physical above all else. Not only does this focus apply to everyone from Nicholas to Kelly, but, more importantly, it turns our attention back to the satisfying labor involved in their cinematic appearances, reframing the Hollywood song-and-dance man in terms of a skilled performative presence (visual and vocal content) that encompasses both the (Black) specialty act and the (white) integrated musical.

Conclusion: Making Room for the Fragmentary

A number like "Mamãe Eu Quero" is a product of all types of musical and industrial labor. It also points to the work that still awaits us, as scholars, educators, and curators, as we continue to cast a critical eye on the classical Hollywood musical. How do we work to make more space for marginalized performers like Harold Nicholas and sequences like "Mamãe Eu Quero" in film scholarship and mainstream film culture? How can we revitalize our exhibition practices and theoretical vocabulary in order to expand the musical canon and "discover the unrealized future of the past"? (Brody 2018). As a solo Black specialty dance staged in the everyday world, "Mamãe Eu Quero" complexly intersects with existing discourses on the musical film in relation to bodily and cinematic labor and freedom. Through its lyrics and choreography, it centralizes notions of work and play, and restages and challenges Jane Feuer's discussion of the genre's overall denial of labor. Ultimately, it highlights that the specialty dance act, especially in relation to the category of the Hollywood song-and-dance man, demands continued theoretical consideration. Finally, in Harold's tour-de-force performance, the sequence provides a productive avenue forward for redefining the category as a more inclusive physical presence in action, allowing multiple types to exist, from Kelly's leading men to Harold within the specialty act. While there remains more theoretical and practical work ahead, "Mamãe Eu Quero" is a playful reminder of how exhilarating and rewarding that labor will be.

Notes

1 Thank you to the editors, Martha Shearer and Julie Lobalzo Wright, for their helpful feedback, and to Aurore Spiers, Carolyn Jacobs, and Jackie Reifer for their rigorous attention to various drafts.
2 See Constance Valis Hill (2000), Arthur Knight (2002), Sean Griffin (2002), Jodi Brooks (2003), and Pamela Grenelle Krayenbuhl (2017).
3 This is no surprise given that *Reckless Age*—a middling, low-budget musical made by a studio other than MGM—is neither a celebrated part of the canon nor easily accessible. A 35 mm print exists at the Library of Congress and in NBCUniversal's archives, and low quality DVD-Rs are available for purchase online. Harold's dance, one of the film's few highlights, is the only scene available on YouTube.
4 For more on Fayard and Harold's careers, from childhood through retirement, see Hill (2000).
5 A provocative parallel is Brooks's discussion of screen tap and the polyrhythmic routines by African American specialty dancers, which she argues play with time in complex ways (2003: 370–1).
6 Bill Robinson's numbers, especially in his films with Shirley Temple where he appeared in servile roles, also typically occur at his place of work.

References

Brody, R. (2018), "The Best Movie Reviews We've Ever Written—*IndieWire* Critics Survey," *IndieWire.com*. June 18. Available online: https://www.indiewire.com/2018/06/best-movie-reviews-ever-written-indiewire-critics-survey-1201975885/ (accessed May 12, 2019).

Brooks, J. (2003), "Ghosting the Machine: The Sounds of Taps and the Sounds of Film," *Screen*, 44 (4): 355–78.

Chaplin, S. (1994), *The Golden Age of Movie Musicals and Me*, Norman, OK: University of Oklahoma Press.
Chumo, P. N. (1996), "Dance, Flexibility, and the Renewal of Genre in *Singin' in the Rain*," *Cinema Journal*, 36 (1): 39–54.
Coelho, J. L. (1998), "Carmen Miranda: An Afro-Brazilian Paradox." PhD diss. New York University, New York.
"Cover Girl" (1944), *Variety*, March 8: 14.
DeFrantz, T. F. (2004), "The Black Beat Made Visible: Hip Hop Dance and Body Power," in A. Lapecki (ed.), *Of the Presence of the Body: Essays on Dance and Performance Theory*, 64–81, Middletown, CT: Wesleyan University Press.
Dyer, R. (1986), *Heavenly Bodies: Film Stars and Society*, London: The Macmillan Press.
Feuer, J. (1993), *The Hollywood Musical*, 2nd edn, Bloomington: Indiana University Press.
Frank, R. E. (1990), *Tap!: The Greatest Tap Dance Stars and Their Stories, 1900–1955*, New York: W. Morrow.
Griffin, S. (2002), "The Gang's All Here: Generic versus Racial Integration in the 1940s Musical," *Cinema Journal*, 42 (1): 21–45.
Hill, C. V. (2000), *Brotherhood in Rhythm: The Jazz Tap Dancing of the Nicholas Brothers*, New York: Oxford University Press.
Knight, A. (2002), *Disintegrating the Musical: Black Performance and American Musical Film*, Durham, NC: Duke University Press.
Knowles, M. (2013), *The Man Who Made the Jailhouse Rock: Alex Romero, Hollywood Choreographer*, Jefferson, NC: McFarland.
Krayenbuhl, P. G. (2017), "Dancing Race and Masculinity across Midcentury Screens: The Nicholas Brothers, Gene Kelly, and Elvis Presley on American Film and TV," PhD diss. Northwestern University, Evanston, IL.
Lippman, T., Jr. (1976), "Song and Dance Man," *The Baltimore Sun*, May 13: A20.
Nepomuceno, R. (1999), *Música Caipira da Roça ao Rodeio*, São Paulo: Ed. 34.
Parker, R. G. ([1991] 2009), *Bodies, Pleasures, and Passions: Sexual Culture in Contemporary Brazil*, Nashville: Vanderbilt University Press.
Petty, M. J. (2016), *Stealing the Show: African American Performers and Audiences in 1930s Hollywood*, Oakland, CA: University of California Press.
"Reckless Age," (1944), *Showmen's Trade Review*, September 9: 55.
Trenka, S. (2014), "Vernacular Jazz Dance and Race in Hollywood Cinema," in L. Guarino and W. Oliver (eds.), *Jazz Dance: A History of the Roots and Branches*, 240–48, Gainesville, FL: University Press of Florida.

Filmography

The Band Wagon, (1953), [Film] Dir. Vincente Minnelli, USA: MGM.
Cover Girl (1944), [Film] Dir. Charles Vidor, USA: Columbia Pictures.
Deep in My Heart (1954), [Film] Dir. Stanley Donen, USA: MGM.
Down Argentine Way (1940), [Film] Dir. Irving Cummings, USA: Twentieth Century Fox.
Duchess of Idaho (1950), [Film] Dir. Robert Z. Leonard, USA: MGM.

The Great American Broadcast (1941), [Film] Dir. Archie Mayo, USA: Twentieth Century Fox.
Lady Be Good (1941), [Film] Dir. Norman Z. McLeod, USA: MGM.
Orchestra Wives (1942), [Film] Dir. Archie Mayo, USA: Twentieth Century Fox.
Panama Hattie (1942), [Film] Dir. Norman Z. McLeod and Roy Del Ruth, USA: MGM.
Pie, Pie, Blackbird (1932), [Film] Dir. Roy Mack, USA: Warner Bros.
The Pirate (1948), [Film] Dir. Vincente Minnelli, USA: MGM.
Reckless Age (1944), [Film] Dir. Felix E. Feist, USA: Universal.
Stormy Weather (1943), [Film] Dir. Andrew L. Stone, USA: Twentieth Century Fox
You're My Everything (1949), [Film] Dir. Walter Lang, USA: Twentieth Century Fox.

11

A Language of Its Own

Mani Ratnam's Experiments with the Song Scene

Aakshi Magazine

> *He asked me to give him abstract images. This is the first time a filmmaker has ever said this to me.*
>
> (MUSIC ALOUD 2013)

The above statement is veteran songwriter Gulzar's description of working with Mani Ratnam for the first time. Gulzar has worked in Indian cinema as a song lyricist since the 1960s, working with different generations of filmmakers including Bimal Roy, Yash Chopra, Hrishikesh Mukherjee among others, so his emphasis on the newness of Ratnam's approach, of this being the "first time" a filmmaker gave such a brief, is significant. It points us toward one of the main arguments of the chapter. While the song sequence has been the norm in the popular Indian film form, Ratnam made the norm his own. In his work, we find a move away from the characteristic of the film song that scholars have identified as a "tendency toward defining the image in the terms set out by the song" (Majumdar 2001: 167). Starting with the relatively marginal space of "regional cinema," and working across languages, in Ratnam's work, the image-song relationship is complex. Moreover, his films often use the song to carry forward narrative, not just when they are integrated into the plot but also when they appear to exist as spectacle, in the process compelling us to complicate the distinction between the two.

The film Gulzar is referring to is Ratnam's first film made in Hindi language, *Dil Se..* (From the heart, 1998). Hindi is the language of India's "national cinema" Bollywood. Before this, Ratnam had made fourteen films in three different languages, all of which constitute "regional" cinema.[1] Two of these earlier films—*Roja* (Rose 1992) and *Bombay* (1995)—had been dubbed in Hindi, and their songs were already popular outside of the Tamil industry. The three films, *Roja*, *Bombay*, and *Dil Se..*, are together known as his political trilogy and are important in his filmography for giving him visibility at a national level in India. Their importance from the perspective of Hindi film music is that music composer A. R. Rahman, who went on to fundamentally change the Bollywood song style, started his career with these films. The two, Ratnam and Rahman, came from the marginal "regional" cinema space and went on to leave a mark on the dominant form of Bollywood. In this chapter, I focus on select songs from the trilogy to show how Ratnam's experimentation with song picturization comes close to giving the film song a cinematic language of its own, where visuals are predominant.[2] At the same time, the songs have an evocative relationship to lyrics too.

In Ratnam's explanation of his "song picturization" process, which is the Indian term used for the process of choreographing prerecorded songs, he talks of the song's lyrics like they are a limitation. Reflecting on the instructions he gives to the song's lyricist, he says,

> You don't want lyrics to say the same thing the film is saying. . . . You want the content and music of the song to add another layer. . . . So my instructions to the lyricist are to keep it broad and not specific to the film. In a sense, I give him everything and then take it away. (Rangan 2017)

This mistrust of words is reflected in the manner in which the mise-en-scène is foregrounded in Ratnam's song sequences; it is perhaps also shaped by the fact that Ratnam has worked in different languages. On his work with a poet like Gulzar in *Dil Se..*, he has said that he did not understand the nuances of the Urdu lyrics (Rangan 2012: 190). The chapter's discussion of the three films explores the resultant complexity of the film song as a narrative device.

Occupying this complex engagement with the song, I focus on the relationship between the Indian film song tradition, song lyrics, and image in select songs to understand the distinct style Ratnam brings to the film song as a storytelling device. While he deviates from some established conventions in his songs, he does not do away with them. His engagement with the song reflects that he works within a film form, historically associated with the Indian popular film, where songs exist at the "heart of the form" (Booth

2013: 35). It is this that makes Lalitha Gopalan comment that his film songs "confidently assert their presence" representing the "possibility of a distinct national style" (2002: 136–7). Ratnam, in fact, is one of the few "regional" directors who made films in the Mumbai film industry.

While gaining visibility at a national level, he continues to work predominantly in Tamil cinema and is highly regarded as one of the most prominent filmmakers both at a regional and at a national level; out of his twenty-six films, only four are in Hindi. The chapter revisits his early career trilogy from the perspective of its songs in order to understand his contribution to innovations in song style.

The Context: Bollywood Song Style, Ratnam, and Rahman

Many of the filmmakers considered important in Indian popular film history have been associated with their own unique style of song picturization.[3] In film analysis, however, both among film critics and in film industry circles, there continues to be a prejudice in considering songs as artistic only if they extend narrative in a literal way, and not exist only as an "attraction." This was famously represented by Satyajit Ray's often quoted dismissal of the Indian film song for going against the "grain of the film" ([1976] 2001: 74–5). In contrast, Ratnam is an example of a filmmaker considered a "cinematic genius" in journalistic and industry circles despite his often spectacular song picturizations ("Abhishek Bachchan" 2012). Gopalan argues that his songs are "carefully" choreographed so as to "heighten viewing pleasure of these attractions as well as their function within the narrative" (2002: 136–7).

Since the 1990s, when the trilogy was made, Ratnam has gone on to direct twenty-six films. The trilogy is a productive case study to understand his song style because of their location both in Ratnam's career and in the time period of Indian film history. The 1990s saw the emergence of Bollywood, a film form and culture industry that emerged post the opening up of the Indian economy (Rajadhyaksha 2003). The political trilogy does not follow this Bollywood style, both in form and in politics. The three films tackle questions of communalism and resistance to the nation-state by those on the fringes, while the more quintessential Bollywood films like *Dilwale Dulhania Le Jaayenge* (1995) and *Hum Aapke Hain Koun . . . !* (1994) were preoccupied with questions of defining Indian culture, modernity, or diasporic identity.

The time period is also important from the perspective of the song for, as Gregory Booth (2013) has argued, it saw the beginning of a change in the Hindi film song style, after a twenty-year-long period of relative continuity. In this change, music composer A. R. Rahman, till then a struggling musician in Chennai who made his debut as a film music composer in *Roja*, is commonly understood to have played a significant role. Jayson Beaster-Jones writes that Rahman "self-consciously tried to change the aesthetics of film music" (2017: 108). This change was in the production process as well as new sound aesthetics particularly "orchestral scoring which was to become one of the stylistic touchstones of contemporary films."

Along with song style, Rahman also contributed to changing the lyric writing style. Till then, Hindi film songs were known for one particular style, having a "refrain-verse structure interspersed with instrumental interludes, and sometimes beginning with a vocal *alap*, or slow, unmetered section" (Morcom 2007: 62). The refrain is called the *mukhda* (face) of the song. Rahman's song composition changed that refrain-verse style; Gulzar has suggested that Rahman brought the film song close to the blank verse (Ramnath 2015).

Interestingly, this ties up with Gulzar's assessment about Ratnam asking him to use abstract images indicating that both were experimenting with a given form: Ratnam with song picturization, Rahman with song style. While the chapter focuses on the lyrics and picturization, emphasizing their role as song scenes in the film, I mention this here to point toward the collaborative nature of the film song.

Song as Transcendence from Cultural Censor in *Roja* and *Bombay*

An "unwritten" prohibition of Indian cinema that film scholars have written about is the absence of the lip-lock; it came into force in the 1940s and started changing in the 1980s. Sangita Gopal argues that in the context of Hindi cinema, "the song sequence rather than the kiss has historically functioned as an engine of couple formation" (2012: 23). Gopalan refers to the cinematic mechanism where the "camera withdraws and the film censors us from seeing any aspect of sexual contact" as "coitus interruptus" (1997: 126). While by the 1990s, the on-screen kiss started making an appearance in films, in the two songs from *Roja* and *Dil Se..* that I analyze, "Rukkumani Rukkumani" and "Hamma Hamma," we find a playful engagement with this long-standing informal "rule" of Indian cinema.

The songs are variations of the "narrational song," defined by Ravi Vasudevan as a song having a narrational authority external to the diegesis (2010: 124). In the song picturization, this external authority lip-syncs the song, in the process commenting on the diegetic characters through the lyrics. The narrational song has a long history in Indian cinema. In the past, the function of the singers has often been to make linkages with mythology, externalize the emotional state of the characters, or legitimize transgressive desires.[4] In the two films, these songs are deployed to engage with cultural and moral censorship—the absence of physical intimacy on-screen. In the former song, the lyrics play an important role; in the latter, we find the primacy of the visual over the aural. As the analysis will show, both song scenes represent a deceptive moment of "coitus interruptus" for these reveal more than they appear to—in *Roja* the song comments on the absence of physical intimacy on-screen; in *Bombay* it evokes the moment of sexual intimacy between the protagonists. While revolving around political issues, both films are centered on romantic plots. In *Roja*, it is the arranged marriage between Roja and Rishi, whose abduction by a Kashmiri terrorist brings the two strangers together. *Bombay* explores the intercommunity marriage of its protagonist couple Shaila Bano and Shekhar, in the context of the 1992 Babri Masjid demolition and Hindu-Muslim communal violence.

"Rukkumani Rukkumani" from *Roja* follows two parallel wedding ceremonies, that of the protagonists Roja and Rishi, and of Roja's sister. In addition, the song picturization places an extra-diegetic group of singer-dancers comprising of elderly women dancing around a young couple who lip-sync the song. Rishi's mother becomes a link between the two set of characters as she is present with the extra-diegetic dancers. Beginning with the words "Rukkumani Rukkumani," the Tamil lyrics go on to describe what the spectator cannot see:

Akkam Pakkam Enna Satham
Kaathu Rendu Koosuthadi
What is this noise in the neighborhood
What is this that I hear

The scenes of the brides getting ready for their wedding are intercut with the group of dancers singing, as quoted above, about the "wedding night" by asking what the "noise" in the neighborhood is. The lyrics go on to state in expressive detail that the source of the noise is the "sound of married couples kissing" and "the cot." This answer is sung, but not shown. What we see instead is only a brief sequence of an empty bedroom, with the decked up "marital bed." The lyrics describe the sexual act, and constantly imply its presence, but the mise-en-scène has no visual signs of this. In fact, the female protagonist Roja looks sad. In the context of the film, this has a narrative reason, for Roja is not getting married out of choice. The song builds a contrast between the enthusiasm of the dancers and the actual relationship between the film's couple which remains unconsummated by the end of the song for when Rishi enters their bedroom at the song's ending, he finds Roja already asleep on the floor, not on the bed that had been prepared for them.

Beyond concerns of taking the plot forward, the cultural implications of this tell but not show, when viewed in the context of coitus interruptus and the absent kiss discussed earlier, become apparent. Here M. Madhava

Prasad's interpretation is relevant too for he views the absence of the kiss as a restriction on representing the private which can otherwise be threatening to a feudal, patriarchal order (1998: 91). The romantic film song, in its long history in Indian cinema, complicates the thesis about the absence of the representation of the private. Prasad writes that in some cases, the songs came to be used as a "public confirmation of a private act" by confining the sexual act to "a zone of privacy while exhibiting the evidence of its consummation" (1998: 91). In this context, "Rukkumani Rukkumani" playfully engages with this long-standing use of the song: its lyrics show evidence of consummation, though not necessarily focused on the couple. (That happens in a later song, "Puthu Vellai," showing the couple falling in love against the backdrop of Kashmir.) The presence of the older women characters, being prodded on by the younger couple to talk about desire, attempts the opposite of confining the act to "a zone of privacy." Toward the end of the song, the extra-diegetic dancers also become diegetic, as the couples enter the frame, and the dancers dance in front of them. The song choreography makes excellent use of Rahman's orchestration by making the dancers match their steps to the music.

"Hamma Hamma" from *Bombay* follows a similar logic of intercutting, but there is a difference: here the passion of the extra-diegetic dancer-couple and that of the main couple parallel each other. This difference can be traced to the narrative, for unlike in *Roja*, here the couple, Shekhar Pillai and Shaila Bano, are in love with each other. Having eloped to Bombay due to their warring Hindu-Muslim families, the song is the moment when they find themselves alone for the first time since they fled their village.

The scenes preceding the song show them walking through a red-light district area, where Shekhar is propositioned by prostitutes, creating the possibility of a diegetic link with the song that will follow. In the next scene as they reach the privacy of their bedroom, Shekhar playfully stops Shaila from entering. As he does this, the diegetic sound of the creaking door leads into the song's instrumental prelude which includes a female aural voice on the soundtrack. The short scene in the domestic space is followed by a tracking shot of a building that gradually stops to reveal a female figure behind a long white curtain.

Dressed in an exotic gold and white dress, this female dancer's face remains hidden behind a white curtained veil in the initial moments of the song. A male dancer is also present, dressed entirely in black, picturized doing cartwheels, accompanied by a group of dancers; the dance is choreographed by Prabhu Deva. They are being watched by an "internal audience" underlining the performative-ness of the dance (Feuer 1993: 27). Once this dancer-couple finally appears together in the same shot, the film cuts to Shekhar pulling Shaila toward him. The song follows this pattern of back-and-forth movement between the dancer-couple outside and the diegetic couple inside the privacy of the bedroom. Interestingly, the longer shots are picturized on the dancer-couple, with the song lip-synced by the male dancer. The main couple has shorter length shots, leaving their activities to the spectator's imagination.

When the dancer-couple are together, the female dancer gradually casts her veil aside, while the male dancer sings the *mukhda* of the song "Hamma Hamma."[5] As they dance to the music of the song, Shaila too jives to the music in the bedroom indicating the possibility that the diegetic couple hear the song too. As the song progresses, they too dance together in their bedroom. Vasudevan has argued that the proximity of the red-light area to their domestic space gives their moment of sexual consummation, though secure in a domestic space, a "peculiar undertone of the illicit and the disreputable" (1996: 13–14). I would, however, emphasize that it is here that the song becomes a deceptive moment of "coitus interruptus," revealing more than it appears to.

As the song proceeds, the dancer-couple change dresses. The changes correspond to the four stanzas of the song, each stanza corresponding to a new stage in the intimacy of the diegetic couple, revealed only in short moments. The pattern of cutting to the extra-diegetic dancers every time we see intimacy between the couple follows the Hindi cinema convention of "inserting extra-diegetic scenes in a romantic sequence to indicate passion through representations of flowing waterfalls, flowers, thunder, lightning and tropical storms" (Gopalan 1997: 126). However, the innovation here is that the song is picturized on the non-diegetic couple. It is the protagonists who are "inserted" into the scene, using short length shots, showing them in various stages of intimacy leading up to the consummation of their relationship.

The song ends with the non-diegetic couple dancing to the last stanza; the last we see of the main couple is them rolling off the bed. While the song is meant as a "coitus interruptus," the interruption is less effective because the scene does transgress the no kiss rule, even if for a split second, and through a veil. This act gains an added transgressive implication in the narrative because of their intercommunal background. The existence of the veiled kiss casts doubt on the song being a "coitus interruptus" for in almost-showing it, the song scene ends up showing more than it appears to. It is only toward the end that it truly fulfills its interruptus function, as the last stanza of the song is shot entirely on the extra-diegetic couple, dancing against a background that is literally set on fire, a metaphoric representation here of the union of the couple of the film (Gopalan 2002). Like in the previous song, therefore, the song engages with cultural censorship around the on-screen representation of sexual intimacy.

Song as Dialogue, Song as Transcendence from Plot in *Dil Se..*

Along with engaging with censorship, another aspect of the examples discussed in the previous section is that adding a non-diegetic moment of interruption in the form of the song opens up a moment of possibility in the plot. Continuing with this possibility of the song scene, in this section I turn to the third film in the trilogy: *Dil Se..*. If we view the song-narrative link in Bollywood as a "type of 'resolution' or interruption to what has come before" (Gehlawat 2010: 2), then most of *Dil Se..*'s six songs, with the exception of one, function in the manner of an "interruption." The "interruption" of the songs has an important role for it makes possible the transgressive romance at the center of the film—between the film's protagonists the radio journalist Amar and the terrorist Meghna/Moina. In other words, without the songs being separate, which Ratnam has cited as a reason for the film's box office failure, the romance would not exist (Rangan 2012). It is only by being separate that the songs become a part of the narrative and take it forward. *Dil Se..*'s songs thus indicate the need to rework this distinction of songs' importance as a narrative device only when integrated into the plot; this would help us better understand the specificity of the Hindi film song.

In their analyses, Anustup Basu (2008) and Ajay Gehlawat (2010) refer to this characteristic. Basu observes that in the songs, "figures 'leave' character behind and incubate in an ecology of the unthinkable" (2008: 161). Likewise, Gehlawat argues that the songs "bifurcate the text and reveal, even as they revel in, these gaps" (2010: 39). The plot follows a more realist logic for the female protagonist Moina, disguised as Meghna to Amar, does not reveal her real identity to him, hidden behind a mask of disinterest to his romantic gestures.

In this absence, Amar (and the spectator) has to imagine the "unthinkable" and it is here that the songs play an important role. Amar's excessive pursuance of her, bordering on harassment and stalking, attains a romantic meaning, due to the songs. I will discuss this further through two songs, one serving as an interruption and the other as resolution: "Satrangi Re" and "Ae Ajnabi."

In "Satrangi Re," which is a rich poetic text with a "sufi quality" written by Gulzar making use of the change in film song style that was mentioned in the beginning of the chapter, Ratnam does not take a passive approach of letting the words do the talking.[6] The song is about the seven stages of love according to ancient Arabic literature, starting from attraction (*uns*) and ending in death (*maut*). Basu calls the entire film narrative a "journey through the seven shades of love" (2008: 166). The striking mise-en-scène of the song, picturized on the barren terrain of Ladakh, often using jerky camera movements, competes with the richness of the poetry. It demands both aural attention (for the spectators who know the language) and visual attention. From the perspective of the narrative, they are in Ladakh so the location is diegetic. However, the placement of the two alone against that landscape creates a powerful stand-alone imagery. During one particular moment, their dance movements evoke the imagery of whirling *dervishes* in a desert storm. The strong winds interfere with their movements, giving an unchoreographed quality to the moment. The jerky close-ups of the camera mirror this quality, before tracking back to leave them alone in that moment. The song's poetry about the madness of love is mapped onto the physical terrain.

Despite both lyrics and visuals being equally powerful, the song scene does not feel like an aural and visual competition, and in this its music comes to the rescue. The song picturization makes use of the orchestral sounds that Rahman is known for, using a mix of drums, flute, and pipes, to act as a connecting thread between the lyrics and the picturization. The picturization maps this change in the changing costumes of the female protagonist through the seven colors, incidentally also the refrain of the song "Satrangi Re," which means the seven-colored one. The dance steps are choreographed by Farah Khan to match the tempo of the music; editing is often cued to the musical (and lyrical) phrases. There are certain moments where the more literal aspects of the song are acknowledged in the dance performance: when the lyrics are about entanglement, we see both of them struggling with a large-sized net. Likewise, when her robe touches him, the lyrics are "Chooti hai mujhe sargoshi se" (Her touch is intoxicating). In this way, we find that the abstract poetry is incorporated into the picturization of the song scene.[7]

In contrast, the song that acts as resolution is "Ae Ajnabi" (O Stranger). The song is present in two versions at different moments in the film: one is early on, right after Amar and Meghna's first meeting, as Amar recounts their meeting on his radio program, playing the song in the process. The second time he repeats the same story and song. The second song scene, however, is longer and is shot in a realist style, resolving the fact that Meghna, who till then has been a mysterious character, does have feelings for Amar.

The song scene identifies the source of the song as the radio that Meghna is listening to. By now, it has been revealed that Meghna is in a terrorist group, and in the scene, she is sitting among her comrades discussing the logistics of their future action. The song, playing on the radio, becomes a reminder of Amar and acts as a disruption to her work, a representation of the main conflict of the film. This makes her walk up to the radio to briefly switch it off only to switch it on again, before finally switching it off for good. The use of the radio in this manner expresses her dilemma and becomes an indication of her feelings.

The song's words are a call from one stranger to another. The male voice sings that without the other both are "incomplete": "Main adhura, tu adhuri, jee rahein hain" (I am incomplete, You are incomplete, We both are living incomplete lives). Here, the song is used in lieu of dialogue and the scene interprets the meaning of the lyrics by connecting the characters who are in separate spaces. It is sung by a male playback singer, with the female singer only singing a few lines.[8] While this realistically shot song is a part of the diegetic world, the memory that it evokes for Meghna is based on the time she and Amar spent in Ladakh in which "Satrangi Re," as discussed earlier, was integral to the development of their romance. Thus, we find that both songs discussed in this section play a role in developing the film narrative—one is picturized as fantasy and the other is integrated into the plot using a more realist style.

A significant characteristic of "Satrangi Re" is the gendered nature of its cinematic gaze. The female protagonist is a spectacle represented by the change in dresses and close-up shots of her bare stomach, with the male protagonist expressing his desire for her through the lyrics and choreography. When she does look at the camera in a direct address and sings the only lines she has in the song, incidentally it is the poetry of the male Urdu poet Mirza Ghalib: "Ishq par zor nahi, Hai yeh woh aatish Ghalib" (No one can come in the way of love, it is that inextinguishable flame, Ghalib). Female agency is glaringly absent from *Dil Se.*. We get to know Moina's side of the story only toward the end of the film, leading up to her final monologue through which she explains her side of the story. This imbalance is reflected in the songs that make their romance possible too for they are from Amar's perspective; the songs therefore reassert this gaze.

This is even more apparent in "Hamma Hamma" from *Bombay* that was discussed in the previous section in a different context. While the song does not have an erotic display of the main female protagonist's body, it is centered on the display of the non-diegetic female dancer's body as spectacle. Though picturized on the dancer-couple, it is not a duet in the tradition of the Hindi film romantic song, but it is a male solo song describing the man's desire for the woman, mentioning her "silk scarf" and comparing her to the "virgin beauty" of the Arabian coast. The song shares some characteristics with what is called the "item number" which was to become a regular feature by the 1990s. The number is centered on the performance of its female dancer, called an "item girl," who would have "no role elsewhere in the diegesis" (Gopal 2012: 40). It is usually a titillating number often used to promote the film as one of the attractions. While the song lyrics share the gendered gaze of the item number, the picturization is more complex. At some moments, it transcends this by not making use of isolated shots focusing on the female dancer's body as has become convention in contemporary Bollywood item numbers. At other moments, like in the beginning of the song, it makes use of these conventions. I make this point here to point toward the limits in the experimentation of the male auteur when it comes to gender politics, even as he is otherwise experimenting with song style and picturization.

Conclusion

The chapter has focused on four songs from Ratnam's political trilogy, which marked his move toward national visibility, showing that the films are an interesting case study of the experiments with song picturization. Working across languages, Ratnam picturized songs in a manner that is not always literal. While in *Roja* and *Bombay*, the narrational song is interpreted in a manner that transcends its usage in Indian cinema in order to expand the representation of sexual intimacy, the songs in *Dil Se..* question the assumption that the song is important to the narrative only when integrated into the plot. The use of songs as a medium to expand the possibilities of the narrative challenges the assumption often made in popular circles in India that songs reflect a nonserious engagement with film and are included only for commercial considerations. Viewed from such a perspective, Ratnam occupies an interesting space that is "commercial" when compared to art cinema and "arty" when viewed in the context of mainstream popular cinema.

Notes

1 These languages included Kannada, Malayalam, Telugu, and, predominantly, Tamil.
2 I owe this observation to a comment made by film scholar Ira Bhaskar in a video interview with Mani Ratnam. Bhaskar says that when she showed *Tu Hi Re* from *Bombay* to her students in New York, she was "stunned" that they understood what was happening in song even though they did not know the language. She says it was the "language of cinema that was communicating to them" (The Big Shot Masterclass with Mani Ratnam 2016).
3 I am thinking here of filmmakers like Raj Kapoor, Guru Dutt, Bimal Roy, Yash Chopra.
4 A famous example of a narrational song is from *Awaara* (1951). This is the song "Ajab teri leela hai girdhari" (Your ways are astounding, O lord), in which extra-diegetic singers compare the situation of the protagonist Leela to Sita's predicament in Ramayana. The song "Aaj sajan mohe ang laga lo" (Embrace me today, my love) from *Pyaasa* (1957) is another example, comparing Gulab's love for Vijay with that of Radha for Krishna.
5 The Hindi version of the song comments on this more directly as its lyrics are "Ek ho gaye hum aur tum" (We both have become one).
6 Gulzar is known to write unpredictable, poetic, and perhaps even "unpicturizable" song lyrics. For instance, he wrote in a song from *Khamoshi* (1970), "Aankhon ki mehekti khusbhoo" (The fragrance of your eyes). In another song from *Bunty Aur Babli* (2005), he wrote "Aankhein bhi kamal karti hain, Personal se sawal karti hain" (Your eyes are astounding, They ask me personal questions).
7 In this context, it is interesting that Ratnam's first language is not Urdu or Hindustani in which the songs are written. As mentioned in the beginning of the chapter, he has said about his work with Gulzar that "I didn't understand the nuances of the lyrics he was writing, but I had to tell him what I wanted" (Rangan 2012: 190).
8 Singers Udit Narayan and Mahalaxmi.

References

"Abhishek Bachchan Hails Mani Ratnam as a Cinematic Genius" (2012), *Hindustan Times*, November. Available online: https://www.hindustantimes.com/bollywood/abhishek-bachchan-hails-mani-ratnam-as-a-cinematic-genius/story-EVjmjzh9MGInCh3j52i7uJ.html (accessed September 16, 2020).

Basu, A. (2008), "The Music of Intolerable Love: Political Conjugality in Mani Ratnam's *Dil Se*," in S. Gopal and S. Moorthi (eds.), *Global Bollywood: Travels of Hindi Song and Dance*, 153–79, Minneapolis: University of Minnesota Press.

Beaster-Jones, J. (2017), "Violence, Reconciliation and Memory: A.R Rahman's 'Bombay Theme,'" in J. Jones and N. Sarrazin (eds.), *Music in Contemporary Indian Film: Memory, Voice, Identity*, 107–20, New York: Routledge.

Booth, G. (2013), "A Moment of Historical Conjuncture in Mumbai: Playback Singers, Music Directors, and Arrangers and the Creation of Hindi Song (1948-1952)," in G. Booth and B. Shope (eds.), *More Than Bollywood: Studies in Indian Popular Music*, 21–38, New York: Oxford University Press.

Feuer, J. (1993), *The Hollywood Musical*, 2nd edn, Indiana: Indiana University Press.

Gehlawat, A. (2010), *Reframing Bollywood: Theories of Popular Hindi Cinema*, New Delhi: SAGE.

Gopal, S. (2012), *Conjugations: Marriage and Form in New Bollywood Cinema*, Chicago: University of Chicago Press.

Gopalan, L. (1997), "Coitus Interruptus and Love Story in Indian Cinema," in V. Dehejia. (ed.), *Representing the Body: Gender Issues in Indian Art*, 124–39, New Delhi: Kali for Women.

Gopalan, L. (2002), *Cinema of Interruptions: Action Genres in Contemporary Indian Cinema*, London: BFI.

Jamuura (2016), *The Big Shot Masterclass with Mani Ratnam : On Films & Much More at BIFFES 2016*, YouTube video, 8 February. Available online: https://www.youtube.com/watch?v=uB9xRsqLtj0 (accessed April 20, 2020).

Majumdar, N. (2001), "The Embodied Voice: Song Sequences and Stardom in Popular Hindi Cinema," in P. Wojcik and A. Knight (eds.), *Soundtrack Available Essays on Film and Popular Music*, 161–85, Durham and London: Duke University Press.

Morcom, A. (2007), *Hindi Film Songs and the Cinema*, Aldershot: Ashgate.

Music Aloud (2013), *Gulzar on A R Rahman, Mani Ratnam and Dil Se..*, YouTube video, 30 September. Available online: https://www.youtube.com/watch?v=MYGudarxlp4 (accessed January 1, 2020).

Prasad, M. M. (1998), *Ideology of the Hindi Film A Historical Construction*, New Delhi: Penguin Books.

Rajadhyaksha, A. (2003), "The 'Bollywoodisation' of Indian Cinema: Cultural Nationalism in a Global Arena," *Inter-Asia Cultural Studies*, 4 (1): 25–9.

Ramnath, N. (2015), "Mozart from Madras: New Documentary Celebrates AR Rahman," *Scroll.in*, 5 January.

Rangan, B. (2012), *Conversations with Mani Ratnam*, New Delhi: Penguin Books.

Rangan, B. (2017), "The Mani Ratnam Interview," *Film Companion*, 6 April. Available online: https://www.filmcompanion.in/the-mani-ratnam-interview-with-baradwaj-rangan/ (accessed January 1, 2020).

Ray, S. ([1976] 2001), *Our Films, Their Films*, Hyderabad: Sangam Books.
Vasudevan, R. (1996), "Bombay and Its Public," *Journal of Arts & Ideas,* 29: 45–67.
Vasudevan, R. (2010), *The Melodramatic Public: Film Form and Spectatorship in Indian Cinema*, London: Palgrave Macmillan.

Filmography

Awaara (1951), [Film] Dir. Raj Kapoor, India: All India Film Corporation.
Bombay (1995), [Film] Dir. Mani Ratnam, India: Aalayam Productions.
Bunty Aur Babli (2005), [Film] Dir. Shaad Ali Saigal, India: Yash Raj Films.
Dil Se. (1998), [Film] Dir. Mani Ratnam, India: Eros International.
Dilwale Dulhania Le Jaayenge (1995), [Film] Dir. Aditya Chopra, India: Yash Raj Films.
Hum Aapke Hain Koun...! (1994), [Film] Dir. Sooraj R. Barjatya, India: Rajshri Productions.
Khamoshi (1970), [Film] Dir. Asit Sen, India: Geetanjali Pictures.
Pyaasa (1957), [Film] Dir. Guru Dutt, India: Guru Dutt Films.
Roja (1992), [Film] Dir. Mani Ratnam, India: Kavithalaya Productions Pyramid.

Music

12

Pianos, Affect, and Memory

Paul Mazey and Sarah Street

When discussing *Casablanca* (1942) and *Brief Encounter* (1945), Pam Cook observes how the fusion of present and past is achieved through piano music and a "particularly interesting and complex use of flashback" (2005: 102). In the case of *Casablanca*, when Rick (Humphrey Bogart) asks Sam (Dooley Wilson) to play "As Time Goes By" on the piano, the music triggers the memory of Paris, and of his love affair with Ilsa (Ingrid Bergman) and her suspected betrayal: "As Sam plays the piano, the camera moves in on Rick's face and a fade leads into the flashback. We know that the memory is in Rick's head, and we take it as an accurate representation of his personal experience" (Cook 2005: 102–3). In *Brief Encounter* Cook observes how a particularly complex representation of time is conveyed when the central character Laura (Celia Johnson) hears a staple of the piano repertoire, Rachmaninov's Piano Concerto No. 2, on the radio. As in *Casablanca*, the piano music heralds a flashback that involves "a deliberate melding of past and present—and, indeed, the future of the characters" (Cook 2005: 104). These observations prompt considerations about other films in which the piano is important, as a trigger for memory or as a visual and emotive signifier for the complex emotions at play in melodrama while sharing affinities with the musical genre. As this chapter details, this is a feature of many British films, but is also found in other national cinemas where the similar connotations of the piano reveal it to be a transnational device relating to status, feeling, and memory.

Some films, most notably Jane Campion's *The Piano* (1993), foreground the instrument's ability to communicate feeling. This point is made by Yvonne Tasker in relation to Ada (Holly Hunter), the film's mute protagonist, whose vocal silence is "counterpointed with her playing, the piano becoming a structuring metaphor for expression" (2007: 69). In other films, like Haneke's *The Piano Teacher* (2001), the passion that can be ignited across the piano keyboard is taken to an extreme in a narrative of sexual repression, rivalry, and fantasy. The piano arouses similar illicit passions in *The Housemaid*, a South Korean melodrama made in 1960 and discussed later in this chapter, where the instrument is a catalyst for the breakdown of a family who employ a housemaid.

The piano's potential, then, has been drawn upon in many film scenarios, especially when located in a domestic arena, away from professional connotations. Perhaps more than most objects in film, it has the capacity to *do something*, to exceed its role as a piece of furniture or a prop to embellish character. Its sounds have the potential to be disruptive, emotive, transformative, and, of course, pleasurable. A piano then is more than an elaborate element of mise-en-scène, it functions differently whether played by a man or a woman; whether in the home or at a public concert, and how its playing relates to the temporalities of narrative, emotion, and memory. In the following examples, we explore these themes in more detail.

In Britain, the piano carries connotations of class and respectability. For the upper classes in the eighteenth and nineteenth centuries, piano playing was one of a number of female accomplishments which both contributed to a young woman's marriageability and confirmed the gentility of her family. In the early twentieth century, the popularity of the domestic piano increased as hire purchase schemes and more affordable imported pianos made the instrument available to the aspirational middle classes (Hardy 2001: 6). The qualities associated with pianism are exploited in British melodrama films, where the piano may act as a symbol and guarantor of gentility and respectability for the woman who plays it.

In addition to marking the feminine decorum of its player, the piano can operate as a conduit to another realm of possibility. Rick Altman (1987: 27) notes that film musicals cater to "fundamental audience desires" to be "somewhere else, someone else, at some other time," and the piano in British melodramas offers similar escapist pleasures as a site where respectable restraint can be cast off and a world of emotional and sexual freedom explored. In *Madonna of the Seven Moons* (1945), Phyllis Calvert plays a woman whose personality splits between that of the respectable wife and mother Maddalena and the free-spirited gypsy Rosanna. Music provides the catalyst for her changes in persona, and an early scene delineates her two sides as she plays the piano. Maddalena starts to play Chopin's Nocturne No. 5 in F Sharp Major, Op. 15, No. 2. The camera moves in to make her the main focus of the image, and the dialogue of the other characters fades from the soundtrack. She appears solemn and concentrates on her hands until she becomes absorbed and the music takes on the lilting melody of the memorable tango tune that composer Hans May repeatedly associates with her Rosanna persona (Figure 12.1). She relaxes her posture, smiles broadly,

FIGURE 12.1 *Piano playing prompts a memory in* Madonna of the Seven Moons.

and looks straight ahead as though recalling a distant happy memory, before she recognizes her momentary wandering and returns to herself and to Chopin. The sequence presages Maddalena's complete return to her Rosanna persona. Significantly, it situates piano playing as an activity in which she may lose herself in the pleasant recollection of her earlier time as the passionate Rosanna, and piano music acts as the trigger for her memory.

A more spectral memory of the past occurs in *A Place of One's Own* (1945). Annette (Margaret Lockwood) is possessed by the ghost of the house's former occupant while giving a rather unmusical performance of Tchaikovsky's "Waltz of the Flowers" from *The Nutcracker* at the piano. As the camera moves into a closer framing of her, she struggles to continue and grows breathless. Annette stops playing, raises her hands to her temples, and watches them move slowly back down to the keyboard as if not in control of them herself.

Then, in a manner greatly more accomplished than before, she plays Chopin's Prelude, Op. 28, No. 4. The piece is significant as it will later signal her possession when she is not at the keyboard, and then briefly enter the underscore at her recollection of the event. As in *Madonna of the Seven Moons*, the camera movement isolates her in the frame and Annette, like Maddalena, ignores her hands and stares straight ahead when she loses possession of herself at the keyboard. Both Annette and Maddalena experience moments of transport, moments where the past intervenes in the present while at the piano, and for both the moment is marked by a change in the tone of the music they play. In both *A Place of One's Own* and *Madonna of the Seven Moons*, as well as confirming the gentility of the women, piano playing acts as a catalyst to memory, possession, and disturbance.

In British melodramas, playing the piano is a gendered activity. While pianism may confer respectability upon the women, its association with the feminized realm of the home may call into question the masculinity and emotional stability of the men who play it. The man whose piano playing is restricted to the domestic sphere tends to be characterized as overly invested in music. An example is the brain surgeon Michael (James Mason) in *The Upturned Glass* (1947). Michael narrates his own story as an anonymous case study for his medical students, and in voice-over describes himself as: "reserved in his personal relationships . . . [with] no close friends. His only relaxation was to sit at home and play the piano." When Michael begins a relationship with Emma (Rosamund John) based on their shared love of music, she is presented as the more competent musician. Whereas Michael's piano playing is always a solitary activity, Emma plays for him. When she does, he gazes at her adoringly, in a gender reversal of the situation described by Heather Laing (2007: 71) in which the male musician exerts a potent attraction for the female listener. Michael's pianism is thus marked as unmanly, obsessional, and his introversion offered as a sign of an unusual nature.

The gender balance of the male musician who attracts the female listener is restored in two further films, *The Night Has Eyes* (1942) and *Dangerous Moonlight* (1941). Significantly, both feature professional pianists, and consequently, their psychological problems are attributed not to the emasculating effects of domestic pianism, but to the trauma of war. *The Night Has Eyes* again stars James Mason, this time as Stephen, a troubled composer living in a remote part of the Yorkshire Moors. "I gave up music for war," he tells Marian (Joyce Howard) at their first meeting and reveals that he had spent time in a psychiatric hospital after his release from a prisoner-of-war camp. Marian hums along when Stephen plays Charles Williams's piano theme, and their growing attachment is mirrored cinematically in the flow of images, strikingly lit by cinematographer Günter Krampf. As Stephen plays the piano and Marian sits across the room, the distance between them is collapsed on-screen as first they are framed individually in profile close-ups before they are united in the intimacy of a two-shot. Stephen reveals that he had not been able to play for almost a year. Marian restores his emotional equilibrium and with it his potential for musical expression.

In parallel with Stephen in *The Night Has Eyes*, the ability of the Polish airman Stefan (Anton Walbrook) to recall and play his music in *Dangerous Moonlight* is equated with his emotional well-being. The film opens with Stefan in hospital after he has crashed his fighter plane, suffering from amnesia and unable to produce more than discordant sounds at the piano. Carol (Sally Gray) hums to him the theme of his fictional composition, Richard Addinsell's Warsaw Concerto. In another room, his physician and a specialist discuss his case. Suddenly, they hear the opening bars of the concerto and rush to observe his recovery. As he continues to play, the specialist comments, "I'd like to know what he's thinking about now," a matter the film quickly resolves. The camera moves at a stately pace into a tight close-up shot of Stefan, and the scene dissolves slowly to reveal his recollection of a war-torn street during a bombing raid, presently confirmed as Warsaw. Stefan's image shares the screen with that of the rubble-strewn street for twenty-three seconds, leaving no doubt that we are sharing Stefan's memory. On the soundtrack, the blasts of the exploding bombs drown out the piano music to leave only the diegetic sound of people rushing to safety. After a moment we hear the Warsaw Concerto again, as Stefan plays it, meets Carol for the first time, and the main narrative unfolds in an extended flashback of his recollection of events. As in both *Casablanca* and *Brief Encounter*, the piano music prompts the flashback memory.

In a romantic formulation, Stefan's piano playing draws Carol to him, and together with his patriotism, she acts as a joint muse in the inspiration of his composition. The Warsaw Concerto is thus a deeply personal expression of Stefan's emotions, a factor magnified by the form of the piano concerto itself. Lawrence Kramer has noted the ability of the romantic piano concerto to create a sense of profound subjectivity through the dual perspective of its dialogue between the "objective" expression of the orchestra and the "subjective" response of the soloist (2007: 100, 101). With its interplay between the piano and the orchestra, the concerto acts as a metaphor for the emotional interaction between the soloist and forces beyond his or her control. This capacity of the piano for subjective emotional expression is exploited in later British melodramas that build their narratives around the composition of piano concertos, notably *Love Story* (1944) and *While I Live* (1947).

In British melodramas, the connotations of musicality and pianism tend to be divided along lines of gender. For the woman, it signifies gentility, while for the man it carries the threat of emasculation, particularly when its performance is limited to the feminized domestic sphere, and the musician's mental balance may be called into question. When the bravado of public performance is involved, musical prowess attests to the emotional sensibility of the composer, although the depth of feeling involved may be accompanied by a measure of inner turmoil and even emotional instability. For both men and women, the piano acts as a trigger for memory, a gateway, whether consciously or unconsciously, to the recollection of earlier times and a deeply subjective means of expression.

To illustrate further some of the complexities and pleasures of pianos, affect and memory we now turn to an American film, *September Affair*

(1950). In this film, Joan Fontaine plays Manina, a single concert pianist, who falls in love with David (Joseph Cotten), a successful but unhappily married engineer, when their flight from Rome to New York is delayed in Naples. In a restaurant, they listen to one of Manina's favorite recordings, Walter Huston singing the Kurt Weill/Maxwell Anderson composition "September Song," and it becomes associated with their romance. When they discover that the onward flight they were due to catch has crashed and they are listed among the dead, they decide to begin a new life together in Florence. Manina's piano teacher Maria (Françoise Rosay), who is preparing her for a concert performance in New York of Rachmaninov's Piano Concerto No. 2, is the only one aware of the deception. However, David's wife and adolescent son discover the truth, and the pull of the couple's former lives overwhelms their desire to be together and they part at the close of the film.

September Affair is redolent with memories—both for the characters and the audience. While it contains no flashbacks, Manina's piano playing is crucial in conveying the conflict she feels between romance and profession. In a key scene, she plays a slow section of the Rachmaninov concerto and, as though unconsciously, the music slips into the first notes of "September Song."

She brings herself back to the Rachmaninov, but again the melody of "September Song" intervenes, as the piano music mirrors her internal conflict between love and duty (Figure 12.2). The bittersweet lyrics of the song, about finding love later in life and how quickly time passes— "It's a long, long while from May to December and the days grow short when you reach September"—are pertinent to Manina's dilemma. Her anguished facial expression conveys the conflict she feels between putting her career on hold while in Italy with David and the pull of the classical music toward her destiny as a concert pianist. Multiple temporalities are thus represented through music and image as Manina's past collides with her present predicament and her concerns for the future. This solitary and private moment contrasts with scenes of her practice sessions with Maria. These demonstrate her commitment to her professional destiny, and they are free of the strains of "September Song" that elsewhere flood the diegetic and non-diegetic soundtrack. In the New York concert performance, however, the dual resonances are retained, although without overt signification in the music. The inner life of personal emotion is conveyed here by focus on Manina's facial expression as we *hear* the music identified with the resuscitation of her career, but we *see* the emotional pull of her desire for David and the personal sacrifice she appears to have made.

We are in no doubt that she will continue as a celebrated concert pianist, but the memories of her affair and the impossibility of its perpetuation suggest an emotional void. As in *Casablanca* and *Brief Encounter*, a complex representation of time is communicated by the piano music and, in this case, by the performer's interaction with it. This highlights Manina's

FIGURE 12.2 *Manina's playing (Joan Fontaine) lapses into "September Song."*

conclusion to David about their experience: "we tried to hide from the past," the implication being that this is impossible. Hoeckner and Nusbaum have observed that cinematic techniques may create "representations that accord more with our experience of using memory" (2013: 241), and this is the case here. Although a flashback is not used, a similar effect is achieved as both character and audience are made aware of simultaneous, multiple temporalities through music and image.

However, the memories in *September Affair* are not confined to the characters. This melodrama exemplifies what Stanley Cavell terms "an autobiography of companions" whereby films not only draw upon our memories of other films but are also themselves part of our autobiographical memory (1979: 3–16). In this case, the film calls to mind earlier films and reveals several intertexts for contemporary audiences and for us today. The inclusion of Rachmaninov's second piano concerto in *September Affair* explicitly references its prominent use in *Brief Encounter* and draws attention to the shared narrative of a couple who are together for a short time but who do not unite at the end. Both films convey a similar sense of romantic longing, of the desire to halt time—to put life on hold—which turns out to be impossible. Manina's career recalls the concert pianists played by Margaret Lockwood and Ann Todd in *Love Story* and *The Seventh Veil* (1945) respectively, films whose narratives are also driven by a central conflict between romance and the demands of a musical profession.

Although not a pianist, Joan Fontaine's role in *Letter from an Unknown Woman* (1948) confers on her an emotional, musical sensibility identified with her desire for Stefan, the concert pianist who is unaware of her feelings but whose music haunts her throughout her life.

A musical sensibility in these films acts as a marker of a character's emotional depth, and piano music expresses and comes to embody the profound feelings with which it is associated. In this way, piano music often keeps alive a treasured memory by expressing the feelings it evokes, a point made by Lawrence Kramer in relation to *Brief Encounter*.

Kramer notes that the film transcends Laura's failure to escape a "repressive social order" because "the lost romance survives in the memory, narrative and music that record its loss" (2007: 93). While the Rachmaninov concerto records the memory of the lost romance in *Brief Encounter*, the memory of David and Manina's time together in *September Affair* is emphatically associated with "September Song." The song is heard more than a dozen times on the soundtrack, far more frequently than the Rachmaninov concerto. It is notable that the classical piece represents Manina's professional life, while her personal feelings are associated with the popular song. Jane Feuer finds that Hollywood musicals typically place elite and popular forms in opposition to each other, a conflict that ends in the "triumphant victory of the popular style" (1993: 56). This privileging of the popular over the classical is reproduced in films outside of the musical genre. Janet Halfyard notes that classical musicians in Hollywood films tend to be linked negatively with high culture and a European identity which are positioned as a threat to popular American culture and American values (2006: 73–85). The Rachmaninov symbolizes for Manina her professional aspirations, while the popular song encapsulates her memory of David, clearly delineated as the two pieces alternate under her fingers at the piano keyboard in the sequence described above. The Rachmaninov concerto thus holds a different meaning in each film. For Laura, it embodies her lost romance; for Manina, it represents the professional aspirations that are an obstacle to her romance.

As an instrument, the piano therefore has many connotations. While piano music clearly embodies treasured emotional memories for the musically sensitive, the act of playing the piano confers qualities of discipline and dedication upon characters who aspire to master it. This sets apart the concert pianists featured in many of the films. In *Dangerous Moonlight*, Stefan's colleagues conspire to keep him from danger in order to serve the higher calling of his musical talent. At the same time, Stefan's patriotic conscience as a Polish national resurfaces in the piano repertoire, specifically the Warsaw Concerto and Chopin's Polonaise in A, that he plays while giving concerts in the United States early in the Second World War, and compels him to return to Europe to do his duty. In *September Affair* Manina continues to practice the piano in her new life with David, working toward her triumphant concert in New York at the end of the film. As such, the instrument is a stringent taskmaster/mistress, requiring a level of discipline and often demanding personal sacrifice. This dedication marks pianists as different and the piano as a prized and enviable possession. Soon after Manina and David settle in their Florentine villa, David surprises her with a gift of a piano in recognition of her profession which unlike the rest of her life cannot be put on hold if she is to progress: "practice makes perfect." Their villa is not complete without it, nor is Manina, although pursuing her career would have ended her secret life had other events not intervened first.

The piano as a prized possession and the special status of the pianist is explored in a different context in *The Housemaid* (1960), a South Korean film melodrama which demonstrates the instrument's transnational cultural significance. In the film, Tong-sik (Jin Kyu Kim) teaches piano to workers in a factory and has a "piano room" in his house. The instrument is a symbol of his family's middle-class status, of rising ambition and achievement. We learn it was paid for in installments, and Tong-sik gives lessons in his home to get a return on his investment. Kyung Hyun Kim notes that the high cost of the piano "fosters the distinctions and class barriers that usher in the tragic plot," and also highlights the piano as "an object of desire, generating fetishistic impulses by virtue of its rarity and delicacy" (2005: 219). Tong-sik's downfall is initiated by the powerful emotions he arouses in the women around him by virtue of his piano playing. Heather Laing observes that the male musician in melodrama is frequently a figure "of female adoration . . . love or even obsession" (2007: 71), and like the male pianists in *The Night Has Eyes* and *Dangerous Moonlight*, Tong-sik inspires strong feelings although he seems oblivious of them. The potential of piano music to forge an erotic connection between performer and listener is described by Lawrence Kramer, whereby the "intimate space" it creates is rendered "libidinally active" as the music gives "tangible form to the movement of desire" (2002: 34). Tong-sik's fall from grace begins when one of his female piano pupils writes him a love letter, and he reports the matter to her work supervisor. Suspended from work and humiliated by his rejection, the woman commits suicide, an act for which he later feels responsible. The woman's friend continues to have piano lessons in his home, and it becomes clear that she is also infatuated with him. As they play a duet, she declares her love, and when he resists her, she tears her blouse and threatens to accuse him of trying to rape her. He throws her out, following which the maid, who has overheard the encounter, plays a few notes on the piano prior to seducing Tong-sik. It is as if the piano is complicit in Tong-sik's downfall, responsible for endowing him with both a particularly attractive musicality and a desirable status. When he succumbs to the sexual relationship with the maid that instigates the family's breakdown, he blames the piano as the cause of their unhappiness since it has provided the funds to employ the maid.

When the maid becomes pregnant and is forced to have an abortion, she resolves to take her revenge, and the film moves into horror territory. In one scene the piano, hitherto the source of harmonic tones and a symbol of refinement and material prosperity identified with Tong-sik, is ravaged by the maid as she thunders down on its keys to produce a cacophonous racket and he fears she will break it. The discordant echoes of these disturbing sounds signify the maid's increasing power over the couple. She murders their child, but they do not turn her in to the police because that would expose Tong-sik's affair, public knowledge of which would destroy his reputation and career.

As a "classic" South Korean melodrama, *The Housemaid* indeed uses the piano in a resourceful and symbolic manner. This is far less the case in an updated version released fifty years later in 2010. While drawing on the same basic plot, the family that employs the housemaid is wealthy and the husband is less of a victim. Instead, he takes sexual advantage of the maid and the family is depicted as exploitative, selfish, and uncaring. The remake tones down the melodramatic ending of the 1960 original, in which the husband dies, repentant, in front of his wife after being forced into a suicide pact with the maid and taking rat poison. In the later film, the husband survives. In lowering the melodramatic intensity, the role of the piano is also reduced, and it plays a less obvious part in the drama in comparison to the earlier film. The husband is no longer a piano teacher, and his occupation is not specified. He plays wonderfully, however, and there is perhaps a nod to the earlier film when the maid is clearly drawn to his musical virtuosity in a scene preceding his seduction of her, perhaps softening her attitude toward him and certainly foregrounding their sexual intimacy. Here, though, rather than being the hapless victim of the adoration he has inspired, the man knowingly initiates the seduction. Focus on the pianist's keyboard dexterity returns in a disturbing reprise as he later touches her body. Like the piano, he manipulates her as a possession of which he is able to take advantage. This resonates with the 1960s film in which the maid and Tong-sik begin their affair in the piano room.

In this way, we are offered a reinterpretation from the perspective of 2010. This suggests a productive way to think about texts that connect with, yet depart from, an iconic "original." This can be applied to a film like *The Housemaid*, with its status as one of the most significant South Korean melodramas of the "Golden Age." While both films feature a piano, their resonances are different with the instrument featuring less as a sign of economic well-being in the remake and more as a source of cultural capital, conferring on the husband an artistic sensibility that sets him somewhat apart from his wife and vindictive mother-in-law. There is another element of cinematic homage in the 2010 version with its inclusion of a mise-en-scène that features many shots of staircases, resonating with the 1960s film in which the house is claustrophobic and "visually suffocating" (Kim 2005:

213). This is another aspect of filmic memory, of how images can reverberate across decades.

As *The Housemaid* remembers its "Golden Age" inspiration, it is also very much located in the director's critique of a society obsessed by wealth and power. The repetition of the piano as both a material and affective symbol suggests its power to serve as a complex and transnationally applied trope in film melodrama. As the notes of a piano take us backward and forward (arpeggio), the remake remodels its source, often into quite a different creature. This resembles memory, the "*Casablanca* effect" that appears to both collapse and stretch time simultaneously.

In bringing to the surface repressed desires and feelings, the piano in cinema is thus capable of conveying complex emotional depths. As these examples have demonstrated, it serves several distinctive functions within melodrama, accentuating the complexities of time, memory, gender, status, and nationality. In this respect, melodramas mobilize affective regimes through music in ways that are more usually identified with musicals. This is achieved through exploiting aural and visual registers: as well as hearing piano music, how we see it being played is also important. This is particularly the case when a character appears to be carried away by the music, even though we know that the actor is not the actual pianist. Our suspension of disbelief is, however, encouraged by facial expression, from Maddalena's visible change of mood in *Madonna of the Seven Moons* to Manina's conflicted emotions in *September Affair*. Camera angles are also significant since the typical strategy is not to show the notes being played. This places emphasis on the protagonist's other physical reactions as in the case of the 2010 version of *The Housemaid*, when a hip-level shot and depth of field permit the housemaid who is listening from afar to be visible in the same shot with the piano and pianist in the foreground (Figure 12.3).

FIGURE 12.3 *The pianist casts a seductive spell in* The Housemaid *(2010)*.

Although other cinematic genres use pianos in perhaps different ways, for melodramas, the piano has been a consistent source of pain, pleasure, and self-discovery. While the encounters may be brief, they are as emotionally resonant as the music with which they are identified.

References

Altman, R. (1987), *The American Film Musical*, Bloomington: Indiana University Press.
Cavell, S. (1979), *The World Viewed: Reflections on the Ontology of Film*, Cambridge, MA: Harvard University Press.
Cook, P. (2005), *Screening the Past: Memory and Nostalgia in Cinema*, London: Routledge.
Feuer, J. (1993), *The Hollywood Musical*, 2nd edn, Basingstoke: Macmillan.
Halfyard, J. K. (2006), "Screen Playing: Cinematic Representations of Classical Music Performance and European Identity," in M. Mera and D. Burnand (eds.), *European Film Music*, Aldershot: Ashgate.
Hardy, L. (2001), *The British Piano Sonata, 1870–1945*, Woodbridge: Boydell Press.
Hoeckner, B. and H. C. Nusbaum (2013), "Music and Memory in Film and Other Multimedia: The Casablanca Effect," in S.-L. Tan, A. J. Cohen, S. D. Lipscomb and R. A. Kendall (eds.), *The Psychology of Music in Multimedia*, Oxford: Oxford University Press.
Kim, K. H. (2005), "Lethal Work: Domestic Space and Gender Troubles in *Happy End* and *The Housemaid*," in K. McHugh and N. Abelmann (eds.), *South Korean Age of Melodrama: Gender, Genre, and National Cinema*, 201–28, Detriot: Wayne State University Press.
Kramer, L. (2002), *Musical Meaning: Towards a Critical History*, Berkeley and Los Angeles: University of California Press.
Kramer, L. (2007), *Why Classical Music Still Matters*, Berkeley and Los Angeles: University of California Press.
Laing, H. (2007), *The Gendered Score: Music in 1940s Melodrama and the Woman's Film*, Aldershot: Ashgate.
Tasker, Y. (2007), "*The Piano*," in P. Cook (ed.), *The Cinema Book*, 3rd edn, London: British Film Institute.

Filmography

Brief Encounter (1945), [Film] Dir. David Lean, UK: Cineguild.
Casablanca (1942), [Film] Dir. Michael Curtiz, USA: Warner Bros.
Dangerous Moonlight (1941), [Film] Dir. Brian Desmond Hunt, UK/USA: RKO Radio Pictures.
The Housemaid (1960), [Film] Dir. Ki-young Kim, South Korea: Hanguk Munye Yeonghwa

The Housemaid (2010), [Film] Dir. Sang-soo Im, South Korea: Sidus.
Letter from an Unknown Woman (1948), [Film] Dir. Max Ophüls, USA: Universal-International.
Love Story (1944), [Film] Dir. Leslie Arliss, UK: Gainsborough Pictures.
Madonna of the Seven Moons (1945), [Film] Dir. Arthur Crabtree, UK: Gainsborough Pictures.
The Night has Eyes (1942), [Film] Dir. Leslie Arliss, UK: Associated British Pictures Corporation.
The Piano (1993), [Film] Dir. Jane Campion, New Zealand/Australia/France: CiBy 2000/Jan Chapman Productions.
The Piano Teacher (2001), [Film] Dir. Michael Haneke, Austria/France/Germany: Arte France Cinéma.
A Place of One's Own (1945), [Film] Dir. Bernard Knowles, UK: Gainsborough Pictures.
September Affair (1950), [Film] Dir. William Dieterle, USA: Hal Wallis Productions.
The Seventh Veil (1945), [Film] Dir. Compton Bennett, UK: Sydney Box Productions.
The Upturned Glass (1947), [Film] Dir. Lawrence Huntington, UK: Triton.
While I Live (1947), [Film] Dir. John Harlow, UK: Edward Dryhurst Productions.

13

Everybody Wants to Be a Cat

Jazz Culture and Disney Animation in the 1960s

Landon Palmer

Among the many forms and genres that the American film musical has taken, both the animated musical and the jazz musical have received relatively limited academic attention as a key component of this tradition.[1] Yet, these subcategories provide opportunities to challenge broader academic conceptualizations of the musical. As Susan Smith argues, due to the tendency of the animated film to feature singing and dancing animals and objects, animated musicals place the performer in a complex relationship to the animated body in contrast to live-action musical performance, as "anything [can] become endowed with a musicality of movement and expression all its own" (Smith 2011: 169). And as several scholars of jazz cinema have shown, on-screen representation of jazz—a genre whose popularization coincided with the rise of sync-sound in American cinema—has demonstrated the inherent tensions between vernacular self-expression and the more calculated efforts of commercial motion picture production, a tendency made most visible in Hollywood's simultaneous embrace of various interpretations of jazz and conditional, marginal casting of African American jazz musicians (see Gabbard 1995; Knight 1995; Chan 2014, and Pillai 2017).

As a film form whose production processes are at odds with the spontaneity embraced by jazz culture, and has had a—to put it mildly—complex history of representing identity, the animated jazz musical puts into motion pervasive issues regarding popular music, cultural identity, and its representation. As with the distinct traditions in which it intersects, limited academic attention to the animated jazz musical is disproportionate to its historical legacy, and much of the established scholarship on this genre focuses on the rich period between the 1920s and the 1940s (see Grant 1989; Goldmark 2005; Shanks 2014, and Sammond 2015). This chapter gives attention to a transitional era at an American animation studio that crossed paths with a marginal period in both jazz and the Hollywood musical: the late 1960s. I investigate the uses of jazz in Walt Disney's first two animated features released after Disney's passing: *The Jungle Book* (1967), the last animated feature with the producer's involvement, and *The Aristocats* (1970), the studio's first animated feature that was largely developed after his death. By examining a troubled period for genres and cultural currents that previously dominated American screens, this chapter seeks to demonstrate how a newly marginal status of commercial and popular entertainment forms and traditions can open up the potential for cultural objects to produce new, even corrective, interpretations of said categories. The newly marginal status of previously dominant popular music genres can create an open field for their signification in the musical—and, as a moving image form that has a complex history of signification, animation is a potent space in which to explore how meaning is made, and remade, from music.

What's notable about the relationship of jazz culture and popular media in the 1960s is both its relative absence in mainstream representation and the conflicted discourses that struggled to locate its place in contemporary popular culture. Within this historical-cultural context, these Disney features produced images that resituated the social meanings of jazz previously established in mainstream American animation. The marginal place of jazz in 1960s popular culture allowed these Disney features to convey an ideology of jazz that was no longer overtly associated with racial panic or contemporary youth culture but gained the status of an enduring art form ostensibly available to "everybody." Such inclusive images of jazz are complicated by their mediation via white vocal performers, indicating that a performatively benevolent reinstatement of white authority is key to Disney's resolution of the social differences that helped define both jazz culture and its contested onscreen representations. Toward this end, the following analysis situates these Disney features within the history of jazz's anthropomorphization on the animated screen.

Jazz Culture, On-screen, and Anthropomorphized

The history of American animation has deep roots in the production and representation of racial and ethnic stereotypes, particularly via performance traditions centered around African Americans that helped to set such stereotypes into motion. American animation's sounds and images of jazz music and musicians cultivated a space in which such stereotypes solidified and cycled, contributing to tensions between jazz culture and its on-screen depiction (Goldmark 2005: 77–106). Such caricatures often took the form of presenting jazz within a tradition of racist images of Black savagery and minstrelsy, as is evident in animated shorts from *Jungle Jazz* (1930) to *The Isle of Pingo Pongo* (1938). As Nicholas Sammond argues, American animation as an industry is "an integral part of the ongoing iconographic and performative traditions of blackface," and its history of racist caricature goes beyond obvious stereotypes and into norms of characterization and performance (2015: 5). "Cartoon minstrels" such as Felix the Cat, Mickey Mouse, and Bugs Bunny, as Sammond goes onto claim, "are distinct from cartoon depictions of African Americans" listed above (28–9). Anthropomorphized animals like the aforementioned characters present a complex terrain for animating cultural, racial, and ethnic identity and stereotypes. As Paul Wells states, animated animals are "able to carry a diversity of representational positions" (2009: 3).

In contrast to the consistently racialized jazz crow in films like Disney's *Dumbo* (1941) and in shorts featuring Max Fleisher's Buzzy the Crow character (1947–54) (Sampson 1998: 72–9; Lehman 2007: 65), the animated cat has functioned as a relatively open signifier in its association with jazz culture and, at times, has been presented as vaguely signifying an "aura" of jazz, displaying a cool, reserved attitude without overt caricature of particular identity tropes. A slang term that connotes "an expert in, or one expertly appreciative of, jazz" that stretches back in popular use to at least the 1930s, "cat" draws a lexical connection between the domestic feline and jazz culture ("Cat" n.d.). This connection arose approximate to, and potentially proceeded, animated depictions of the cat as jazz aficionado. For example, *Felix the Cat*, a series of shorts initially produced throughout the 1920s and into the 1930s, is widely interpreted as embodying and satirizing jazz culture (Tom 1996). Cartoonist George Herriman's Krazy Kat, a character who originated in newspaper comic strips in 1913, grew into a jazz signifier first in John Alden Carpenter's ballet *Krazy Kat: A Jazz Pantomime* (1922) and subsequently in the animated short film *Birth of Jazz* (1932) ("John Alden Carpenter"). The latter depicts the titular feline inventing the genre: Krazy falls from a stork's blanket into a room full of sentient musical instruments from which the character leads an orchestra that flies around the world, spreading the musical innovation. Following these examples, animators continued employing cats to signify and anthropomorphize jazz culture, as evinced by the short *The Zoot Cat* (1944), the animated opening credits sequences for the *Pink Panther* series (1963–2009), and the adult-oriented feature *Fritz the Cat* (1972).[2] Two 1940s films, one from Warner

Bros. and the other from Disney, demonstrate American animation's racial, social, and moral perspectives on jazz as articulated via jazz cats.

Warner's short form *Tin Pan Alley Cats* (1943), which was withdrawn from syndication in 1968 because of its racist imagery, was one of many Warner Bros. cartoons to utilize the star image of African American pianist Fats Waller (Sampson 1998: 148). A feline caricature of Waller is presented here in service of a moralistic denunciation of a perceived social degradation associated with jazz culture. The short finds a cat resembling Waller encountering a group of gospel musicians on his way to a jazz club who warn him of the "wine, women, and song" that await inside. While onstage, his music partner, perhaps meant to resemble an anthropomorphized Louis Armstrong (Sampson 1998: 214), delivers an escalating trumpet solo that transports Waller-cat to a strange, hedonistic netherworld full of surreal imagery including, in a sign of the times, Josef Stalin repeatedly kicking Adolf Hitler. Waller-cat becomes so panicked by this experience that, upon his "comedown," he joins the churchgoers in a rendition of "Gimme That Old Time Religion" outside the club. "Tin Pan Alley Cats" revisits much of the condemnation of jazz culture leveled by previous animated shorts, specifically in its implied criticism of recreational drug use and associated interpretation of jazz as an African American cultural practice degrading to mainstream society (Goldmark 2005: 98–9; Lehman 2007: 81–2).

Other examples of mainstream animation, however, interpret cat-characterized jazz culture as a harmless youth diversion. The segment "All the Cats Join In" from Disney's musical package feature *Make Mine Music* (1946) follows the adventures of a young man who, inspired by a song played on a jukebox, calls up his friends and drives them to a malt shop for an evening of dining and dance. Following the opening credits' still images of cats, the film's narrative begins with images of a sketchbook as a pencil independently jumps up and dances toward it. The pencil writes on the first page, "This concerns a . . . ," then flips the page to reveal an image of a jukebox, then writes "and a" on the next page, and, on the following page, draws a cat, erases it, and replaces it with a white teenager who comes to life and begins his good, clean jazzy evening (Figures 13.1 and 13.2). "All the Cats Join In" literally illustrates the feline as metaphor for the jazz culture participant, visually rendering jazz slang in representing contemporary youth culture. Disney's concomitant ethnic and cultural representation on display here is notably distinct from Warner's *Tin Pan Alley Cats*: the young man and his friends are all white, and they are consumers, not producers, of jazz, with their fun depicted as a harmless youth activity.

Respectively, *Tin Pan Alley Cats* and "All the Cats Join In" point to jazz as a component of urban African American cultural production and white youth socialization, but not both simultaneously. American animation's use of jazz cats reveals divergent perspectives and moral claims about the meanings of jazz culture, and such "representational positions"—to return

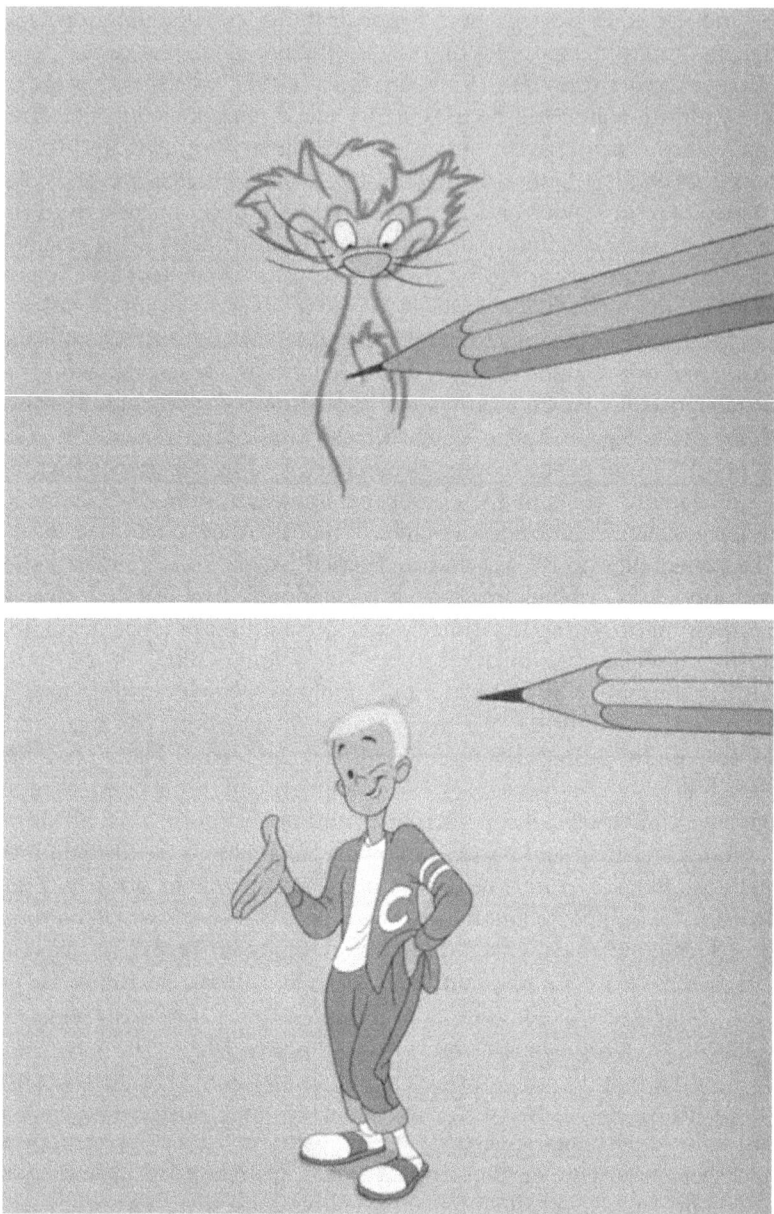

FIGURES 13.1 AND 13.2 *A connection is drawn between a cat and a young, white jazz fan.*

to Wells's phrasing—extend to the decisively noncontemporary jazz cats of *The Aristocats*, which updated ideas about who is included in jazz culture (2009: 3).

The 1960s Jazz Culture and Disney Animation

In "The Modern Scene," jazz critic Amiri Baraka, then writing as LeRoi Jones, asserts that hard bop by the 1950s provided little more than an exercise of musical knowledge, diverging from jazz's political legacy as a nonconformist form of African American expression (1963: 217). This led, the author attests, to the modern jazz scene of the 1960s that arose alongside a severing of the relationship between jazz artists and working-class African American consumers (Jones 1967: 69–73). Baraka's contemporaneous writings reflect a larger uncertainty about the place of jazz in American culture by the midcentury, particularly in the oscillation between its commercial value and its challenges to the status quo, a conversation complicated by persistent questions about who jazz is for. Such questions have been a subject of inquiry by cultural studies scholars. Citing saxophonist Archie Shepp's controversial assertion that "Other people may have an intuitive working class instinct but it takes the intelligentsia to give that order and to make it meaningful," Amy Abugo Ongiri sees the disconnect between modern jazz and working-class African American audiences as evidence of "a general anxiety about the preservation of African American cultural production ... in the face of a desegregation imperative" (2010: 129). More broadly, Paul Lopes chronicles the contradictory state of jazz by the 1950s and 1960s in which the music became, at once, a "major art tradition" reflected by its formation into an art world and a genre diffused across a variety of subcategories (cool jazz, hard bop, etc.) (2002: 1). While not having meaningfully lost its commercial appeal and ability to evolve, the status of jazz by the mid-1960s occupied a contradictory space in American popular culture as both a marginal musical practice and an entry of growing importance in the American musical canon.

The travel of jazz to the margins of both popular music and political relevance was evident in live-action feature films. While jazz enjoyed a continued on-screen representation throughout various facets of feature filmmaking in the early part of the decade—across the major Broadway musical adaptation (*West Side Story* [1961]), Hollywood's European sojourns (*Paris Blues* [1961]), the independent film (*The Connection* [1962]), the modest studio production (*Too Late Blues* [1961]), the documentary (*Jazz on a Summer's Day* [1960]), and the European import (*All Night Long* [1962])—depictions of jazz culture had fallen off-screen by the middle of the decade. In his review of *A Man Called Adam* (1966), critic Bosley Crowther opened with the observation, "Few film dramas these days bother to explore the world of jazz musicians" (1966: 24).³ It was in this discursive context, with pronounced uncertainty about the role of jazz within American culture and its relative absence on American screens, that *The Aristocats* and *The Jungle Book* depicted jazz as severed from contemporary cultural production.

The Aristocats

The Aristocats posits a contrasting framework between dominant culture and jazz culture, but not an oppositional one. The film takes place in Paris in 1910 and follows a group of privileged cats who, after being abandoned by the butler of their manor so that he may claim their inheritance, are adopted by a group of streetwise alley cats. The high social and cultural status of the film's central family (indicated by the title's portmanteau) is established early in the film when Duchess (voiced by Eva Gabor) directs her kittens to sing "Scales and Arpeggios" on an ornate piano holding a Georges Bizet songbook. This song demonstrates the aristocats' traditional, tutored, and cultured understanding of music, as the lyrics instruct the norms of "proper" musical knowledge: "Every truly cultured music student knows/You must learn your scales and your arpeggios." Notably, when the youngest cat, Berlioz (Dean Clark), performs a piano slide, his sister, Marie (Liz English), characterized as snobbish, tells on him, indicating a stifling of improvisatory instincts that are later let loose by the alley cats' jazz.

"Scales and Arpeggios" provides the groundwork for the musical-cultural shift of "Ev'rybody Wants to Be a Cat," the film's centerpiece number that is introduced when the aristocats arrive at the jazz-playing alley cats' apartment. The alley cats' band displays an integrated, multicultural vision of jazz production unavailable in previous works of American animation, although the feline musicians' ethnicities are stereotypically rendered. The band features a Russian double bassist, a Chinese drummer (depicted especially offensively), an Italian accordion player, an English hippie acoustic guitarist, and a trumpet player named Scat Cat voiced by African American entertainer Scatman Crothers—all performing in a "pad" owned by O'Malley the Alley Cat, voiced by Disney regular and white Dixieland jazz musician Phil Harris. Although *The Artistocats* continues American animation's tradition of illustrating stereotypes, it neither utilizes the jazz cat to present jazz as a segregated cultural activity nor incorporates overtly racist images of African Americans. Instead, *The Aristocats*' use of song as musical pedagogy and the film's surface-level depiction of multicultural musical connection echo an earlier Disney work that, to adopt Ella Shohat and Robert Stam's terms, exemplifies the tendency of Hollywood musicals to stage harmony among an ethnic and racial multiplicity specifically for a "dominant White group" (1994: 223–30). In the short *Toot, Whistle, Plunk and Boom* (1953), Professor Owl (Bill Thompson) delivers to a classroom an abbreviated lecture on the entire human history of musical sounds. As part of the "Boom" (percussion) section, the film displays an array of bells and drums used by a procession of orientalist caricatures, culminating with an appearance by a white jazz drummer. Unlike early twentieth-century animated works featuring jazz, both *The Aristocats* and *Toot, Whistle, Plunk and Boom* seek to create a benevolent, celebratory image of human connection through music that transcends cultural difference in the name of musical education; but like such earlier animated works, these films do so through employing stereotypical images as a representational shorthand that forms the basis for such connection.

As with *Toot, Whistle, Plunk and Boom*, musical education in "Ev'rybody Wants to Be a Cat" is delivered via a white-coded authority figure in the form of O'Malley. Beyond the character's Irish surname, Reitherman told journalists that O'Malley was modeled after studio-era screen star Clark Gable ("The Aristocats for Christmas" 1970: 28). Harris's voice imbues O'Malley with a friendly presence akin to his other voice performances as genial and loyal yet buffoonish bears in *The Jungle Book* and *Robin Hood* (1973), but functions in *The Aristocats* as more of a father figure and traditional male lead rather than a trusty sidekick. As the audience's point of entry into the alley cat scene, O'Malley is able to cogently move between the aristocats' high-culture world and the subterranean hip scene of his bandmates. In contrast to the conspicuous rasp of Crothers's Scat Cat (a role for which Disney initially cast Louis Armstrong [Thomas 1968: 22]), Harris's voice performance code-switches between sharing jazz slang with his bandmates and competently conversing with Duchess, thereby providing a white pathway between the refined aristocats and his multicultural social scene on the margins of Paris.

In contrast to "Scales and Arpeggios," "Ev'rybody Wants to Be a Cat" does not provide overt instructions for enculturation into a certain type of music. Instead, O'Malley and Scat Cat "teach" the act of becoming a hip "cat" as acquiring a status of being and knowing. In Phil Ford's cultural history of hipness, he explains why hipness is a form of knowledge that cannot be instructed: "If no one can tell you what is hip, then no one can tell anyone else, either" (2013: 4). "Ev'rybody Wants to Be a Cat" echoes this understanding of hipness, defining hip cat identity as a mode of adaptive cultural positioning rather than tutored cultural knowledge, defined by the lyrics as "know[ing] where it's at" and "pickin' up on the feline beat." Hip cat identity is further described in the song by its opposite: "a square in the act," the lyrics assert, "can set music back . . ." These lyrics point to hipness as a stance against that which it is not, defined by Ford thusly: "Hipness is not an idea, style, or habit, but rather a stance toward the square, uptight, unfree world" (2013: 4). It would seem, then, that the film's upper-class protagonists could not possibly acquire such cultural positioning, having come from the "square" social context that performances of hipness are defined against. But Marie joins in singing alongside O'Malley and Scat Cat by the third verse, showing an adaptive enculturation into the alley cats' hip attitude.

The aristocats are automatically included in, and successfully perform, the hip jazz cat lifestyle and mode of expression, signified by their musical competence with "Ev'rybody Wants to Be a Cat" that involves scatting, dancing, jazz instrumentation, and even an implied reference to recreational drug use (Figure 13.3). The aristocats' "stance toward the square, uptight, unfree world" is acquired swiftly, without intercultural tension, fear of moral consequence, class conflict, or even a resolution of the contradiction that they are the products of that uptight, square world. This lack of resolution is further illustrated at the film's conclusion, when O'Malley and the other alley cats see no problem in accepting life under the roof of the aristocats' gilded household. *The Aristocats* illustrates a breakdown of the racial, cultural, and generational distinctions that previously characterized American animation's interpretations of jazz culture. Yet, in Disney's efforts to "depoliticize" the genre, they replace resonances of jazz as a form of African American vernacular expression with a mutable system of inclusion led by a white figure of authority.

"Ev'rybody Wants to Be a Cat" also contains a temporal dimension to support its rhetoric of hipness, asserting "everything else" besides "that feline beat . . . is obsolete" and that square musicians "can set music back/

FIGURE 13.3 *Echoing recreational marijuana use, Scat Cat, under psychedelic lights, instructs Toulouse (Gary Dubin) on how to "be a cat" by blowing a horn.*

to the caveman days." Such temporal distinctions (hip is new, square is old) continue the song's definition of hipness as an oppositionally defined state of being, yet such cultural cues stand in contrast to the ahistorical pastiche of the film's setting. *The Aristocats*' Belle Époque Paris features a Swinging London cat immersed in psychedelic fashion, kittens adopting contemporaneous terms like "groovy" as part of their hip enculturation, and a proliferation of the sounds and rhetoric of jazz before ragtime was exported to France during the First World War. Such anachronisms present the notion that, in contrast to prior animated depictions of jazz, jazz culture is no longer a distinctly contemporary phenomenon, but exists among of a legacy of cultural references that can communicate hipness. The rhetoric delineating hip from square still persists, but without a clear indication as to whether any cat, at any place or time, cannot learn to be hip.

The Jungle Book

The inclusive message of "Ev'rybody Wants to Be a Cat" echoes similar themes of cross-cultural transcendence expressed in Disney's previous animated feature, *The Jungle Book*, which lays the groundwork for *The Aristocats*' narrative of mobilizing jazz identity into the mainstream and vice versa. "I Wanna Be Like You (The Monkey Song)" features orangutan King Louie—voiced by Italian American jazz vocalist Louis Prima as a character invented for this adaptation of Rudyard Kipling's writing—who makes a deal with the human Mowgli (Bruce Reitherman), declaring that if Mowgli teaches him how to make fire, Louie will teach Mowgli how to stay in the jungle, singing in the chorus that "Someone like me [an ape]/Can learn to be/Like someone like you [a 'man-cub']." As the studio later repeated with *The Aristocats*, Disney initially sought to cast Louis Armstrong in this supporting role (hence the character's name), but changed direction due to the likely controversy over casting a Black performer as an ape (Weinert-Kendt 2013). Despite casting Prima in the role, King Louie is still a jazz-singing ape, an image that echoes American animation's early twentieth-century legacy of representing jazz through anthropomorphized racist stereotypes. While the production actively sought to avoid reinforcing such connections, its pursuit of a more inclusive image of jazz culture resonates on top of this history. "I Wanna Be Like You" conveys Louie's desire to pass from his circumscribed position, to "elevate" from animality to humanity, from a jazz-singing monkey to the top of a hierarchy of creatures. The racial implications of King Louie's aspirations are augmented by the fact that the character was voiced by a singer bearing audible signifiers of white-ethnic performance while Mowgli, despite being a South Asian character, speaks with a generically white young American voice.

As Baloo the Bear (Harris, again) and Bagheera the Panther (Sebastian Cabot) plan to rescue Mowgli, Baloo becomes entranced by King Louie's

FIGURE 13.4 *Baloo "apes" King Louie.*

music. Disguised as an orangutan using a coconut and leaves, Baloo joins the chorus, scats, and dances with King Louie, bringing to life the orangutan's lyrics about "learn[ing] to be like someone like you" (Figure 13.4). But Baloo's guise no longer convinces once his costume comically falls apart. Like the kittens of *The Aristocats*, Baloo successfully, albeit momentarily, imitates King Louie's signifiers of jazz culture, specifically in his vocal, physical, and sartorial imitation of the ape. This song, about learning how to acquire new cultural knowledge and transcend into a different community, is turned on its head by Baloo, a friendly but "square" bear, who pivots its meaning from becoming knowledgably human to becoming convincingly hip. Baloo fleetingly demonstrates the possibility that authentic hipness can be a successfully learned and imitated performance. The bear's failure comes from his outing as an imposter—an unconvincing performer of embodied hipness—and the character's resulting comic embarrassment arises from this incongruity, revealing that Baloo has transformed the orangutan's identity into a costume. The Harris-voiced Baloo is able to briefly move between different identities; his participation in jazz culture is based on his ability to perform certain signs and codes that he can freely, if fleetingly, adopt and abandon. This is something King Louie cannot do, for the jazz-playing orangutan's circumscription is the basis for his musical inspiration. In this way, "I Wanna Be Like You" conveys ideas about cultural transcendence while presenting a scenario that resembles white appropriation of African American jazz culture. In *The Aristocats*, Harris's character conveys no similar risk of fraudulence in his adoption of a jazz identity, and is instead the film's leading authority figure on how to be a hip cat, instructing the aristocats that, regardless of difference (whether that be class, nationality, or culture), the successful imitation of certain codes is sufficient for entry into jazz culture.

If jazz culture's marginal phase in the 1960s permitted more elastic patterns of animated representation, what at this time had replaced jazz in contemporary relevance? In "The Modern Scene," Baraka asserts that rock 'n' roll provided a new, albeit limited, means of countercultural expression (Jones 1963: 223). As Matt Brennan shows, by 1970, strains of mainstream jazz were perceived by the music press as having "abandon[ed] swing rhythm for a straight rock feel," effectively subordinating itself to this dominant popular music genre (2017: 180). The categories of music that Disney opted not to use in these mainstream features speak to this shift in popular music culture. In *The Jungle Book*, Mowgli encounters a group of vultures clearly intended to resemble the Beatles. The vultures serenade Mowgli with a barbershop-quartet-style tune titled "That's What Friends Are For (The Vulture Song)." The song was originally written and recorded as a mock-up of the Beatles' style of rock 'n' roll, but this plan was abandoned during production due to Walt Disney's fears that the number would badly date the film ("Lost Character: Rocky the Rhino" 2007). That there was no similar perceived threat for "I Wanna Be Like You" demonstrates the differences in the studio's perceptions of jazz and rock 'n' roll at this time, perceptions that indicate the distinct positions that each genre had developed in 1960s American culture: jazz is continually relevant cultural wallpaper, but the "British invasion" style of rock 'n' roll is an of-the-moment fad. Stefan Kanfer of *Time*, in a qualified positive review of *The Aristocats*, observed that "other animations" like the Beatles' *Yellow Submarine* (1968) show "more audacity" than the safe-playing Disney feature—a distinction that indicates the rock-facing shift in the popular culture landscape that Disney himself feared could "date" the animated musical (1971: 65).

Conclusion

While animated features like *The Jungle Book* and *The Aristocats* are rarely included in crisis histories of the late-1960s Hollywood musical, these films participated in the efforts of their counterparts in engaging with ideas about old and new amid this marginal period of the genre (see Kessler 2010 and Kennedy 2014). As Martha Shearer shows, with the "death and metamorphosis" experienced by the Hollywood musical during this period, the genre "reinforce[ed] ideas of the musical as reliable, old-fashioned entertainment" (2016: 193–6). Such reinforcement involved producing images of what "old-fashioned entertainment" looks and sounds like, and these Disney features offer an illustration of how jazz came to be included in such a category. Like the similarly anachronistic representation of jazz in Louis Armstrong's performance of the title song in 20th Century Fox's live-action musical adaptation of *Hello, Dolly!* (1969), jazz culture in these Disney features travels across temporal and narrative contexts, anchored by an employment of previous swing and big band styles rather than the genre's contemporaneous developments, toward a transcendence of previous representational connections between jazz and racial, social, and cultural specificity. Jazz in these two films became represented as, in a paradoxical byproduct of the genre's marginal place in contemporary American popular culture, part of an American musical repository, resulting in an image of jazz culture in which "everybody" wants to be a cat and providing the tools by which they can. Such inclusion was manifested by de-centering jazz as a historically African American form of cultural production in order to ignore cultural differences and social distinctions toward a colorblind invention of connections across class, taste, and music.[4]

Notes

1 For example, Rick Altman acknowledges the American film musical's "long history of attention to jazz" but discusses animation almost exclusively in terms of its incorporation into live-action musicals (1987: 55, 58, 71, 241).

2 Parodying *Dumbo*, *Fritz the Cat* also features crow characters stereotypically coded as Black.

3 American cinema's view of jazz as having little contemporary relevance continued in early 1970s films that focused on the genre's past and future, such as the Billie Holiday biopic *Lady Sings the Blues* (1972) and Sun Ra's afro-futurist science-fiction film *Space Is the Place* (1974). However, jazz scores, first popularized in the mid-1950s, reemerged in 1970s films noir including Jerry Goldsmith's score for *Chinatown* (1974) and Bernard Herrmann's score for *Taxi Driver* (1976).

4 The author extends his appreciation to Colleen Montgomery and this volume's editors for their constructive feedback in the formation of this chapter.

References

Altman, R. (1987), *The American Film Musical*, Bloomington: Indiana University Press.
"The Aristocats for Christmas" (1970), *The Ottawa Citizen*, 19 December: 28.
Brennan, M. (2017), *When Genres Collide: Down Beat, Rolling Stone, and the Struggle Between Jazz and Rock*, New York: Bloomsbury.
"Cat" (n.d.), *Oxford English Dictionary*. Available online: https://www.oed.com/view/Entry/28649#eid10061368 (accessed May 17, 2019).
Chan, H. M., ed. (2014), special issue on jazz and film, *The Soundtrack* 6 (1–2).

Crowther, B. (1966), "A Man Called Adam," *The New York Times*, 4 August: 24.
Ford, P. (2013), Dig: *Sound and Music in Hip Culture*, New York: Oxford University Press.
Gabbard, K. (1995), "Introduction: Writing the Other History," in K. Gabbard (ed.), *Representing Jazz*, 1-10, Durham: Duke University Press.
Goldmark, D. (2005), *Tunes for 'Toons: Music and the Hollywood Cartoon*, Berkeley: University of California Press.
Grant, B. K. (1989), "'Jungle Nights in Harlem': Jazz, Ideology and the Animated Cartoon," *Popular Music and Society*, 13 (4): 45-57.
"John Alden Carpenter" (n.d.), *Encyclopaedia Britannica*. Available online: https://www.britannica.com/biography/John-Alden-Carpenter#ref1179745 (accessed June 27, 2019).
Jones, L. (1963), *Blues People: Negro Music in White America*, New York: William Morrow and Company.
Jones, L. (1967), "The Jazz Avant-Garde (1961)," in *Black Music*, 69-73, New York: William Morrow and Company.
Kanfer, S. (1971), "Review: The Aristocats," *Time*, 25 January: 65.
Kennedy, M. (2014), *Roadshow!: The Fall of Film Musicals in the 1960s*, New York: Oxford University Press.
Kessler, K. (2010), *Destabilizing the Hollywood Musical: Music, Masculinity and Mayhem*, New York: Palgrave Macmillan.
Knight, A. (1995), "*Jammin' the Blues*, or the Sight of Jazz, 1944," in K. Gabbard (ed.), *Representing Jazz*, 11-53, Durham: Duke University Press.
Lehman, C. P. (2007), *The Colored Cartoon: Black Representation in American Animated Short Films, 1907-1954*, Amherst: University of Massachusetts Press.
Lopes, P. (2002), *The Rise of a Jazz Art World*, Cambridge: Cambridge University Press.
"Lost Character: Rocky the Rhino" (2007), *The Jungle Book* DVD, Burbank, CA: Disney.
Ongiri, A. A. (2010), *Spectacular Blackness: The Cultural Politics of the Black Power Movement and the Search for a Black Aesthetic*, Charlottesville: University of Virginia Press.
Pillai, N. (2017), *Jazz as Visual Language: Film, Television and the Dissonant Image*, London: I.B. Tauris.
Sammond, N. (2015), *Birth of an Industry: Blackface Minstrelsy and the Rise of American Animation*, Durham: Duke University Press.
Sampson, H. T. (1998), *That's Enough Folks: Black Images in Animated Cartoons, 1900-1960*, Lanham: The Scarecrow Press.
Shanks, C. (2014), "Of Mice and Music: Image, Soundtrack and Historical Possibility," *The Soundtrack*, 6 (1-2): 67-81.
Shearer, M. (2016), *New York City and the Hollywood Musical: Dancing in the Streets*, London: Palgrave Macmillan.
Shohat, E., and R. Stam (1994), *Unthinking Eurocentrism: Multiculturalism and the Media*, New York: Routledge.
Smith, S. (2011), "The Animated Film Musical," in R. Knapp, M. Morris and S. Wolf (eds.), *The Oxford Handbook of the American Musical*, 167-78, New York: Oxford University Press.

Thomas, B. (1968), "First Cartoon Minus Disney," *The Ottawa Citizen*, 3 August: 22.
Tom, P. V. (1996), "Felix the Cat as Modern Trickster," *American Art*, 10 (1): 64–87.
Weinert-Kendt, R. (2013), "Cutting through a Cultural Thicket," *The New York Times*. June 20. Available online: https://www.nytimes.com/2013/06/23/theater/the-jungle-book-comes-to-the-stage.html (accessed June 29, 2019).
Wells, P. (2009), *The Animated Bestiary: Animals, Cartoons, and Culture*, New Brunswick: Rutgers University Press.

Filmography

All Night Long (1962), [Film] Dir. Basil Dearden, UK: Roberts Pictures.
The Aristocats (1970), [Film] Dir. Wolfgang Reitherman, USA: Disney.
Birth of Jazz (1932), [Film] Dir. Manny Gould and Ben Harrison, USA: Charles Mintz Productions.
Chinatown (1974), [Film] Dir. Roman Polanski, USA: Paramount Pictures.
The Connection (1962), [Film] Dir. Shirley Clarke, USA: Allen-Hodgdon Productions.
Dumbo (1941), [Film] Dir. Ben Sharpsteen, Norman Ferguson, Wilfred Jackson, Bill Roberts, Jack Kinney, and Samuel Armstrong, USA: Disney.
Fritz the Cat (1972), [Film] Dir. Ralph Bakshi, USA: Fritz Productions.
Hello, Dolly! (1969), [Film] Dir. Gene Kelly, USA: Twentieth Century-Fox.
The Isle of Pingo Pongo (1938), [Film] Dir. Fred Avery, USA: Leon Schlesinger Studios.
Jazz on a Summer's Day (1960), [Film] Dir. Bert Stern, USA: Galaxy Productions/Raven Films.
The Jungle Book (1967), [Film] Dir. Wolfgang Reitherman, USA: Disney.
Jungle Jazz (1930), [Film] Dir. Harry Bailey and John Foster, USA: Van Beuren Studios.
Lady Sings the Blues (1972), [Film] Dir. Sidney J. Furie, USA: Motown Productions.
Make Mine Music (1946), [Film] Dir. Jack Kinney, Clyde Geronimi, Hamilton Luske, and Joshua Meador, USA: Disney.
A Man Called Adam (1966), [Film] Dir. Leo Penn, USA: Trace-Mark Productions.
Paris Blues (1961), [Film] Dir. Martin Ritt, USA: United Artists.
Robin Hood (1973), [Film] Dir. Wolfgang Reitherman, USA: Disney.
Space is the Place (1974), [Film] Dir. John Coney, USA: North American Star System.
Taxi Driver (1976), [Film] Dir. Martin Scorsese, USA: Columbia Pictures.
Tin Pan Alley Cats (1943), [Film] Dir. Bob Clampett, USA: Leon Schlesinger Studios.
Too Late Blues (1961), [Film] Dir. John Cassavetes, USA: Paramount Pictures.
Toot, Whistle, Plunk and Boom (1953), [Film] Dir. Ward Kimball and Charles A. Nichols, USA: Disney.
West Side Story (1961), [Film] Dir. Jerome Robbins and Robert Wise, USA: The Mirisch Company.
Yellow Submarine (1968), [Film] Dir. George Dunning, UK/USA: Apple Films.
The Zoot Cat (1944), [Film] Dir. Joseph Barbera and William Hanna, USA: MGM.

14

Short-form Pop Music Films in 1960s Britain

Richard Farmer

The relationship between British cinema and 1960s pop music has most often been understood in terms of feature-length films. From Cliff Richard's *The Young Ones* (1961) and *Summer Holiday* (1963), which borrowed something from the narrative and aesthetic conventions of Hollywood musicals, via compendium "juke box" movies like *Live It Up* (1963) and *Gonks Go Beat* (1964), to exploitation vehicles which sought to cash-in on the fame of an act such as Herman's Hermits or Gerry and the Pacemakers, and on to the more jaundiced, skeptical pictures appearing in the latter part of the decade—for example, *Privilege* (1967) or *Performance* (1970)—British cinemagoers and pop fans were offered access to their favorite musicians via films made in a range of different styles. These films have received extensive attention from scholars, who have both tracked their evolution in relation to the changing status of popular music in the UK and also sought to understand them, in collective terms, as "pop musicals."[1]

However, just as the markets for popular music in Britain were heterodox and overlapping—at the start of the 1960s, a number of musical styles, most importantly pop and jazz, were deemed to be "equally influential" and as such provided the impetus for diverse cinematic productions (Mundy 2007: 172; Mitchell 2013: 209–10)—so the range of films understood as "pop music" movies was equally varied. In some instances, productions with only a slight musical connection were marketed as pop music films: *A Place to Go* (1963) was described by fan magazine *Pop Weekly* ("More movie plans": 8) as a "major" pop music film because it featured Mike Sarne, an actor with a few successful novelty records to his name (and who is shown singing the title song under the opening credits). More importantly for this chapter, the "pop music film" can be, and often was at the time, recognized as a cinematic production of any length or form that grows out of and seeks to exploit popular music as a commercial product. Fiction and nonfiction shorts, newsreels and cinemagazines emerged from the same cultural moment as feature-length pieces and shared similar intentions in that they sought to cater to and exploit the tastes and desires of a specific and increasingly valuable set of consumers. Shorter forms of cinema were cheap to make and quick to produce, making them easier to fit into crowded touring schedules in a period where much of an artist's income was derived from live performance. As such, shorter films were better placed than feature films to exploit current fads while they were still at, or near, flood tide. As Robin Bean noted in *Films and Filming*, that part of the production sector dedicated to the feature film often needed time "to adjust to ever changing moods and whims. Sometimes by the time it makes up its mind to take the plunge the water's drained away" (1964: 9).

It would, of course, be incorrect to claim that every appearance on celluloid by a popular musician constitutes a hitherto overlooked pop music film, let alone a pop musical. An item about Tommy Steele moving house from Bermondsey to Catford in an August 1957 edition of Pathe News, or a February 1969 Movietone piece on Lulu's marriage to Maurice Gibb, is simply a story about a musician in the public eye, even if it makes clear the increasing prominence of certain stars whose fame emerged from, but extended beyond, their music. However, many music-focused shorts foreground the musician as performer, and, moreover, are alive with the energy and spectacularity of performance and the pleasures of spectatorship, whether the spectator is present at the time of filming or watching later, at the cinema.[2] Many of these *can* be understood as pop musicals, or perhaps pop musical films, especially if, following Rick Altman (1995: 294), a separation is drawn between "a musical" and "a musical film," with the former term used to describe films conforming to the formal and ideological conventions of a particular Hollywood genre, and the latter held to mean "a film with a significant amount of diegetic music . . . some produced by principle characters."[3] It is these often marginalized parts of the cinema program that I will explore in this chapter, investigating their production and consumption, but also thinking about how they functioned aesthetically and as intermedia/transmedia texts.

There are myriad intriguing and enjoyable short musical films, relating to a range of different popular musics and made in a number of different styles. Program fillers featuring big-band leaders such as Ted Heath and Eric Delaney suggest that in the early 1960s, at least, youthful tastes had not yet swept all before them, whereas as a host of shorts featuring artists such as Chris Barber, Dill Jones, Tony Kinsey, and Ray Ellington sought to capitalize on the short-lived but widespread popularity of "trad" (and other forms of) jazz at the start of the decade. Some of these films moved beyond the filming of live or as live performances, introducing fictional or fictionalized sections to link the different songs that tended to constitute the bulk of the running time. In *The Johnny Leyton Touch* (1962, ten minutes), released in time to promote his single "Son, This is She," the eponymous drama-school-graduate-cum-pop-singer demonstrated the acting chops that would see him land roles in *The Great Escape* (1963) and *Guns at Batasi* (1964). In *Four Hits and a Mister* (1962, fourteen minutes), "a showmanlike short that definitely digs," jazz clarinetist Acker Bilk donned a different costume and adopted a different persona for each of the songs that he performed for the camera with his Paramount Jazz Band (*"Four Hits"* 1963: 14). If Bilk's versatility was impressive, the Shadows' presence in the thirty-minute *Rhythm 'n Greens* (1964), in which the group clown and play their way through British history from the Stone Age to the rock 'n' roll age, was singled out for decidedly faint praise: "better acting . . . than one might expect from a musical group, but their range is still very limited" (*Rhythm 'n Greens* 1964: 166). The release during the second half of the 1960s of films such as *The Pretty Things* (1966, fourteen minutes) or *The Bee Gees* (1968, six minutes) suggests that there was still perceived to be a market for music shorts although, as John Mundy notes, production became "seriously curtailed" as the decade wore on (2007: 184).

As interesting and important as such films are, the remainder of this chapter will focus in the main on three short color films produced by Pathe, and issued as part of the Pathe News program, in an attempt to exploit the popularity of the then current "beat boom." Each of these films—"The Beatles Come to Town" (December 1963, six minutes), "The Dave Clark Five" (February 1964, six minutes), and "Rolling Stones Gather Moss" (October 1964, five minutes)—was dedicated to capturing and communicating the excitement of live performances given by a leading beat group. Each of the films conforms to a similar template, presenting material shot preshow and backstage and building to a musical climax by way of live performance and fan reaction. Although contemporary records suggest the importance of these films to pop fans and performers at the time of their production and release, and while their popularity might have provided the impetus for the subsequent production of longer, more expensive films, they have received little attention from film scholars. While I would not seek to downplay the central importance of the feature-length narrative film to the cinematic reputations of the Beatles (*A Hard Day's Night*, 1964; *Help!*, 1965; etc.) and the Dave Clark Five (*Catch Us If You Can*, 1965), or of the longer-form nonfiction/documentary to the Rolling Stones (*Charlie Is My Darling*, 1966; *One + One/Sympathy for the Devil*, 1968; *Gimme Shelter*, 1970), drawing attention to shorter form films has the potential to extend and augment our understanding of the ways in which pop music circulated via the cinema. What's more, such films also allow us to reconsider how the film industry tried to package pop for its own ends and how pop music consumers used the cinema to access their idols, thus imbricating the medium within the experience of musical fandom.

Newsreel producers were interested in pop music for a number of reasons. By the start of the 1960s, Pathe News and British Movietone were all that remained of the "big five" companies that had dominated the golden age of British newsreels, and despite their increasingly anachronistic nature, they were still regular features of the program in many venues (McKernan 2002: x). The rapid growth of TV ownership during the 1950s allowed British consumers to watch daily news bulletins at home, and in response, newsreel companies came to focus on less time-sensitive "human interest and travelogue" stories (Pronay 1993: 9; Young 2005: 237–8; "Half of UK cinemas" 1961: 22). Focusing on topical and apolitical general interest items, the newsreels came increasingly to resemble cinemagazines such as *Pathe Pictorial* (first issued in 1918, relaunched in color in 1955) or Rank's *Look at Life*, which had arisen phoenix-like from the ashes of the Universal and British Gaumont newsreels in 1959 as the Organisation's cinemas had sought to bolster the nonfiction elements of its programs. The novelty, energy, and strong visual identities of many pop singers and beat groups were ideal fodder for the cinemagazines and remaining newsreels, as were the enthusiastic reactions and spending power of youthful fans, leading one publication associated with Pathe News to claim that the newsreel had devised a strategy to become "top of the pop coverage by scooping the groups" ("How the Five" 1964: 32).

Both Pathe and Movietone issued newsreels containing stories centered on pop musicians. To give just a few examples: in the spring of 1964, both companies presented footage shot at the *NME*'s Poll Winners Concert; while in August that year, Pathe ran a piece which showed Manfred Mann performing "Do Wah Diddy Diddy" at the Mecca Palais in Edinburgh; and the following February, a piece on the Rolling Stones' arrival in Sydney showed them playing "Not Fade Away" to an audience of excited Australian fans. The sartorial trends associated with the new music also provided an excuse for a story. In November 1963, Movietone featured a piece on youth fashion in which the Swinging Blue Jeans played while two female models danced in clothes patterned after the band's distinctive look. The next month an edition of *Pathe Pictorial* called "Beau Modern" (1963, eight minutes), which took as its subject the increasing flamboyance of contemporary male fashions, ended with a lengthy sequence showing the Searchers, smartly suited and booted, playing "Sugar and Spice" in a recording studio. As mentioned previously, numerous other stories focused on musicians as personalities, rather than performers.

Furthermore, the precipitous decline of cinema ticket sales in Britain from their 1946 peak did not affect all age groups equally, and brought about a more pronouncedly youthful audience: by 1965, one survey claimed that almost half of all female cinemagoers were aged sixteen to twenty-four.[4] This encouraged the newsreel companies to include stories that pandered to the perceived interests of their most regular customers, in the expectation that this would make their product, and the cinema as a whole, more popular. So strong did exhibitors believe the earning potential of "The Beatles Come to Town" to be with pop fans that Pathe secured additional bookings for its newsreel on the strength of this one film alone (Stroller 1963: 4), while one chain of news cinemas advertised in the *New Musical Express* to let readers know that they could watch the Beatles at their theaters (Advertisement 1963: 2). Yet, although the Pathe films were careful to show the groups *as* groups, they also worked to differentiate the individuals that comprised them: each member of the Beatles, the Dave Clark Five, and the Rolling Stones is named and afforded a close-up, either backstage or while performing (and often both). The brevity of the films, and the lack of synchronous dialogue, means that there is less opportunity to capture and present individual personalities to the viewer than there is in, say, a feature such as *A Hard Day's Night*, which takes care to show John, Paul, George, and Ringo as possessing quite distinct characters and traits. However, this is not to say that the Pathe films present the band members as indistinguishable or interchangeable, and individual personas do emerge, for instance, as Charlie Watts sticks his tongue out at the camera, John Lennon pulls faces, or Dave Clark demonstrates his privileged position by adjusting Lenny Davidson's tie. Here, the films seem intent on providing satisfaction to those fans interested in, and excited by, the musician as much as they were the music that they made.

The commercial linkages between the burgeoning pop music sector and the British majors—Associated British Picture Corporation (ABPC) and Rank—had the potential to make interaction mutually beneficial. Sales of Helen Shapiro's "Walkin' Back to Happiness," for example, were boosted considerably by the song's appearance in an edition of *Look at Life* titled "For the Record" (September 1961, 9 minutes), which, as part of a wider story on the pop industry, showed the track being recorded, promoted, and distributed. Rank's willingness to promote "Walkin' Back to Happiness" in this way was almost certainly linked to the fact that it had obtained the rights to publish the song through its Filmusic subsidiary. In return, EMI, which released the single, agreed to promote *Look at Life* when advertising the disc both at point of sale and via broadcasters such as Radio Luxembourg ("Record prizes" 1961: 6; see also Schroeder 2016: 47–50).

ABPC, on the other hand, owned both Pathe News and the ABC cinema chain, so it comes as little surprise that "The Beatles Come to Town" and "Rolling Stones Gather Moss" were shot at ABC venues in Manchester and Hull, respectively, thereby allowing the films to advertise these cinemas as sites where pop performances could be enjoyed either on stage or on screen. In a feature on its readers' positive response to "The Beatles Come to Town," *ABC Film Review*—the circuit's fan-oriented promotional magazine, which in this period was taking an increasing interest in pop music—stressed the role that ABC cinemas had played in allowing fans to see the band play live. The magazine described "the incredible reception the Beatles were given when they appeared on the stages of ABC cinemas up and down the country" and claimed that each concert was "preceded by a full-scale 'military' operation by the police in co-operation with ABC managements" (Taylor 1964: 17–18). Although "The Dave Clark Five" was shot at the Royal Ballroom in Tottenham—the band's "home" venue and one of the Mecca chain's premiere dancehalls—*ABC Film Review* was eager to use its article on the film to promote a forthcoming tour in which ABC cinemas would feature prominently: "After their appearance on ABC cinema screens, Dave and his boys will be seen in person on the stages of twelve ABC cinemas during April and May" ("How the Five" 1964: 32).

For the pop stars, and their managers, the newsreels and cinemagazines—like feature films—were potential sources of direct and indirect revenue. Musicians were often paid to appear (Lewisohn 1992: 129),[5] but short films also worked to maintain, or increase, an act's profile, or to promote a particular record. In "The Dave Clark Five," for example, the band plays current hit "Glad All Over," which at the time of the film's release was still competing for the top spot in the charts. Perhaps even more excitingly for pop fans, though, the film also shows the band performing their *next* single: "For the first time, even before the disc is on sale, here's their new number, 'Bits and Pieces.'" While this was quite a coup for Pathe, it was an exceptional promotional opportunity for the DC5, and the film is constructed to present "Bits and Pieces" to its best advantage. The film offers fewer cutaways to the audience than do the Rolling Stones or Beatles films, and so focuses even more on the band and its music. No doubt boosted by Pathe's interest, "Bits and Pieces" entered the chart at number nineteen on February 26, 1964, and peaked at number two a couple of weeks later.

The cinema could promote artists using a number of technological attractions not then offered by television, a medium which had itself sought to jump on the popular music bandwagon with shows such as *Six-Five Special* (1957–8), *Thank Your Lucky Stars* (1961–6), *Ready, Steady, Go* (1963–6), and *Top of the Pops* (1964–2006). Author David Hepworth remembered that seeing the Beatles on the vast expanse of the cinema screen, with its high-resolution images, was "enthralling" precisely because it showed them "on a screen *yay* high and brought them up *this* close. Nothing had done that before. TV still had end-of-the-pier production values so we had never seen them via a medium that matched their splendor" (2018: 24–5). Hepworth's recollections relate specifically to *A Hard Day's Night* and so do not mention "The Beatles Come to Town," which offered two further attractions not then available on British television: widescreen and color. Combining these two processes in a newsreel was unprecedented, a consequence of the Beatles' elevated cultural profile and status and a further attempt to differentiate the film's aesthetic from television ("The Beatles in 'Scope" 1963: 7). "The Dave Clark Five" and "Rolling Stones Gather Moss" were not widescreen presentations, but they were shot in color "as if . . . a royal tour" (Chaplin 1964: 14). Because British television was transmitted solely in black and white until 1967, each of the three Pathe films most likely constituted the first publicly accessible color moving images of the groups concerned.[6] Indeed, "The Beatles Come to Town" was all the more exciting because, to quote Alun Owen, who wrote the script for the (monochrome) *A Hard Day's Night*, to most fans "the boys are essentially black and white people," most frequently seen on television or in the newspapers (quoted in Glynn 2013: 83).[7] Pathe's decision to shoot in widescreen and/or color spoke to what Rick Altman (1995: 295) has shown to be a tradition of using musical films to "showcase" technological innovation, presenting such innovation as a spectacle in its own right, while simultaneously using its aesthetic potentialities to associate music and movement with pleasure and sensation.

However, whereas color had frequently been used in the Hollywood musical in a more or less fantastical way—to help separate the world of the film from the world of the viewer—the three short Pathe "beat" films under consideration used it to help construct a vision of reality, that is, in an attempt to collapse some of the distance between the cinemagoer and the events transpiring on the screen. Here, the nature of the cinematic image combined with the cinema's capacity for louder and higher-fidelity sound, and the fact that in some cases the cinema in which the film was watched acted as an analogue for the cinema in which the film was shot, to more closely approximate than could television the experience of seeing a band perform live. "The Beatles Come to Town" was said by one newspaper to give fans "an opportunity to see the group in action" ("The Beatles in Color" 1963: 7), while an 8 mm copy of the film—"with soundtrack"—was offered as a prize (alongside a projector) in a competition run by the *People* newspaper, and was said to provide "the excitement, frenzy and . . . ecstasy of a real live Beatle show!" ("Free! Must be won" 1964: 7). "The Dave Clark Five," meanwhile, was said by one critic to communicate "the good authentic glow of watching a real performance" (Chaplin 1964: 14).

Moreover, each of the three films contains shots that seem to have been included specifically to excite and thrill, to move the viewer to a place where they can be overwhelmed by the physical nature of performance and, linked, take pleasure in the embodied aspects of musical fandom and spectatorship. We are shown the Beatles' head-shaking harmonies ("ooohs" during "She Loves You," "aaahs" during "Twist and Shout"), Mick Jagger dancing in all his tight-trousered glory during an instrumental break in "Around and Around," and several "beautifully timed breaks for the stamping of those five stylish pairs of boots" as the DC5 play "Bits and Pieces" (Chaplin 1964: 14).

It is at these moments that the films come closest to offering unadulterated sensation, where the excitement of a live show is most effectively captured, amplified, and communicated back to the cinema audience.

Although the Pathe films might have felt like pale imitations of actually attending a concert, they did afford certain compensations. From a purely logistical standpoint, tickets for the cinema were easier to obtain than were tickets for a concert. Not only were there more of them, available at a wider range of venues, but they were also more likely to be generally affordable (Hepworth 2018: 24–5). This allowed *ABC Film Review* to claim that "millions of fans" had seen "The Beatles Come to Town" in the weeks after its release, whereas the film itself stresses that the demand for tickets to watch the "Fabulous Four" in concert far outstripped the number that were available (Taylor 1964: 17). Furthermore, the sound—either recorded live at the venue or synchronized with a prerecorded version of a song (Wyman 1990: 259)—was mixed to increase the volume of the bands relative to the noise made by fans "scream[ing] at the tops of their piercing voices," even though the fans' reactions remained an important element of the sound design of each of the films (Grant 1964: 43). This meant that the cinemagoer could "actually hear" the music (Grant 1964: 43), something that was not always possible at a concert, given the relatively primitive nature of contemporary amplifiers and PA systems (Babiuk 2001: 102).

The films manipulate the reality of the typical concert-going experience in other ways, too. All three start outside the venue, and thus from a spatial position which aligns them with the ordinary fan's perspective. However, they all move inside *before* the doors are opened to the eager throng (both Beatles and DC5 films contain shots looking out through the doors toward the expectant crowd), and in so doing take the viewer beyond what the ordinary concertgoer might expect to see for the price of their ticket. Thus, for all that they function as actuality films, documenting the beat boom as it happened and mediating it according to the norms and conventions of the newsreel (most notably through the commentary that accompanies each film), they also, crucially, augment reality. They do this by offering a private view of the concert as experienced not simply by the fan but also, crucially, by the artists and their intimates. Spending time with the band as they answer reporters' questions, or get dressed or brush their hair not only works to show us a "day in the life" of a pop star but more importantly constructs a teenage dreamscape in which the viewer is welcomed backstage and provided with access of a kind that spoke not to the world as they might experience it, but rather as they might wish it to be.[8]

The newsreel musicals are thus aligned with backstage musicals, in that both intersperse and diegetically motivate their production numbers with behind-the-scenes sequences. This alignment can also be seen in their echoing of what Feuer (1977) has identified as the backstage musical's tendency to refer self-referentially to the production of the very entertainment that viewers are being asked to enjoy, or in the playful way, for instance, that the Stones's concert is temporarily imperiled by their inability to get to Hull. However, the Pathe shorts diverge from the tropes of the backstage musical in other ways. In "The Beatles Come to Town," "The Dave Clark Five," and "Rolling Stones Gather Moss"—and also in similar newsreel items featuring other groups—there are no rehearsals, no sense of "the maturation of the show" (Feuer 1977: 313). The ability to whip the audience into a frenzy of excitement is, therefore, not shown as being arrived at through practice and hard work—traits that might be associated with a job or a profession—but is, rather, presented as being innate. These musicians' skills appear to emerge solely, and fully formed, as the result of the symbiotic relationships they have with their fans. Indeed, films such as *Sympathy for the Devil* or *Let It Be* (1970) that showed the tedious and repetitive labor that went into the production of popular music would only emerge later, and would often adopt the more self-consciously "intellectual" form of the documentary, as befitting the supposed seriousness of the more adult rock sound.

Cutting between multiple camera positions allows the viewer to see the bands from a wider range of perspectives than they would have been available from their seat. True, some shots approximate an audience member's view of the stage, but these are combined with close-ups and reaction shots of the audience in order to present musical performance in an omnipresent manner, and occasionally from a view similar to that which the artists had of the audience. Whereas *A Hard Day's Night* seems to mimic a televisual aesthetic and so position the Beatles' first feature in relation to the moving-image medium through which they were perhaps most commonly accessed, "The Beatles Come to Town"—as are the Stones and DC5 films—is more interested in providing a more cinematic sense of grandeur and spectacle, within the limitations imposed by the newsreel format. The concert as seen in these films, therefore, exists *only* in these films, *only* as a cinematic event that positions the viewer at once inside and outside the body of the corporeal spectator, attempting to balance the real and the fantastical. As such, while the Pathe films record and reproduce concerts by the Beatles, the DC5, and the Rolling Stones, they also give a sense of what it felt like to be at these concerts, and, incoherently and incompletely, an insight into what it was to be a fan of these groups.

Short-form pop films constitute intriguing attempts by the British film industry to express cinematically the cultural prominence of popular music, and so associate the cinema with the excitement that surrounded the pop music phenomenon. They also speak to the wider commercial and cultural intersections between pop music and the cinema in Britain at this time, demonstrating the film and music industries' attempts to work together for their mutual financial benefit. Admittedly, such films do not constitute pop musicals in the conventional sense—their brevity allows for little or, most often, no narrative development. But this *lack* of narrative perhaps works in the films' favor: musicians are not (or are only rarely) actors, and in these shorts, they are not expected to be. Rather, they are simply asked to perform as themselves, thereby allowing the films to concentrate almost exclusively on the spectacular nature of performance. The success of feature films starring Cliff Richard, Tommy Steele, or the Beatles shows that longer films could successfully find ways to accommodate and exploit pop personalities and their music, but shorter films functioned as exciting musical experiences that permitted fans to engage cinematically with their favorite acts, and so operated alongside longer films as important elements of the relationship between pop music and the moving image.

Notes

1. To take but a few examples, see Glynn (2013), Medhurst (1995), Caine (2004), James (2016: esp. 126–82, 255–85), Donnelly (2001).
2. Some newsreel stories also worked anthropologically, introducing viewers to the nature of contemporary pop fandom. In the *Tatler*, for example, Elspeth Grant noted that she was "greatly indebted to Pathe News" for a story that afforded her access to a phenomenon, Beatlemania, that she would not otherwise have engaged with: "I found the short film a most illuminating and alarming experience" (1964: 43).
3. A similar distinction is made by Mundy (2007: 8).
4. History of Advertising Trust: J. Walter Thompson Archive: 50/1/531/2/3/13: Clover Southwell to Brian Squires, December 20, 1965.
5. On film's importance as a source of revenue for the Beatles, see Neaverson (2000: 151).
6. BBC2 began regular color broadcasts in July 1967; BBC1 and the ITV stations in November 1969. Many television sets were not able to reproduce color pictures until well into the 1970s.
7. Color images of the band did circulate via magazines, posters, and LP covers.
8. In this, the films might be understood to speak to Richard Dyer's notion of musicals offering the viewer a utopian vision. See Dyer (1992).

References

Advertisement for Jacey News Theatres (1963), *New Musical Express*, 20 December: 2.
Altman, R. (1995), "The Musical," in G. Nowell-Smith (ed.), *The Oxford History of World Cinema*, 294–303, Oxford: Oxford University Press.
Babiuk, A. (2001), *Beatles Gear*, San Francisco: Backbeat Books.
Bean, R. (1964), "Keeping up with the Beatles," *Films and Filming*, February: 9–12.

Caine, A. (2004), *Interpreting Rock Movies: The Pop Film and Its Critics in Britain*, Manchester: Manchester University Press.
Chaplin, S. (1964), "World of the Pops," *Guardian*, 8 February: 14.
Donnelly, K. J. (2001), *Pop Music in British Cinema*, London: BFI.
Dyer, R. (1992), "Entertainment and Utopia," in R. Dyer, *Only Entertainment*, 2nd edn, 19–35, London: Routledge.
Feuer, J. (1977), "The Self-reflective Musical and the Myth of Entertainment," *Quarterly Review of Film & Video*, 2 (3): 313–26.
"*Four Hits and Mister* Review" (1963), *Kinematograph Weekly*, 28 March: 14.
"Free! Must Be Won This Week!" (1964), *Daily Mirror*, 6 January: 7.
Glynn, S. (2013), *The British Pop Music Film: The Beatles and Beyond*, Basingstoke: Palgrave Macmillan.
Grant, E. (1964), "On films," *Tatler*, 8 January: 43.
"Half of UK cinemas play Rank color mag" (1961), *Variety*, February 15: 22.
Hepworth, D. (2018), *Nothing Is Real*, London: Bantam Press.
"How the Five Found Fame and Fortune" (1964), *ABC Film Review*, April: 32–3.
James, D. E. (2016), *Rock 'n' Film: Cinema's Dance with Popular Music*, Oxford: Oxford University Press.
Lewisohn, M. (1992), *The Complete Beatles Chronicle*, London: Pyramid Books.
McKernan, L. (2002), "Introduction – British Newsreels: Past and Present," in L. McKernan (ed.), *Yesterday's News: The British Cinema Newsreel Reader*, viii–x, London: British Universities Film and Video Council.
Medhurst, A. (1995), "It Sort of Happened Here: The Strange, Brief Life of the British Pop Film," in J. Romney and A. Wootton (eds.), *Celluloid Jukebox: Popular Music and the Movies since the 50s*, 60–71, London: BFI.
Mitchell, G. A. M. (2013), "From 'Rock' to 'Beat': Towards a Reappraisal of British Popular Music, 1958–1962," *Popular Music and Society*, 36 (2): 194–215.
"More Movie Plans for Groups" (1964), *Pop Weekly*, w/e 25 January: 8.
Mundy, J. (2007), *The British Musical Film*, Manchester: Manchester University Press.
Neaverson, B. (2000), "Tell Me What You See: The Influence and Impact of the Beatles' Movies," in I. Inglis (ed.), *The Beatles, Popular Music and Society: A Thousand Voices*, 150–62, London: Palgrave Macmillan.
Pronay, N. (1993), "British Film Sources for the Cold War: The Disappearance of the Cinema-going Public," *Historical Journal of Film, Radio and Television*, 13 (1): 7–17.
"Record Prizes in *Look at Life* Contest" (1961), *Kinematograph Weekly*, 21 September: 6.
"*Rhythm 'n Greens* Review" (1964), *Monthly Film Bulletin*, January: 166.
Schroeder, J. (2016), *All for the Love of Music*, Kibworth Beauchamp: Matador.
Stroller (1963), "Longshots," *Kinematograph Weekly*, 12 December: 4.
Taylor, N. (1964), "The Beatles Come to Town," *ABC Film Review*, February: 16–19.
"The Beatles in Color Production" (1963), *Coventry Evening Telegraph*, 21 December: 7.
"The Beatles in 'Scope from Pathe" (1963), *Kinematograph Weekly*, 12 December: 7.

Wyman, B., with R. Coleman, *Stone Alone: The Story of a Rock 'n' Roll Band*, London: Viking.
Young, C. (2005), "The Rise and Fall of the News Theatres," *Journal of British Cinema and Television*, 2 (2): 237-8.

Filmography

The Beatles Come to Town (1963), [Film] UK: Pathe.
Beau Modern (1963), [Film] UK: Pathe.
The Bee Gees (1968), [Film] Dir. unknown, UK: Associated-London.
Catch Us If You Can (1965), [Film] Dir. John Boorman, UK: Bruton Film Productions.
Charlie Is My Darling (1966), [Film] Dir. Peter Whitehead, UK: ABKCO Films.
The Dave Clark Five (1964), [Film] UK: Pathe.
For the Record (1961), [Film] UK: Rank.
Four Hits and a Mister (1962), [Film] Dir. Douglas Hickox, UK: Parkside Productions.
Gimme Shelter (1970), [Film] Dir. Albert Maysles, David Maysles, and Charlotte Zwerin, USA: Maysles Films.
The Great Escape (1963), [Film] Dir. John Sturges, USA: The Mirisch Company.
Gonks Go Beat (1964), [Film] Dir. Robert Hartford-Davis, UK: Titan Film Productions.
Guns at Batasi (1964), [Film] Dir. John Guillermin, UK: Twentieth Century-Fox.
A Hard Day's Night (1964), [Film] Dir. Richard Lester, UK: Proscenium Films.
Help! (1965), [Film] Dir. Richard Lester, UK: Walter Shenson Films/Subafilms
The Johnny Leyton Touch (1962), [Film] Dir. Norman Harrison, UK: Robert Stigwood Productions.
Let It Be (1970), [Film] Dir. Michael Lindsay-Hogg, UK: Apple Films.
Live It Up! (1963), [Film] Dir. Lance Comfort, UK: Three Kings.
Performance (1970), [Film] Dir. Donald Cammell and Nicholas Roeg, UK: Goodtimes Enterprises.
Place to Go (1963), [Film] Dir. Basil Dearden, UK: Excalibur Films.
The Pretty Things (1966), [Film] Dir. Caterina Arvat and Anthony West, UK: Morrison and West Associates.
Privilege (1967), [Film] Dir. Peter Watkins, UK: Rank Film Distribution.
Ready, Steady, Go (1963–66), [TV program] ITV.
Rhythm 'n' Greens (1964), [Film] Dir. Christopher Miles, UK: ABPC.
Rolling Stones Gather Moss (1964), [Film] UK: Pathe.
Six-Five Special (1957–8), [TV program] BBC.
Summer Holiday (1963), [Film] Dir. Peter Yates, UK: Ivy Films.
Sympathy for the Devil (1968), [Film] Dir. Jean-Luc Godard, UK: Cupid Productions.
Thank Your Lucky Stars (1961–6), [TV program] ITV.
Top of the Pops (1964–2006), [TV program] BBC.
The Young Ones (1961), [Film] Dir. Sidney J. Furie, UK: ABPC.

15

"Good Evening, Pasadena!"

Fantastical Performance Spaces in the Rock Documentary

Richard Wallace

This chapter examines the rock documentary as a mode of film musical. It is not my main concern to argue that music documentaries *are* musicals; others (de Seife 2007: 54–60; Caine 2008) have begun to do this work, with David E. James in particular suggesting a generic fluidity between fictional rock-based musicals and documentary depictions of rock and pop music (2016: 15). Although the documentary approach might instinctively feel like the musical's antithesis, they share key characteristics that are not limited to their mutual incorporation of musical sequences, and this chapter explores some of the ways in which existing theoretical approaches to the musical are pertinent to the operational mechanics of the rock documentary. Like the musical, the music documentary opens up utopian cinematic spaces in which the musical performance sequences are enacted, and it does this through aesthetic and narrative conventions that it shares with its fictional counterpart.

In the rock documentary, the deliberate deployment of particular shooting and editing techniques transforms live performance into a specifically filmic experience that is concordant with, but ultimately separate from, the original event—usually a live concert.

Phillip Auslander calls the product of this transformation a "mediatized performance," because the live event is "circulated on television, as audio or video recordings, and in other forms based in technologies of reproduction" (1999: 5). Although generally thought of as being secondary to the concert and live album (Donnelly 2013) because of their dependence on that original context for their existence, we can think of concert films as stand-alone cultural artifacts in their own right and focus our attention on how the musical performances are constructed as cinematic moments, separate from the live original. Furthermore, the cinematic techniques that are employed for effect in the music documentary are frequently the same as those found in and around the musical numbers of classical Hollywood musicals. Although this analysis offers a range of observations which are widely applicable to the music documentary, space precludes a detailed survey of this expansive (and expanding) field. The focus of this chapter is, therefore, restricted to one film in particular, *Depeche Mode: 101* (1989), so as to provide a focused account of how thinking about this film in terms of the musical offers some alternative ways of understanding it as a documentary text.

101 chronicles the American leg of British electro-rock band Depeche Mode's 1988 tour in support of their album *Music for the Masses* (1987) and continues D. A. Pennebaker's interest in filming musicians previously seen in *Dont Look Back* (1967), *Monterey Pop* (1968), and *Ziggy Stardust and the Spiders from Mars* (1979). At this point in time, Depeche Mode comprised singer Dave Gahan and musicians Andy Fletcher, Martin Gore, and Alan Wilder, with their roles in the band characterized by Fletcher in the film as follows: "Martin's the songwriter, Alan's the good musician, Dave's the vocalist . . . and I bum around." The first two-thirds of the film establish the band and its music and detail the arrangements for the tour's climactic final gig at the Pasadena Rose Bowl in Los Angeles in front of 65,000 people, thus situating that concert as the central focus of the documentary. We see live sequences from a number of concerts on the tour framed by documentary footage of behind-the-scenes activities, including a sound check, media appearances, and backstage discussions. These sequences accrue to provide a sense of the labor required to put on a tour of this scale, and are punctuated in turn by a subplot, engineered for the film, in which a group of competition-winning Depeche Mode fans shadow the band's progress on a separate tour bus.[1] The final third of the film is then dedicated to the Pasadena performance—the tour's 101st.

Although this three-act structure is, as K. J. Donnelly argues, "similar to the backstage musical" because of the oscillation between off-stage "preparation" and on-stage "performance" sequences (2013: 173), these performance sequences have as much in common with the integrated musical form. We can, therefore, approach the on- and off-stage performative spaces of the rock documentary (and the variety of performance modes we find in them) through theoretical frameworks which address the shift between registers that occurs when the musical film moves between "real" and "fantasy" spaces, such as Altman's conceptualization of the "audio dissolve" (1987), Dyer's notion of "expansion" ([1998] 2012), and Feuer's formulation of the musical's "myth of entertainment" (1977). By doing so, we can begin to think about the placement, sequencing, and transition into (and out of) live performances in the rock documentary—and the fantastical performance spaces they frequently inhabit/project—as being like the transitions between similarly constructed spaces within the musical genre more generally. Three of the most important textual strategies deployed for this purpose that will be addressed here are: the movement from off- to on-stage performance modes by the band members, and particularly by front-man Gahan; how the transformation into and out of this fantastical performance space is managed textually; and the impact that the structure and shape of the final concert have on the viewing experience.

"Going on Stage" as Performative Transition

Jonathan Romney has argued that although the backstage space of the rockumentary is usually "imagined as a far more 'real' space than the stage on which the artists do their work," it remains the case that "particularly when cameras are present, [it] is no less a space of display" (1995: 86). This is evident in a sequence that takes place backstage at the Pasadena Rose Bowl, where Gahan is deep in discussion with Wilder, Gore, and the band's production director Andy Franks about how best to welcome the audience to the show. The scene initiates the final third of the film and opens in medias res, with Wilder offering a suggestion of "Hello Pasadena," delivered in a self-consciously silly voice that suggests both an awareness of the camera's presence and the clichéd nature of his suggestion.[2] Gahan responds immediately: "No, I don't think I should say Pasadena. I've been thinking about this today; it's been playing on my mind." At stake for Gahan here is the professionalism of live performance: the important balance between saying the right thing and feeling confident in his ability to deliver the words in an authentic and seemingly spontaneous manner. It is the most overt example of the band directly interrogating their own performative presence in the film, and it establishes a clear distinction between "backstage" and "on-stage" as performance spaces.

The sense of backstage performativity remains, however, due to the occasional awkwardness of the conversation. As well as the funny voice, Wilder over-performs a version of reassurance, dismissing Gahan's insecurities in an overly jokey fashion, patting his colleague's shoulder and saying, "Dave, I wouldn't let it play on your mind" before looking toward the camera with a knowing smirk (Figure 15.1). This performance of backstage banter is picked up by Gahan who adopts another comical voice—this time excessively flat and emotionless—to suggest that he might instead say "Good

FIGURE 15.1 *Alan Wilder (left) smirks at the camera, while Dave Gahan (center) and Andy Franks (right) discuss the band's entrance.*

evening, everybody." He quickly declares this as sounding "terrible," and similarly vetoes Franks's suggestion of "Good evening everyone. Welcome to the concert for the masses," by exclaiming, "Who do you think I am, fucking Wordsworth?"

Keith Beattie suggests that "conceptions of truth in the rockumentary are located within and emerge from the revelation of an authentic self within (on-stage and backstage) performances" (2005: 27), rather than by the documentary approach successfully stripping away these performative elements. Backstage in Pasadena, Depeche Mode perform an off-stage version of themselves in which Gahan's working-class Basildon accent sits incongruously within the mise-en-scène of an American football changing room. It is a highly performative (and deliberately comic) moment, but one that creates a space against which Gahan's on-stage persona can be judged, and it sits in stark contrast with its on-stage counterpart which appears ten minutes later. After taking to the stage and performing a rousing rendition of their recent hit single and regular show-opener "Behind the Wheel," the filmmakers cut to a night-time aerial shot of the Rose Bowl, illuminated by hand-held lighters as Gahan thanks the crowd with a rasping yell of "Good evening, Pasadena!" In contrast to his nervous uncertainty backstage, here

Gahan is assured and confident and gets a raucous response from the crowd.

This moment demonstrates two interlinked concerns that are common to both the musical and the music documentary: the movement from "real" to "fantastic" performance spaces that characterize the musical numbers; and what Jane Feuer has called the "myth of entertainment" that facilitates this shift. For Feuer, backstage musicals are self-reflexive in that they "give pleasure to the audience by revealing what goes on behind the scenes" of a musical production, and in doing so "demystify the production of entertainment" (1977: 315). The backstage sequences of *101* highlight the creative and physical labor that goes into "putting on the show," something that can be seen in numerous other music documentaries including *Gimme Shelter* (1970), *Woodstock* (1970), and *Homecoming* (2019). In *101* there are numerous sequences where the band or their team are seen making key strategic decisions about how the gig will be staged: Franks is observed negotiating the position of the stage within the Rose Bowl; we see the lights being rigged under the guidance of Jane Spiers, the stage and lighting designer; Wilder demonstrates how he programs his keyboards; and the merchandise crew can be seen dealing with the logistics of program and T-shirt sales (and counting the money).

However, Feuer argues that backstage musicals simultaneously "remythisize . . . that which they set out to expose" because "[t]he musical desires an ultimate valorization of entertainment; to destroy the aura, reduce the illusion, would be to destroy the myth of entertainment as well" (1977: 315). Part of this process is the simultaneous showing and hiding of the labor that goes into a performance. Feuer argues that only "unsuccessful performances are demystified" (1977: 315), whereas it remains unclear how the successful performances that resolve the narrative are attained. Gahan's on-stage exclamation of "Good evening, Pasadena!" feels effortless, and through it, he demonstrates his command of the stage, of the live audience, and—through the shooting and editing—the audience in the cinema as well. This is a "successful" performance that is quite at odds with the insecure backstage iteration. That earlier version gestures toward the kind of mental and performative labor that goes into producing the appearance of spontaneity, another key element of the classical Hollywood musical that Feuer argues is both "technically the most complex type of film produced in Hollywood" and "the genre which attempts to give the greatest illusion of spontaneity and effortlessness" (1977: 318).

As Feuer elaborates, "spontaneous performances that mask their technology have been calculated too—not for audiences within the films but for audiences of the film" (1977: 318), and while we see some of the work that goes into Gahan's creation of his on-stage persona, we remain none-the-wiser as to how the transformation from one to the other actually occurs. Gahan's successful performance of spontaneity is, in part, a product of cinematic manipulation, and the erasure of labor occurs because he inhabits two differently formulated performance spaces, both of which have their referents in the real world but which are also constructed by the film. The first is the flawed space of "backstage," where rehearsals and soundchecks offer partial performances, and which are signaled as being congruent with the "real" through their performative and stylistic roughness (though they *are* still performances). The second is a more polished cinematic space, where only accomplished performances occur and where the experience is one of utopian fantasy. Here, Gahan is not the slightly clumsy Basildonian but is transformed into the messianic figure of the charismatic rock star with a powerful voice and a commanding, yet nimble, stage presence which incorporates elements of balletic dance alongside standard rock and roll posturing.

This transformation matches those found within the musical, where the "reality" of the everyday world of the characters gives way to the utopian space of the number. The slippage is not precisely the same, of course. *101*'s documentary nature means that however much it is shaped, the source material remains grounded in real events over which the filmmakers have limited control, and—with some limited exceptions, such as *Led Zeppelin: The Song Remains the Same* (1976)—the utopian spaces can't ever defy the laws of nature, gravity, or architecture as they frequently do in the musical. The documentary starts off "more real" and ends up "less fantastical" than most musicals do. However, the transition is still an important factor in the effectiveness of the musical sequences where a stage is set—both literally and through the cinematic apparatus—for a more fantastical mode of performance than was evident at the original concert.

This transition from one performative space to another, and from the real to the fantastical, is not something that we are able to observe in any tangible way in the music documentary, in part because this is as much a psychological process that takes place within the head of the performer as it is a physical one. In the 2014 documentary *20,000 Days on Earth*, Nick Cave suggests that before a performance "you can't really understand how you can do the show," but that "something happens on-stage that takes you away from that" and creates "a place that you can forget who you are and become somebody else." Thomas Austin argues that such interiority "presents a particular hermeneutic dilemma for documentary" (2016: 415); however, it is gestured toward in the "going-on-stage" moments common to many rock documentaries, including *101*.[3] This is not to say, however, that we are unable to gain affective, experiential knowledge of this transition, and I wish to suggest that in the rock documentary, this real/fantasy dichotomy is frequently combined with a simultaneous transition between different regimes of documentary knowledge acquisition. More specifically, we are moved from a focus on the real/factual, where the documentary image is "rich in [factual] visual information" (Plantinga 2013: 41) as to how a concert is staged and which cultivates knowledge of that process, to the fantastic/experiential, where the provision of factual information is displaced by a focus on knowledge that is "subjective, affective, visceral and sensuous" (Beattie 2005: 23). This shift in focus is congruent with the pleasures and textual strategies through which the musical moves between similar registers. In particular, Rick Altman's concept of the "audio dissolve" is used throughout *101* to navigate the transition from the factual documentary reality of "backstage" to a fantastical, emotive documentary space "on-stage."

From Fact to Feeling: The Documentary Audio Dissolve

Altman suggests that musicals operate across two distinct realms, the "real" and the "ideal" and that "[w]hat distinguishes the musical is its tendency to dissolve one realm into another" (1987: 77). This perceptual, cognitive, and textual dissolve is gradual and occurs within both the sound and image tracks, but not necessarily synchronically, and so it is with *101*'s transitions from an evidentiary knowledge regime to one characterized by feeling and emotion. The loss of distinction between "realms" is frequently anticipated by the soundtrack, and Altman argues that "in the musical film there is a constant crossing-over" between the diegetic soundtrack and non-diegetic music, and that the audio dissolve works by "[superimposing] sounds in order to pass from one sound track to another" (1987: 63).

It is common for there to be a diegetic source which acts as a lead into the transition, and on several occasions in *101*, we are shown a large deck containing a reel-to-reel tape that plays a crucial part in Depeche Mode's live set, providing the underlying rhythm track on top of which the four band members add their various sonic textures. About twenty minutes into the film, Gore and Wilder are seen sound-checking the song "The Things You Said." The location is a brightly lit sports hall, devoid of audience, but busy with road crew and a number of fans who are sitting at the back. The tape is started and on the soundtrack we hear a sparse rendition of the song's introduction, accompanied by the loud chatter of the crew.

The camera's focus on the tape deck performs an evidentiary function that is more-or-less in line with the traditional knowledge-gathering role of documentary, and there is the suggestion that we are learning something about Depeche Mode's process of music-making and live performance. We get a sense of the methods through which the sound in the venue is tested, of how the musicians interact with the automated elements of their apparatus, and of how they perform when they are not before a vast crowd. The evidentiary character and roughness of this moment are highlighted when the unsteady hand-held camera that circles around Gore as he steps up to the microphone to sing captures him missing his cue in a moment of imperfection emblematic of one of Feuer's "unsuccessful" performances.

However, the sonic space quickly becomes divorced from this documentary reality, because as the instrumental introduction builds, the nonmusical components of the soundtrack are gradually diminished until the only remaining elements are the tape, Wilder's keyboard, and Gore's voice. The manipulation of the soundtrack continues as we are relocated to the back of the hall, the camera finding interest in one of the fans (Chris Hardwick) playing with their camera, and the sound of crowd noise is gradually introduced. The next image is a reverse shot of the stage, taken from roughly the same position that the camera shooting the fan had been occupying, but now the stage is fully dressed, the house lights are down, and Gore is in his stage costume, held by a spotlight as he performs the song to a packed house. The backing tape provides continuity between the two sonic spaces, and the preemptive introduction of aural elements from the live footage over images of the rehearsal means that the visual transition does not jar. Taken together, these stylistic shifts signal that we are now in the emotive, fantastical space of the live performance, and the factual exploration of how the show is produced has given way to an affective and embodied engagement with the live performance. I will return to Dyer's arguments regarding the nature of the musical and "utopia" in the final section of this chapter; however, this shift from a focus on the processes of a performance to an attempt to convey its experiential qualities is congruent with his notion that the musical offers audiences a view of "what utopia would feel like rather than how it would be organised" ([1977] 1985: 222). It is this shift from organization to feeling that is captured in these moments.

Structure and Chronology: The Rockumentary as Dual-focus Narrative

Another way in which the Pasadena show is framed as the climax of the film's narrative is by a judicious process of song selection. Although a variety of Depeche Mode songs are seen being performed live throughout the first half of the film, the coverage of the Pasadena show itself is distilled to a handful of—at that time—the band's most well-known hits: "Behind the Wheel," "Strangelove," "Everything Counts," "Just Can't Get Enough," and "Never Let Me Down Again." The Pasadena sequence, therefore, acts as both a greatest hits compilation and a crowd-pleasing encore to the rest of the film.

Furthermore, Pennebaker et al. sequence the performances so as to place maximum emphasis on the final moments of a spirited performance of "Never Let Me Down Again." Strict chronology is eschewed in favor of sequencing which maximizes the internal emotional logic of the film; in reality, the song was followed by two encores, selections from which are placed earlier in the concert sequence. This is a technique Pennebaker uses very successfully elsewhere, most notably in *Monterey Pop*, where the performances were edited out of sequence so as to emphasize Ravi Shankar's set, which Pennebaker viewed as the festival's lynchpin, and thus a logical climax to the film. Jonathan Demme's 1984 concert film *Stop Making Sense* takes an alternative approach to editing by constructing a single sixteen-song Talking Heads concert from footage taken from four separate twenty-song performances at Hollywood's Pantages Theatre.

This re-sequencing positions "Never Let Me Down Again" as the logical conclusion to the various narrative strands that have been unfolding throughout the film. Altman has argued that the American musical should be understood as embodying a "dual-focus narrative" in which the linear, cause-and-effect connections between the male and female protagonists—whose coming together drives the narrative—should be seen as secondary to the idea of "parallelism" (1987: 17). As he argues, "[t]his dual-focus structure requires the viewer to be sensitive not so much to chronology and progression—for the outcome of the male/female match is entirely conventional and thus quite predictable—but to simultaneity and comparison" (Altman 1987: 19). We find this logic at work throughout *101* in the oscillation between Depeche Mode's tour across America (presented as a series of live performances) and the parallel activities of the fans on the tour bus, with the Pasadena Rose Bowl presented from the outset as both groups' inevitable final destination.

Benjamin J. Harbert has noted that "Pennebaker's music documentaries are distinctive in how they defeat the division between the stage and audience floor, creating a synchronicity of performers and audience members" (2018: 159). However, he also suggests that *101* offers a narrative of "social estrangement" in which "[t]he tacitly separate worlds of the traveling Depeche Mode fans and the band provide a palpable sense of alienation" (Harbert 2018: 159)—from one another and from their own relationships with wider society. In contrast to this establishing duality, Harbert argues that "the final half hour brings the two worlds of the band and the fans together, providing a celebratory finale that suspends the tensions established earlier" (Harbert 2018: 160). Although I agree with this last point, my view of the film's overall structure is somewhat different. Harbert argues that the band and the fans are kept separate throughout the film, and indeed that their distance *increases* as the film progresses. However, it is my contention that the opposite is true and that as the film moves closer to Pasadena, the distance between the fans and the band is gradually lessened as they become more entangled within the fantastical cinematic musical spaces.

Footages from early dates on the tour and sequences on the fans' bus and in hotel rooms are alternated during the first half of the film to suggest their interconnectedness, and that their individual meanings are to be found in their interrelationship. This is literalized just after the half-way point of the film, when the footage of Depeche Mode's on-stage performance of the song "Nothing" is intercut with the fans dancing to the same song on their bus. This marks a noticeable development from earlier portions of the film because for the first time the spaces of fan/band are shown to overlap, momentarily bringing the band and the fans into proximity with one another. Though they are depicted as occupying separate physical and temporal spaces—the band are on-stage in the evening, the fans are on the road during the day—they are brought together cinematically within "the space of the song" (Dyer 2012). The distance between fans and band continues to lessen as the film progresses. The fans are shown in various configurations at a number of concerts, and during the "A Question of Time" sequence, a couple of the fans watch the live performance from the back of the venue. Though they are a long way from the stage, their separation from the band is collapsed further when a jump cut connects footage of one of Gahan's balletic spins with one of the fans performing a less accomplished rendition of the same maneuver, the match on action merging two separate performance fragments by two different people into one complete motion.

It is during the performance of "Never Let Me Down Again" where the two narrative strands finally come together in a sustained way, articulated through the film's visual style. As the song's lengthy instrumental coda begins, a series of shots moves us rapidly out from a privileged on-stage position to create a space that is more inclusive. It offers a clear example of what Dyer refers to as the "motif of expansion" ([1998] 2012: 101), a key element of the utopian effect created within musicals, whereby "a number develops outwards from its moment in the narrative, opening up spatially and temporally" and that the feeling produced is "utterly blissful" (Dyer [1998] 2012: 101). As the coda to "Never Let Me Down Again" begins, the proximity of the camera moves outwards, expanding the visual field from a medium shot of Gahan to an extreme long shot filmed from the back of the arena using a telephoto lens which brings the audience into the picture as it zooms back still further. This shot is held for twenty-five seconds and follows the singer as he strides across the stage from his central position, disappearing into the darkness of an unlit portion of the stage. The filmmakers stay with the shot as Gahan reappears, lit from the back by bright footlights and from the front by a spotlight, and positioned on a central runway that stretches out into the crowd, who remains unseen in the darkness.

The intensity of the musical bridge continues to rise in anticipation of the final breakdown, and Gahan raises his hands into the air in accord with the tension created by the music. As this musical tension is resolved, and the band play through a final, spirited instrumental version of the song's chorus, Gahan waves his arms in an energetic twisting-side-to-side motion before gesturing to the audience to do the same. As he stands on the stage, a shining white specter surrounded by blackness, the floodlights come up to reveal 60,000 Depeche Mode fans mirroring his actions (Figure 15.2). It is a moment of direct interaction and unity between performer and audience that is so startling—and emotionally striking—that as the concert (and the film) draws to a close, the attention of the camera moves away from Gahan and the rest of the band, fascinated by the communal performance of the crowd, but connecting the two in a single panoramic shot that lasts for forty-eight seconds that is reminiscent of the "communal gaze" that Julie Lobalzo Wright (2013: 73) has argued emphasizes the communal aspects of the crowd in *Woodstock*.

This pan away from the stage enacts one final process of expansion that fulfills the communalistic function of the musical as articulated by Feuer: "successful performances will be those in which the performer is sensitive to the needs of his audience and which give the audience a sense of participation in the performance" and furthermore, that "promoting audience identification with the collectively produced shows ... seeks to give the audience a sense of participation in the creation of the film itself" (1977: 321). Wright has argued that the notion of "the crowd as contributors"

FIGURE 15.2 *The audience responds to Gahan's invitation to dance and the floodlights reveal a sea of arms waving in unison.*

(2013: 79) can be found in *Woodstock*, where they are unified with the on-stage performers "through the musical spectacle that both produce" (2013: 78), and the same can be seen in this climactic moment of *101*. There are multiple audiences in play here: the crowd at the show watching the band; the performers on the stage watching the crowd; the documentary crew observing (and being observed by) both; and the audience in the cinema. However, at the finale, any separation between them is collapsed into one collective experience. This is enacted during the conclusion of "Never Let Me Down Again," but the possibility of it is unlocked a few minutes earlier during the performance of "Just Can't Get Enough," when Gahan gestures directly to the camera, to Pennebaker, and to the cinema audience to join him in his dance (Figure 15.3). This brief moment reconfigures the spectator/participant relationship by positioning the film viewer as part of both the watching audience and the observing film crew (and therefore as part of the filmmaking process) *and* as a participant in the on-stage and on-screen spectacles.

In *101* the opening out of the performance space at the film's conclusion, from one enclosed by medium-close ups of the band on venue stages and tour buses to the expansive field of a long-shot containing thousands of individuals moving as one, is utopian for both the on-screen audience and

FIGURE 15.3 *Gahan invites the cinema audience to participate.*

the audience in the cinema, and it contains all of the utopian solutions that Dyer argues are fundamental to the musical ([1977] 1985). The shift between shot lengths, Gahan's aural and gestural incitement to participate, and the camera's (and editor's) focus on the community of the audience rather than the individuality of the singer (though also connecting the two in the long takes) works as examples of the kind of "nonrepresentational signs" that Dyer ([1977] 1985) argues are the textual mechanics from which musicals fashion their utopias. The "dual-focus narrative" of *101* is resolved, and the sense of a direct coming together of performer and audience which the film has been building toward is palpable. Significantly, this is also a moment that gains much of its power through its transformation into cinema.

Conclusion

This chapter has suggested that thinking about the music sequences in the rock documentary as emotive cinematic moments—rather than as moments of documentary evidence-gathering—opens up some alternative avenues of exploration for these films. The shift from factual to experiential regimes of documentary knowledge replicates some of the transitions common to the musical and offers instructive ways to begin to conceptualize these moments. This discussion is necessarily limited and does not address, for instance, the aesthetics *during* the performances. However, it suggests some alternative ways of conceptualizing a form that is often maligned because it sits between two competing poles, those of serious documentary enquiry and the commercial imperatives of a mainstream entertainment product. This approach goes some way toward bridging this gap by suggesting some ways in which we can conceptualize the documentation of entertainment in an emotionally enlightening way.

Notes

1 This subplot emerged from the notorious international following that had emerged around Depeche Mode, explored in more detail in Jeremy Deller and Nicholas Abraham's *The Posters Came from the Walls* (2008).

2 It is, after all, dangerously close to the famous shouts of "Hello Cleveland," uttered by band members in the mockumentary *This Is Spinal Tap* (1984) when parodying the formulaic aspects of rock 'n' roll stage-craft.

3 Ironically, the most insightful example of this might be *This Is Spinal Tap*'s mockumentary iteration, where the band gets lost backstage and bass player Derek Smalls (Harry Shearer), fired up and ready for his entrance, is left shouting "Hello Cleveland!" to a bemused boiler-room attendant. I have argued elsewhere that the parody is particularly effective because it makes visible

that which the music documentary frequently fails to reveal: the moment of performative transition, rendered as comedy here due to its juxtaposition with the unsuitable space of its articulation and the absence of an audience (Wallace 2018: 83–4).

References

Altman, R. (1987), *The American Film Musical*, Bloomington: Indiana University Press.
Auslander, P. (1999), *Liveness: Performance in a Mediatized Culture*, London; New York: Routledge.
Austin, T. (2016), "Interiority, Identity and the Limits of Knowledge in Documentary Film," *Screen*, 57 (4): 414–30.
Beattie, K. (2005), "It's Not Only Rock and Roll: 'Rockumentary,' Direct Cinema, and Performative Display," *Australian Journal of American Studies*, 24 (2): 21–41.
Caine, A. (2008), "Can Rock Movies be Musicals?" in L. Geraghty and M. Jancovich (eds.), *The Shifting Definitions of Genre: Essays on Labeling Films, Television Shows and Media*, 124–41, Jefferson: McFarland.
de Seife, E. (2007), *This Is Spinal Tap*, London: Wallflower Press.
Donnelly, K. J. (2013), "Visualizing Live Albums: Progressive Rock and the British Concert Film in the 1970s," in R. Edgar, K. Fairclough-Isaacs and B. Halligan (eds.), *The Music Documentary: Acid Rock to Electropop*, 171–82, New York; London: Routledge.
Dyer, R. ([1977] 1985), "Entertainment and Utopia," in B. Nichols (ed.), *Movies and Methods Volume II*, 220–32, Berkeley; Los Angeles London: University of California Press.
Dyer, R. ([1998] 2012), "The Space of Happiness in the Musical," in R. Dyer (ed.), *In the Space of a Song: The Uses of Song in Film*, 101–13, London; New York: Routledge.
Dyer, R. (2012), *In the Space of a Song: The Uses of Song in Film*, London; New York: Routledge.
Feuer, J. (1977), "The Self-reflexive Musical and the Myth of Entertainment," *Quarterly Review of Film & Video*, 2 (3): 313–26.
Harbert, B. J. (2018), *American Music Documentary: Five Case Studies of Ciné-Ethnomusicology*, Middletown, CT: Wesleyan University Press.
James, D. E. (2016), *Rock 'N' Film: Cinema's Dance with Popular Music*, Oxford: Oxford University Press.
Plantinga, C. (2013), "'I'll Believe it When I Trust the Source': Documentary Images and Visual Evidence," in B. Winston (ed.), *The Documentary Film Book*, 40–7, London: BFI/Palgrave Macmillan.
Romney, J. (1995), "Access All Areas: The Real Space of Rock Documentary," in J. Romney and A. Wootton (eds.), *Celluloid Jukebox: Popular Music and the Movies since the 50s*, 82–92, London: BFI.
Wallace, R. (2018), *Mockumentary Comedy: Performing Authenticity,*, Cham, Switzerland: Palgrave Macmillan.

Wright, J. L. (2013), "The Good, The Bad and The Ugly '60s' The Opposing Gazes of *Woodstock* and *Gimme Shelter*," in R. Edgar, K. Fairclough-Isaacs and B. Halligan (eds.), *The Music Documentary: Acid Rock to Electropop*, 71–86, New York; London: Routledge.

Filmography

20,000 *Days on Earth* (2014), [Film] Dir. Iain Forsyth and Jane Pollard, UK: Corniche/BFI/Film4/JW/Pulse.
Depeche Mode: 101 (1989), [Film] Dir. David Dawkins, Chris Hegedus, D. A. Pennebaker, UK/USA: Mute Film/Pennebaker Associates.
Dont Look Back (1967), [Film] Dir. D. A. Pennebaker, USA: Leacock-Pennebaker.
Gimme Shelter (1970), [Film] Dir. Albert Maysles, David Maysles, Charlotte Zwerin, USA: Maysles Films.
Homecoming (2019), [Film] Dir. Beyoncé Knowles-Carter, USA: PRG.
Led Zeppelin: The Song Remains (1976), [Film] Dir. Peter Clifton, Joe Massot, UK/USA: Swan Song.
Monterey Pop (1968), [Film] Dir. D. A. Pennebaker, USA: John Philips-Lou Adler/Leacock- Pennebaker.
The Posters Come from the Walls (2008), [Film] Dir. Jeremy Deller and Nicholas Abraham, UK: Hudson Productions/Brown Owl Films.
Stop Making Sense (1984), [Film] Dir. Jonathan Demme, USA: Talking Heads.
This is Spinal Tap (1984), [Film] Dir. Rob Reiner, USA: Spinal Tap Prod.
Woodstock (1970), [Film] Dir. Michael Wadleigh, USA: Wadleigh-Maurice.
Ziggy Stardust and the Spiders from Mars (1979), [Film] Dir. D. A. Pennebaker, UK: Mainman/Bewlay Brothers/Miramax.

Musicals across Media

16

Live Musical Spectaculars

Eventizing Network Television in the Post-Network Age

Anthony Enns

The social importance of network television in late twentieth-century American culture is often attributed to the fact that it represented an electronic public forum that effectively unified the nation. By the end of the twentieth century, however, the major networks had suffered a tremendous loss in ratings due to competition from cable channels, and the more recent trend toward time-shifting technologies and on-demand streaming services has made the traditional concept of TV broadcasting virtually obsolete. Nevertheless, the networks have not gone away; instead, they have attempted to adapt to a changing media ecology by playing to their greatest strength—namely, their ability to facilitate shared communal experiences in real time—through the expansion of news and sports offerings and the creation of new kinds of media events that encourage "appointment viewing"—a new term for the old practice of watching a particular program at a particular time.

One of the earliest methods of "eventizing" network television, which is currently experiencing a tremendous resurgence, is the production of live musical spectaculars. These live broadcasts have proven to be remarkably successful in promoting "appointment viewing," yet they are also highly complex and ambiguous texts. On the one hand, they appear to reflect a nostalgic desire to return to the broadcast era, which is romanticized as a simpler time when audiences were more socially and politically unified.

On the other hand, they also appear to extend this nostalgic fantasy to the webcast era by depicting social media as the continuation of television broadcasting by other means. The following chapter will examine this recent trend by exploring how live musical spectaculars function as a site where the past, present, and future of television is currently being negotiated. While it is clearly an attempt on the part of producers to return to the social, political, and economic conditions of the network age—a time when television was perceived as fostering a sense of social cohesion and collective identity—it is also an attempt to reinvent television for the post-network age, as this sense of social cohesion is now attributed to new online platforms that allegedly provide the same kinds of communal experiences for contemporary media users.

Live musical spectaculars are also significant because they have been largely ignored in studies on musicals. It is important to note, for example, that live musical spectaculars were first produced on television in the early 1950s, when families typically watched television together and programmers sought to develop genres that would appeal to the widest possible audience. One of the first strategies they developed was to expand the existing audience by co-opting other media, such as radio, film, and theater. In 1944, for example, theater designer Robert Wade (1944: 728) described the new medium as "radio with sight, movies with the zest of immediacy, theatre (intimate or spectacular) with all seats about six rows back and in the center, tabloid opera and circus without peanut venders." When NBC hired Sylvester "Pat" Weaver as head of programming in 1949, he similarly sought to capture "light viewers" (i.e., those who would not normally watch television) by featuring productions that capitalized on television's ability to recreate the energy of theatrical performances (Baughman 2007: 6). This strategy led to the creation of *Musical Comedy Time* (1950–1), the first TV series to feature musical numbers adapted from Broadway stage productions, and *The Ford Fiftieth Anniversary Show* (1953), which aired on both NBC and CBS to ensure the largest possible audience (some cities did not have local affiliates for both networks). *General Foods 25th Anniversary Show* (1954) took this strategy even further, as it was aired on all four major networks (NBC, CBS, ABC, and DuMont). NBC then introduced the monthly programs *Max Liebman Presents* (later renamed *Max Liebman Spectaculars*, 1954–6) and *Producers' Showcase* (1954–7), which featured a series of well-known Broadway musicals. The most successful episode of *Producers' Showcase* was a live performance of *Peter Pan* (1955), which was shot in the same theater where the stage musical was performed and attracted an estimated audience of sixty-five million. This was the largest audience for any TV program at the time, and it was so well-received that it was restaged the following year with the same cast, sets, and costumes. Weaver attempted to replicate this success with a production of *The King and Mrs. Candle* (1955), which featured music by the same composer, and a production of *Annie Get Your Gun* (1957), which featured the same star (Mary Martin). Not to be outdone, CBS aired a live production of Richard Rodgers and Oscar Hammerstein's *Cinderella* (1957)—their only musical written specifically for television—which attracted more than a hundred million viewers (for more on this musical, see Stilwell 2018: 55–78). The tremendous success of these live musical spectaculars thus challenges the assumption that the declining popularity of musicals coincided with the rise of television (see, for example, Barrios 1995: 3). As Kelly Kessler (2020: 14) points out, musicals actually played a key role in establishing the identity of television as a live medium, as producers "sought to absorb both the sweeping popularity and the cultural legitimacy of the musical genre."

Despite their initial success, there was a decline in the production of live musical spectaculars following the rise of time-shifting technologies. In 1956, for example, NBC employed the first magnetic videotape system to prerecord a musical number for *The Jonathan Winters Show* (1956–7), and the networks soon replaced much of their New York-based live programming with Los Angeles-based taped programming. The rise of home video recorders and on-demand streaming services introduced an additional delay that disrupted the notion of TV reception as a shared communal experience. For example, Jane Roscoe (2004: 364) points out that "our experience of contemporary media is fragmented rather than unified or centralized," and Amanda Lotz (2014: 5–6) similarly notes that "the U.S. television audience now can rarely be categorized as a mass audience and is instead more accurately understood as a collection of niche audiences." Live television has not entirely disappeared, as it still persists in the coverage of news, sports, award shows, and public ceremonies, yet contemporary critics tend to focus on the importance of media events rather than televisual liveness. For example, Daniel Dyan and Elihu Katz (1992: 15) argue that televised ceremonies enable "social integration of the highest order," and this function also applies to other kinds of events, like the Super Bowl (Real 1975) and the Olympics (Rothenbuhler 1988), which attract large audiences precisely because they are broadcast live. Jérôme Bourdon (2000: 553) also argues that this strategy represents an attempt to preserve the unique "aura" of television, which is "related to the need to know others are watching at the same time." The concept of liveness thus remains relevant to discussions of the post-network age because the increasing significance of media events still depends on television's ability to facilitate shared communal experiences.

The desire on the part of network programmers to create media events that draw viewers back to the traditional broadcast schedule has recently culminated in the return of the live musical spectacular. The decision to resuscitate this format was largely due to the success of several made-for-television musicals in the early twenty-first century, including *High School Musical* (2006–8), *Glee* (2009–15), and *Smash* (2012–13), which demonstrated the appeal of musicals—particularly among millennial viewers. Ryan Murphy, the creator of *Glee*, also organized the concert tour *Glee Live!* (2010–11), which reportedly earned $40 million from forty shows, and produced *Glee: The 3D Concert Movie* (2011), which attempted to capture the experience of attending these concerts in person. This was followed by the first modern live musical spectacular, *The Sound of Music Live!* (2013), which was produced for NBC by Craig Zadan and Neil Meron. Zadan and Meron had financed a series of made-for-television musicals in the 1990s, including *Gypsy* (1993), *Cinderella* (1997), and *Annie* (1999), as well as several successful film musicals, including *Chicago* (2002) and *Hairspray* (2007). They returned to television as producers on the musical series *Smash*, but their live spectacular proved to be an even greater success with a total of 18.6 million viewers (the highest Thursday night viewership since the cancellation of *Friends* in 2004). In the following years, they also produced *Peter Pan Live!* (2014) and *The Wiz Live!* (2015), which effectively established the live musical spectacular as an annual event. These spectaculars would not be considered "media events" according to Dayan and Katz's definition of the term, as they were produced by networks rather than organizations outside of the TV industry, they were not ceremonial or presented with any sense of reverence or awe, the networks did not preempt commercial interruptions, and the audiences were comparatively small. From the perspective of network programmers, however, these pseudo-events are far more profitable than genuine events, as the networks are free to monetize the programs through advertising revenue as well as the sale of DVDs, soundtrack albums, and digital downloads.

Other networks soon began to adopt this strategy. The first network to compete with NBC was Fox, whose production of *Grease: Live* (2016) succeeded in attracting 12.2 million viewers. This musical was also significant in that it reflected a sense of nostalgia not only for the music and fashion of the 1950s but also for the era of early live television. In fact, the musical was originally inspired by the first nationally televised teen dance show, *The Big Beat* (1957), which was hosted by disc jockey Alan Freed (widely known as the "father of rock 'n' roll"). The show was canceled after the first month because a Black performer was shown dancing with a white woman from the studio audience (Jackson 1991: 168), but its tremendous popularity among younger viewers convinced ABC to produce *American Bandstand* (1952–89), which soon became a national institution (see Jackson 1997). Freed was the inspiration for the character of Vince Fontaine in the musical (a celebrity who hosts a fictional TV show called *National Bandstand*), and the climax features a teen dance competition that is broadcast live on television. The musical can thus be understood as a direct response to the emergence of live television and its promotion of teen culture, as it allowed teenagers to develop their own style of music, clothing, dancing, etc. As Stuart Hall and Paddy Whannel (2018: 273) point out, television played a significant role in the emergence of teen culture because it offered "an area of common symbols and meanings, shared in part or in whole by a generation, in which they can work out or work through not only the natural tensions of adolescence, but the special tensions of being an adolescent in our kind of society." Thomas Doherty (2002: 68) also points out that the final scene in *Grease* was directly inspired by the teen films of the 1950s, which often featured live TV finales that testified "to the powerful role the new medium played in the popularization of rock 'n' roll and to TV's centrality for the new generation." In other words, the musical dramatizes how television allowed teen viewers to begin learning from each other rather than relying on established institutions, such as schools, churches, families, etc.

During the live performance, the studio audience consisted primarily of teens who were incorporated into the finale as on-stage extras. Production designer David Korins explained that this strategy was designed to capture the "feeling" of early TV dance shows, as there was "an energy and an undeniable vitality that real humans give back to real humans that are performing" (Rooney 2015). This kind of self-reflexivity is also an inherent part of the musical genre, which is often described as a reaction to the decline of the "folk art" of traditional rural music halls, in which everyone participated equally in the production and consumption of musical entertainment, and there was no clear separation between performers and audiences (see Hall and Whannel 2018: 45–65). While the "folk art" of music halls was gradually displaced by the "mass art" of cinema, which introduced a clear separation between performers and audiences, Jane Feuer (1993: 26) argues that film musicals compensated for this loss by featuring audiences within the performances, which "makes of the movie audience a live audience." By blurring the boundaries between performers and audiences, the film musical thus creates the illusion that it is still a "folk art" produced and consumed by the same community, which serves to conceal the alienating aspects of mass-produced consumer culture. This argument clearly anticipates many of the claims made in this chapter, as television musicals similarly employ self-reflexive strategies to disguise their attempt to establish media dominance as an attempt to foster social integration. The key difference is that television musicals more often represent the technology of live television as compensating for the decline of "folk art," as it similarly enables shared communal experiences and collective social identities. *Grease* was thus an ideal property for a live musical spectacular precisely because of its nostalgic depiction of live television as the medium responsible for creating and nurturing an authentic teen culture.

Grease: Live also emphasized the importance of social integration by depicting an integrated high school in Chicago in 1959. In reality, desegregation plans were not proposed in Chicago until 1966, and these plans were quickly abandoned following a series of hostile demonstrations organized by white residents. In the 1970s, many of these residents moved to the suburbs, and the number of white public-school students fell by

75 percent. By the time a court-mandated desegregation plan was finally imposed in 1980, there were almost no white students left, which made desegregation virtually meaningless. *Grease: Live* thus presented a utopian vision of social integration, which was made possible in part by television's ability to facilitate shared communal experiences between viewers from different social groups.

In an effort to compete with Fox, NBC's next live musical spectacular was *Hairspray Live!* (2016), which similarly targeted millennial viewers by focusing on rock 'n' roll music, incorporating live audiences, and emphasizing television's importance for the development of teen culture. The musical was based on John Waters's 1988 film, which was set in Baltimore in 1962, and it provides a behind-the-scenes look at the production of *The Corny Collins Show*—a fictionalized version of *The Buddy Deane Show* (1957–63), which was broadcast live on WJZ-TV, a local ABC affiliate station. Like *American Bandstand*, *The Buddy Deane Show* was designed to showcase the latest styles in teen music, clothing, and dancing, and Waters (1990: 89) was a devoted follower of the show because it taught viewers "how to be a teenager." However, it was also racially segregated, as it only allowed Black teens to attend once a month on "Negro Day." In 1963 an integrationist group challenged this policy by obtaining tickets for white and Black teens to attend the show at the same time, and the station received so much hate mail that it was immediately canceled.

The inspiration for Waters's film reportedly came from one of the performers on *The Buddy Deane Show*, who attempted to downplay the problem of racial segregation by emphasizing the exclusion of overweight women: "A black girl could have gotten on easier than a fat girl. No fat girls even came on to apply" (Heller 2011: 53). Waters's film focuses on precisely this scenario by depicting an overweight girl named Tracy Turnblad, who dreams of becoming a dancer on *The Corny Collins Show*. After achieving this goal, she immediately starts working to integrate the program—a goal that is eventually realized, unlike the outcome of the attempts to integrate *The Buddy Deane Show*. *Hairspray* thus explicitly promotes the power of television to bring people together, and Dana Heller (2011: 103) describes it as "one of the twentieth-century's most celebratory films about television's transformation of everyday life and consciousness." While Heller (2011: 112) notes that this celebratory tone is ultimately undermined by the film's camp aesthetic and its overt critique of consumerism, she also adds that this critique is largely absent from the musical adaptation, as "the Broadway production of *Hairspray* is not a camp rewriting of popular memory, or an attempt to critically engage with the pieties of national mythology, but a sincere celebration of those pieties." The musical thus transformed Waters's ironic satire into a feel-good story of racial integration, and it proved to be far more successful, as it appealed to a younger audience that was not familiar with either the original film or its source material.

Like *Grease: Live*, *Hairspray Live!* also demonstrated the socially integrating function of live television by incorporating the studio audience into the performance, but producers went a step further by featuring live audiences in other cities, including Baltimore, Atlanta, Philadelphia, and Houston. These segments helped to convey the idea of the live musical spectacular as an event that was being experienced simultaneously across the country, much like the New Year's Eve celebrations at Times Square in New York City, which were first broadcast live on NBC in the 1940s. *Hairspray Live!* also included live commercials for various products, such as Oreos, Reddi-wip, and Toyota, which functioned as both an ironic commentary on early advertising techniques and genuine advertisements that demonstrated how these primitive techniques might solve the problem of advertising in the post-network age (as time-shifting technologies and on-demand streaming services are making the traditional commercial break virtually obsolete). In other words, these commercials did not simply function as non-diegetic interruptions of the actual live broadcast; rather, they were also incorporated into the narrative as diegetic interruptions of the fictional live broadcast, which gave added weight to their placement within the plot. For example, following the song "Ladies Choice," during which white and Black teens were shown dancing on separate sides of a rope at a school dance, the performer playing the role of Corny Collins presented a live advertisement for Oreo cookies, which functioned as both a diegetic advertisement for a sponsor of the fictional program *The Corny Collins Show* and a non-diegetic advertisement for a sponsor of the actual program *Hairspray Live!* The advertisement was thus seamlessly incorporated into the narrative, as the performer remained in character throughout, and there were no cuts to signal the commercial break. By positioning the advertisement within the context of the character's attempts to resist the program's policy of racial segregation, which had just been vividly demonstrated in the previous number, his colorful description of dark chocolate wafers and white creamy filling also served as both a genuine advertisement for the product and a metaphor for racial integration. The musical's celebration of the socially transformative power of live television was thus extended to the live commercials, as they appeared to promote consumer capitalism as well as social equality; indeed, these two goals effectively became one and the same, as the unifying power of live television was equated with mass advertising.

Hairspray Live! was also promoted using various social media platforms, which allowed viewers to interact with the performers and each other. For example, NBC's digital team created a special Snapchat lens, Twitter hashtags, and Instagram stories, and they invited key social media influencers to generate content during the broadcast itself. Critics frequently note that social media platforms enable a kind of liveness that resembles live television. For example, Nick Couldry (2004: 356) describes "online liveness" as a sense of "social co-presence . . . made possible by the Internet," and Philip Auslander (2012: 6) similarly argues that social media platforms convey "a sense of always being connected to other people." Tim Highfield, Stephen Harrington, and Axel Bruns (2013: 317) also note that the practice of "enveloping"—that is, inviting audience members to interact with one another during a broadcast—helps to enhance television's socially integrating function, as social media platforms provide "a communal space where audience members can come together to discuss and debate, in real-time, their responses to what they are watching." Instead of seeing social media as a rival to television, critics like Jonathan Gray and Amanda Lotz (2012: 3) thus conclude that these platforms merely provide supplementary activities. These supplementary activities also have the potential to boost ratings, as the posts written by influencers during *Hairspray Live!* reportedly generated more than 3 million interactions on Twitter and Instagram and more than 5.5 million interactions on Facebook, which resulted in a 3.6 percent ratings bump for female viewers between the ages of eighteen and twenty-four and a 3.3 percent ratings bump for female viewers between the ages of twelve and seventeen. One social media influencer, Becca Pallack, even claimed that "the social media elements add another dimension to the show since we're all watching it together . . . [and] it connects all of us" (Hamedy 2016). NBC thus succeeded in attracting millennial viewers, in part, by convincing them that the kinds of communal experiences facilitated by social media platforms were a natural extension of live television.

Given the fact that social media strategies have become essential to the production of live musical spectaculars and that the most successful spectaculars often reflect their own conditions of mediality, it is no surprise that these platforms have also been incorporated into subsequent productions, such as *Jesus Christ Superstar Live in Concert* (2018). This performance, which was broadcast live on NBC on Easter Sunday, attracted 9.6 million viewers, which made it the most-viewed program in its time slot. The musical was originally written as a concept album that presents the story of Jesus as a parable about the modern media age and the rise of celebrity culture. Just as *Grease* focused on the youth culture of the 1950s and *Hairspray* focused on the youth culture of the 1960s, *Jesus Christ Superstar* also focused on the youth culture of the 1970s, as the original 1971 stage production and Norman Jewison's 1973 film adaptation portrayed Jesus and his followers as hippies whose values were directly opposed to those of the previous generation. Subsequent productions have updated the costumes to reflect the youth culture of their own time. The 2000 Broadway revival, for example, was set in the graffiti-strewn underpass of an urban bridge and featured costumes inspired by grunge fashion, thus drawing parallels between the tremendous popularity and sudden death of Jesus Christ and Kurt Cobain. The live performance in 2018 followed the same pattern by depicting Jesus and his followers as punks with spiked hair, torn jeans, and combat boots. As with *Grease: Live* and *Hairspray Live!*, the local studio audience was also incorporated into the production as Jesus's adoring fans, and they were actively encouraged to react loudly, as if they were attending a rock concert. When John Legend first appeared as Jesus and began shaking hands with various audience members, it was thus unclear whether their enthusiasm represented a performative simulation of Jesus's followers or a genuine response to the presence of a contemporary pop star, which was clearly the point.

This conflation of biblical and modern media culture was particularly apparent during the musical number "The Arrest," in which Jesus was surrounded by reporters asking questions. The use of reporters during this number was not new, as a similar technique had already been used in the *Jesus Christ Superstar* arena tour in 2012. In *Jesus Christ Superstar Live in Concert*, however, the TV cameras entered the stage, and several reporters spoke directly to the viewing audience, thus replicating the style of live TV news coverage. Several "citizen journalists" also filmed the arrest using smart phones, which was an obvious reference to the countless videos posted online featuring African Americans harassed by white police officers—an intertextual reference that was made even more explicit by the casting of an African American performer in the role of Jesus. The incorporation of TV cameras and smart phones thus not only served to conflate television and social media as complementary technologies due to their ability to facilitate shared communal experiences, which was directly associated with Jesus's message of social integration, but it also represented these technologies as socially transformative by suggesting that they could be used to expose and resist social inequality and injustice.

Fox's most recent live musical spectacular, *Rent: Live* (2019), similarly featured rock 'n' roll music, a multiethnic youth subculture, and the incorporation of media technologies. The musical, which was based on Giacomo Puccini's opera *La bohème* (1896), focuses on a group of impoverished young artists struggling to survive in Lower Manhattan's East Village during the HIV/AIDS epidemic in the early 1990s, and it specifically refers to the 1988 riot in Tompkins Square Park, which was the result of conflicts between urban gentrifiers and local residents. Artists were often involved in anti-gentrification activism at this time (Abu-Lughod 1994: 258), and the characters in the musical similarly express a sense of solidarity with the squatters and homeless people who are being displaced. Maureen, for example, is a performance artist who stages a live show to protest the eviction of the homeless, and Mark is an amateur filmmaker who records the ensuing riot and is subsequently offered a job at a tabloid television news show called *Buzzline*. Mark also records a series of episodes in the lives of his friends, and at the end of the musical, he screens a film that encapsulates their experiences over the past year—experiences that reflect the various scenes within the musical itself. John Istel (1996: 17) interprets

Rent as a "comment on how technology can alienate us," as Mark always "puts his camera between himself and those closest to him," yet his live coverage of the riot clearly serves to expose the plight of the homeless and his closing film effectively brings the characters together as an integrated community. Eleonora Sammartino (2017) also points out that the sense of community fostered by media technologies is closely related to the musical's recurring theme of living in the present, as "past, present, and future are sedimented in the same moment here and now thanks to Mark's film." While the closing footage does not represent a live broadcast in the traditional sense, the musical effectively becomes a live performance of Mark's footage, which is similarly designed to generate a sense of solidarity among viewers of different races and sexualities. *Rent* is another ideal property for a live musical spectacular, in other words, because it once again illustrates the ability of mass media technologies to facilitate shared communal experiences in real time.

The value of live musical spectaculars clearly lies in their ability to draw viewers back to the traditional broadcast schedule. They also incorporate this media strategy into their narratives by depicting how media events serve to facilitate shared communal experiences that have the potential to unify an otherwise heterogeneous audience, and they achieve this goal in two different ways. On the one hand, they sometimes depict the network age as a time when society was more unified and integrated—an idea that is frequently associated with the emergence of teen culture, which is shown to be a direct result of the communal viewing experiences made possible by live television. On the other hand, they also extend this idea to the post-network age by depicting the communal experiences facilitated by social media platforms as a natural continuation of the broadcast era. Contemporary live musical spectaculars thus represent a complex case of remediation, as network television initially sought to establish its social relevance by remediating older media forms, like musical theater, and it is now seeking to maintain its continued relevance by remediating newer media forms, like social media.

Critics often note that TV producers use social media to extend their own power and influence. For example, Inge Ejbye Sørensen (2016: 386) argues that TV networks use social media to "build and amplify the sense of their own importance and centrality in the mediation of live events," and Karin van Es (2017: 115) similarly claims that the collaboration between TV networks and social media "functions as a mechanism of control, a way that media institutions exert their dominance over the production and distribution of media content." Within the narratives of live musical spectaculars, however, television and social media are more often conflated because they are both perceived as fostering a sense of social cohesion and collective identity. In other words, these technologies tend to be represented as catalysts for positive social and political change because of their mutual ability to facilitate shared communal experiences. The contemporary resurgence of live musical spectaculars can thus be understood as a strategy that serves to reinforce the social and economic power of TV networks by promoting the idea that live television was essential for democratic consensus-building during the broadcast era and that it could continue to perform the same function today as long as viewers are willing to watch at the appointed times.

References

Abu-Lughod, J. (1994), *From Urban Village to East Village: The Battle for New York's Lower East Side*, Oxford: Blackwell.
Auslander, P. (2012), "Digital Liveness: A Historico-Philosophical Perspective," *PAJ: A Journal of Performance and Art*, 34 (3): 3–11.
Barrios, R. (1995), *A Song in the Dark: The Birth of the Musical Film*, Oxford: Oxford University Press.
Baughman, J. L. (2007), *Same Time, Same Station: Creating American Television, 1948-1961*, Baltimore: Johns Hopkins University Press.
Bourdon, J. (2000), "Live Television Is Still Alive: On Television as an Unfulfilled Promise," *Media Culture & Society*, 22 (5): 531–56.
Couldry, N. (2004), "Liveness, 'Reality', and the Mediated Habitus from Television to the Mobile Phone," *The Communication Review*, 7 (4): 353–61.
Dayan, D., and E. Katz (1992), *Media Events: The Live Broadcasting of History*, Cambridge, MA: Harvard University Press.
Doherty, T. (2002), *Teenagers and Teenpics: The Juvenilization of America Movies in the 1950s*, Philadelphia: Temple University Press.
Feuer, J. (1993), *The Hollywood Musical*, Bloomington: Indiana University. Press. Gray, J., and A. D. Lotz (2012), *Television Studies*, Cambridge: Polity.
Hall, S., and P. Whannel (2018), *The Popular Arts*, Durham, NC: Duke University Press
Hamedy, S. (2016), "Here's How NBC Made 'Hairspray Live' Shine on the Second Screen," *Mashable*, 8 December. Available online: mashable.com/2016/12/08/hairspray-live-nbc-digital-efforts/ (accessed September 16, 2020).
Heller, D. (2011), *Hairspray*, Oxford: Wiley-Blackwell.
Highfield, T., S. Harrington, and A. Bruns (2013), "Twitter as a Technology for Audiencing and Fandom," *Information, Communication & Society*, 16 (3): 315–39.
Istel, J. (1996), "Did the Author's Hyper-Romantic Vision Get Lost in the Media Uproar?" *American Theatre*, 13 (6): 13–17.
Jackson, J. A. (1991), *Big Beat Heat: Alan Freed and the Early Years of Rock & Roll*, New York: Schirmer.
Jackson, J. A. (1997), *American Bandstand: Dick Clark and the Making of a Rock 'n' Roll Empire*, Oxford: Oxford University Press.
Kessler, K. (2020), *Broadway in the Box: Television's Lasting Love Affair with the Musical*, Oxford: Oxford University Press.

Lotz, A. D. (2014), *The Television Will Be Revolutionized*, New York: New York University Press.
Real, M. (1975), "Superbowl: Mythic Spectacle," *Journal of Communication*, 25 (1): 31–43.
Rooney, D. (2015), "Fox's *Grease: Live* to Incorporate Studio Audience," *Hollywood Reporter*, 17 December. Available online: www.hollywoodreporter.com/live-feed/foxs-grease-live-incorporate-studio-849706 (accessed September 16, 2020).
Roscoe, J. (2004), "Multi-Platform Event Television: Reconceptualizing Our Relationship with Television," *The Communication Review*, 7 (4): 363–9.
Rothenbuhler, E. W. (1988), "The Living Room Celebration of the Olympic Games," *Journal of Communication*, 38 (4): 61–81.
Sammartino, E. (2017), "Challenging 'La Vie Bohème': Community, Subculture, and Queer Temporality in *Rent*," *European Journal of American Studies*, 11 (3). Available online: journals.openedition.org/ejas/11720.
Sørensen, I. E. (2016), "The Revival of Live TV: Liveness in a Multiplatform Context," *Media, Culture & Society*, 38 (3): 381–99.
Stilwell, R. J. (2018), "The Television Musical," in R. Knapp, M. Morris, and S. Wolf (eds.), *Media and Performance in the Musical: An Oxford Handbook of the American Musical, Volume 2*, 55–78, Oxford: Oxford University Press.
van Es, K. (2017), *The Future of Live*, Cambridge: Polity.
Wade, R. J. (1944), "Television Backgrounds," *Theatre Arts*, 28 (12): 728–32.
Waters, J. (1990), *Crackpot: The Obsessions of John Waters*, London: Fourth Estate.

Filmography

American Bandstand (1952–1989), [TV program] ABC.
Annie (1999), [TV program] ABC, November 7.
The Big Beat (1957), [TV program] ABC.
The Buddy Deane Show (1957–1963), [TV program] WJZ-TV.
Chicago (2002), [Film] Dir. Rob Marshall, USA: Miramax.
Cinderella (1957), [TV program] CBS, March 31.
Cinderella (1997), [TV program] ABC, November 2.
The Ford Fiftieth Anniversary Show (1953), [TV program] NBC/CBS, June 15.
Friends (1994–2004), [TV program] NBC.
General Foods 25th Anniversary Show (1954), [TV program] NBC/CBS/ABC/DuMont, March 28.
Glee (2009–2015), [TV program] Fox.
Glee: The 3D Concert Movie (2011), [Film] Dir. Kevin Tancharoen, USA: 20th Century Fox.
Grease: Live (2016), [TV program] Fox, February 3.
Gypsy (1993), [Film] CBS, December 12.
Hairspray (2007), [Film] Dir. Adam Shankman, USA/UK: New Line.
Hairspray Live! (2016), [TV program] NBC, December 7.
High School Musical (2006), [TV program] Disney Channel, January 20.

High School Musical 2 (2007), [TV program] Disney Channel, August 17.
High School Musical 3: Senior Year (2008), [Film] Dir. Kenny Ortega, USA: Disney.
Jesus Christ Superstar (1973), [Film] Dir. Norman Jewison, USA: Universal.
Jesus Christ Superstar Live in Concert (2018), [TV program] NBC, April 1.
The Jonathan Winters Show (1956-7), [TV program] NBC.
Max Liebman Presents/Max Liebman Spectaculars (1954-6), [TV program] NBC.
Musical Comedy Time (1950-1), [TV program] NBC.
Peter Pan Live! (2014), [TV program] NBC, December 4.
Producers' Showcase (1954-7), [TV program] NBC.
Rent: Live (2019), [TV program] Fox, January 27.
Smash (2012-13), [TV program] NBC.
The Sound of Music Live! (2013), [TV program] NBC, December 5.
The Wiz Live! (2015), [TV program] NBC, December 3.

17

Camp and the Celebration of the Popular Song in *RuPaul's Drag Race* "Lip Sync for Your Life"

Julie Lobalzo Wright

This chapter argues that there are implicit connections to the musical in *Ru Paul's Drag Race* (LOGO, 2009–16; VH1, 2017–present) (*RPDR*) and *Ru Paul's Drag Race All-Stars* (*All Stars*) (LOGO 2012–16, VH1, 2018–present) "Lip Sync for Your Life" (LSFYL) segments. The links between the musical genre and LSFYL were crystalized when Hollywood musicals icon, Debbie Reynolds, was a guest judge in season 2, episode 8 of *RPDR*, commenting after a lip sync performance that Raven (*RPDR* contestant) was good at lip syncing, a necessary skill for performers in classical Hollywood cinema. Reynolds included the caveat that while many fans assumed the performers sang live on-set, they actually sang to their own prerecorded records. In the case of Reynolds, this comment is complicated by the fact that one of her most famous roles was in *Singin' in the Rain* (1952), a film that exploited technology in order to integrate sound and image (Cohan 2000: 59) through various means, including the dubbing of Reynolds's singing performances by Betty Noyes and costar Jean Hagen.[1]

Lip synching is experiencing a televisual boom at the moment through the various *Drag Race* and worldwide *Lip Sync Battle* (Spike/Paramount Network, 2015–present) permutations, while concurrently, numerous contemporary musicals have adopted on-set, live singing (*Les Misérables* [2012] is a recent example) in order to retain the performer's "authenticity." Reynolds's statements on *Drag Race* highlight that lip synching has been a central aspect of media-based musical performances since the industrial adoption of sound technology. Parallel to film, lip synching is frequently a vital component of musical performances on TV variety programs, music chart shows, and music videos. This chapter argues part of their appeal lies in their connection to the classical Hollywood musical.

Musical moments are prominent on *RPDR* amid the *LSFYL* segments in addition to the maxi-challenge Rusicals (such as season 10's "Cher: The Unauthorized Rusical" based on the icon's life and career) and the multitude of musical icons impersonated on the *Snatch Game* (Liza Minelli, Carol Channing, Bernadette Peters, etc.).[2] In tandem with runway moments and the continuing "maxi-challenge" *Snatch Game*, LSFYL is one of the most exportable parts of *Drag Race* owing to sharing performances on social media and, therefore, known by audiences beyond simply *Drag Race* fans.

Drag is an exploration of sexuality and gender through performance styles that can be comedic, dramatic, slapstick, and political, among many other types. Drag performances may include live singing, but *RPDR* is generally known for the lip sync of songs in the elimination round where two contestants are pitted against each other. There is a long history of lip synced drag performances, reviewed at length in Fitzgerald and Marquez (2020), arising in the 1950s and varying in content throughout the decades from spoken word comedic pantomimes to cabaret performances and celebrity impersonations. *RPDR* is mainly aligned with lip syncs that combine fidelity to the song and the type of artifice expected in drag performances. The LSFYL holds an important position in the reality show, determining which Queens move on in the competition and, ultimately, assists in determining who wins the title of "America's Next Drag Superstar" in the finale. The LSFYL merges drag performance, musicals, and reality television, combining these areas in a program that is presented as a more "'earnest' reality" program because of its talent contest framework (Brennan and Gudelunas, 2017: 2), alongside series like *Project Runway* (Bravo, 2004–8, 2019–present; Lifetime, 2009–17) and *Top Chef* (Bravo, 2006–present). *RPDR* can also be considered, as argued by Kevin J. Donnelly and Beth Carroll, as part of a "larger peripheral market of music focused on audio-visual entertainment and audience engagement" (2018: 2), such as *The X Factor* (ITV, 2004–present)/*The X Factor* (US) (Fox, 2011–13) and *Strictly Come Dancing* (BBC, 2004–present)/*Dancing with the Stars* (ABC, 2005–present) that, while not traditional musicals, are part of the twenty-first-century musical landscape. This chapter aims to illustrate that the fusion of these vivacious genre and performance types has configured a complex form of entertainment indebted to classical Hollywood musicals through their camp value, celebration of the popular song, and the dual-focus and dual-register structure.

Dual Focus, Dual Register, and Narrative

There are numerous narrative strands that take place within *RuPaul's Drag Race*, comprising contestant story arcs, the knock-out formula of the competition, and familiar *Drag Race* formulations. These competing storylines can influence the final lip sync in various ways, including contestants appearing to concede defeat on the runway (e.g., in season 9 when Charlie Hides barely mustered a lip sync performance; or, also in season 9, when Valentina was told to remove her face mask) or employing their disappointment of being in the bottom two to deliver a spectacular performance (as Chi Chi DeVayne did twice in season 8). In a similar fashion to classical Hollywood musicals, the relationship of the LSFYL to narrative indicates that these moments progress the larger narrative (who will win the competition) while also impeding any narrative progress (everything stops for two contestants to lip sync). According to Cohan, "since the musicals were for the most part still understood as narratives, numbers served contradictory purposes: even when they moved the story, they stopped it momentarily as spectacle" (2005: 64). The LSFYL serves a similar function, but its existence within reality television indicates that various formal strategies are utilized, such as editing, to follow the "rhythm of emotional climaxes familiar from soap operas" (Kavka 2012: 79). Fundamentally, the lip sync is the emotional climax of each *Drag Race* episode, but the multiple narratives can compete leading to different registers that audiences follow due to, for example, their allegiance to a specific Queen or how swayed they are by the producer's vision, exhibited through editing. Therefore, it is through the LSFYL that the multiplicity of readings takes place, further connecting these moments to the classical Hollywood musical, as will be argued later in the chapter.

The duality of musicals has been discussed by Steven Cohan and Rick Altman. Cohan argues the musical engages in shifts in register that break away from codes of realism, often through the movement between dreams and reality within the diegesis (Cohan 2010: 3), whereas Altman claims the dual focus of musicals arise from the union of the couple. There are explicit and inherent ways LSFYL moments draw on the musical genre's duality, frequently through parallel narratives and shifts in register. Of importance to the LSFYL context is Rick Altman's contention that the "dual-focus structure requires the viewer to be sensitive [. . .] to simultaneity and comparison" (1987: 19). This structure is applicable to the lip sync because the text compels the audience to compare and contrast the performances by cutting between shots of the two contestants and the other members of the studio—the judges and "safe" contestants. As noted, the competing narratives have a bearing on the reception of the performance, both for the studio and for the home audience, but the fact that the dual-focus structure "derives from *character*" (Altman 1987: 21) assists in highlighting the personal aspects of the performance, from their performance style to their overall standing in the knock-out competition.

The cast of season 5 included Alyssa Edwards and Coco Montrese, professional rivals since 2010 when Edwards was stripped of her title as "Miss Gay America" and replaced by First alternate, Montrese. Episode 1 of season 5 teased this rivalry by having Montrese enter the workroom last, followed by slow-motion shots of Edwards and Montrese's shocked faces, interspersed with their observations about their conflict. There were arguments throughout the season between the two in addition to comments relating to the other's success or failures in the competition. Their storylines were not always presented in parallel to each other; however, a comparison was frequently made with one another and coming to a head in episode 9 when Edwards and Montrese were forced to lip sync for their life. This particular LSFYL transformed these dual paradigms through Edwards's comment that this performance would be the "tie-breaker" in relation to "all the drama" from the pageant experience. The theme of the song (Paula Abdul's "Cold Hearted Snake") and their deliberate gestures to one another throughout the performance bonded this performance to their shared past, but also the fact that the show presented the contestant's storylines as parallel to one another from the very beginning.

Camp

There is also a double function inherent in camp due to its style and the employment of camp as a "strategy of passing" (Cohan 2005: 9). As defined by Cohan, camp is "the ensemble of strategies used to enact a queer recognition of incongruities arising from the cultural regulation of gender and sexuality" (Cohan 2005: 1). Camp "allowed for the ironic, self-reflexive style of gay men passing as straight, who kept a 'straight face' so as not to let outsiders in on the joke, while simultaneously winking at the initiated in shared acknowledgement of it" (Cohan 2005: 1). According to Esther Newton, camp helps create a "double stance" toward performance through the desire to put on a good show, while also indicating distance by exposing the show (qtd. in Cohan 2005: 11). It is notable that Newton specifies that camp and drag are prone to this duality, while Cohan extends these ideas to argue for camp's presence in MGM's musical films through the genre's "incongruous binary logic" that underpins the oscillation between narrative and musical number (2005: 21). Altman (1987) states that this dual focus is related to the genre's overwhelmingly heteronormative narratives, even as, in later work, he acknowledges the musical's "homosocial" project through the genre's eradicating of homosocial bonds (2010).

What is pertinent to this discussion of *Drag Race* is the excess of the musical number through an intense and emotional "performance style that theatricalizes transparency and then naturalizes the theatricality" (Cohan 2005: 2). As Jack Babuscio articulates, camp concerns itself with the "*intensities* of character, as opposed to content" through a performance style that exhibits a "heightened sensitivity to aspects of a performance which others are likely to regard as routine or uncalculated" (2004: 126). Emotion underpins these performances because they frequently exhibit extreme feelings and that "little something extra" (Altman 1987: 266). Richard Dyer argues that musicals express utopianism through emotion and "what utopia would feel like rather than how it would be organized" (1992: 18), feeling like energy, intensity, and community. Therefore, camp musical performances are emotionally heightened through their transparently theatrical style that conceals and reveals that the audience is, ultimately, watching a show.

The LSFYL from season 4, episode 3 between The Princess and DiDa Ritz is a useful example to consider these ideas. After receiving negative comments from the judges for their "maxi-challenge" infomercial performances, The Princess and DiDa Ritz are told they are up for elimination with this moment enhanced through RuPaul's threatening reminder to not "fuck it up." The two contestants begin to lip sync to guest judge Natalie Cole's "This Will Be (An Everlasting Love)." While The Princess begins the lip sync with subtle gestures, DiDa is more animated, gesturing to Cole sitting at the judge's table and expressing the joy, excitement, and romance that underlies the love song. DiDa's intensity and "confidence" (Vesey 2017: 597) is communicated through her continued focus on Cole, overextended mouthing of words, and exuberant body by snapping her fingers, shuffling her feet, and bobbing her head. The camerawork and editing confirm this perception by affording The Princess hardly any attention from the third verse onward with the camera almost solely focused on DiDa. Furthermore, the episode cuts to a voice-over from DiDa explaining that she does not want Natalie Cole "to leave saying that Drag Queen did a terrible job of my song." Coming soon after this comment is a close-up of RuPaul delighting in the performance and Cole shouting her approval, especially during the vocal breakdown when DiDa flails her arms and shuffles her body to the beat of the song. As the song comes to a close, there are more cuts to the judges table with various judges singing along and all waving their approval, ending with a voice-over from fellow contestant, Latrice Royal, exclaiming, "That is what a lip sync for your life is, baby. That is high drag at its finest." This one performance demonstrates how LSFYL moments are deliberately theatrical and emotionally uncalculated, with the editing assisting in building to the climactic moment when DiDa Ritz is saved and The Princess leaves the competition. It is evident that DiDa gave that "little something extra" through a performance that flaunted how joyful love feels.

It is important that this type of camp performance is indebted to the classical musical, specifically Judy Garland's performance of "The Man That Got Away" in *A Star Is Born* (1954). This musical performance has been analyzed by numerous scholars including Altman (1987) and Dyer (1991). Cohan also applies a camp reading of "The Man That Got Away" in *Incongruous Entertainment* with the performance acting as one of his foundational examples of camp in classical Hollywood musicals. According to Cohan, what is camp about Garland's performance is not the "authenticity of her singing or its emotional content, but its theatricality," confirmed post-performance when Norman Maine (James Mason) gushes about her "display of stylish, professional expertise" (2005: 29). The LSFYL is only able to authenticate the display of emotion, and this must be theatrical because it is measured by the audience in the studio and at home. Subtlety can be mistaken for a bland performance, something that is not conducive to the LSFYL position in the episode's climatic moments.

The DiDa Ritz versus The Princess example also relies on the existence of an audience, consisting of the judges and other contestants who watch the lip sync from the back of the stage. Their reactions are often seen and heard in explicit ways through cutaway shots, voice-overs, or subtitles for muffled comments. Later seasons of *Drag Race* have held the finals in front of a live audience, encouraging a greater amount of crowd participation evident in season 7's penultimate lip sync where audience members loudly cheered and stood on their feet when (eventual winner) Sasha Velour lifted her wig and flower peddles fell onto the stage. While there is not a voting element to this competition as compared to other reality shows like *American Idol* (Fox, 2002-2016; ABC 2018–present), *Drag Race*, in a similar fashion to classic musicals, encourage spectators to "identify with a spontaneous audience which has actually participated in the performance" (Feuer 1993: 34). While there are clear spaces that separate the studio audience with the judges sitting at a long table directly in front of the stage and the "safe" contestants standing at the back, the implication is that these spectators are taking part in the performance.

"This Will Be (An Everlasting Love)" can be compared to "By Strauss" in *An American in Paris* (1951), Jane Feuer's example of a musical "narrative audience" (Feuer 1993: 31–4). While "By Strauss" begins with only three participants (Gene Kelly, Oscar Levant, and George Guétary), as the song progresses, the camera changes its focus through editing and movement, revealing a larger audience inside and out of the cafe. LSFYL varies from this in that the viewing audience is aware of the presence of the judges and contestants from the beginning. However, a similar process takes place through the participation in and the celebration of the performance. DiDa Ritz's performance featured shouts from the judges and cheering from the contestants, in addition to cutaways and voice-overs added in postproduction. Quite simply, the performance would have been less spectacular without the studio audience's contribution. What is celebrated in both examples is the performance and the song, bridging the gap between performer and audience.

Celebration of the Popular Song

Kelly Kessler writes that the musical is a genre where "self-expression supersedes everyday means of communication" (2010: 7). Accordingly, the LSFYL with its connections to the musical genre becomes the final place where contestants are able to communicate with both the audience in the studio and the one at home. As the abovementioned example illustrates, dual registers and a camp performance style figure in LSFYL moments, but, in a similar fashion to the classical Hollywood musical, they also celebrate the popular song. Feuer indicates that the MGM studio institutionalized the "power of music," utilizing the song as a "more expressive realm" than nonmusical language (Feuer 1993: 52). The type of music celebrated is popular music, the low arts, as opposed to high cultural arts like classical music. It is through this celebration that popular music is elevated with a similar process taking place on *Drag Race* by frequently promoting the music of female artists, validating female performances and the emotion conveyed. The LSFYL is analogous, expressing, borrowing from Dyer, the "feelings" utopianism embodies (1992: 18). Again, as Cohan argues, what moves audiences watching these performances is the intensity of the performance, but this occurs as much through the bodily performance as it does through the bond between performer and popular song.

There is a separation between the voice and body that is unique to individuals that lip sync to other people's songs. The relationship between pop music and *RuPaul's Drag Race* is complex due to its reflection of RuPaul's career as a pop cultural icon that includes a strong musical legacy. Alyxandra Vesey raises the issue that while contestants on the program are often filtered by their ability to lip sync, when they leave the competition they are expected to create original music even though there are limitations for pop stardom, especially due to race (2017: 589–604). The lip syncs are frequently sound tracked by music from pop divas, such as Madonna, Judy Garland, and Ariana Grande, producing a commonality between drag performers and these female icons by expressing the "significant degree of labour" involved in femininity (also echoed in RuPaul's famous catchphrase, "you better work") (Brown 2019: 66).

Merrie Snell writes in her study of lip synching that the "voice is set free" (2020: 3) from the body when individuals lip sync, an essential context for the layered voices and bodies represented in *Drag Race*. Frequently, LSFYL performances draw on the performers' "own embodiment" of the song, deriving from, habitually, their place within the competition, performance style, and subject and/or mood of the song. Therefore, DiDa Ritz's lip sync embellished the contestant's desire to stay in the competition and preserve their reputation through a virtuoso performance (Vesey 2017: 598). At the same time, DiDa's body conveyed a buoyancy that was absent from their "maxi challenge" as a spokesperson for RuPaul's Greatest Hits album, suggesting that the LSFYL became a space for DiDa to embody determination, resiliency, and ecstasy (confirmed when RuPaul told DiDa she was safe and "that's the Queen I want to see from now on").

A similar process takes place in season 2, episode 4 of *Pose* (F/X, 2018–present), the TV series about ballroom culture in New York City in the late 1980s/early 1990s.[3] In the episode, Candy's (Angelica Ross) wish to have a lip sync category introduced at the ball is rejected by the ballroom council. Subsequently, Candy is murdered and the council decide to instate the category in her honor, naming it "Candy's Sweet Refrain." The episode mainly takes place at her funeral where Candy's spirit interacts with friends and family before her casket is taken away to the ballroom setting. Eventually emerging from the casket in a fringed red dress, Candy performs "Never Knew Love Like This Before" by Stephanie Mills to a rapturous crowd. While the character was presented as a living spirit throughout the episode, there is a tonal shift that takes place through the hoots and hollers from the ballroom crowd that are aurally equal to Mills's song. Candy effortlessly moves throughout the surrounding crowd, pausing for extended goodbyes with close friends. These goodbyes are extensions from the lip sync with Candy emphasizing that she "never knew love like this before" through her body as much as through the precision of her lip sync.

This performance illustrates Snell's contention that lip syncs allow individuals to find their "voice through others" (2020: 67). Snell includes many cinematic examples in her study, including Ferris Bueller lip synching to The Beatles' "Twist and Shout" in a downtown Chicago parade in *Ferris Bueller's Day Off* (1986) and, alone in her apartment, Bridget Jones's alcohol-induced performance of "All By Myself" by Celine Dion in *Bridget Jones' Diary* (2001). While an embodiment takes place in these examples, the multiplicity of registers through narrative and gender performance in *Pose* and *Drag Race* presents a complexity in drag lip synching that is unequalled in examples of same-sex vocal and bodily performances. In a similar manner to DiDa Ritz, Candy's performance exhibits the labor involved in femininity, the resilience Candy had to exhibit as a transgender woman in New York City (as a sex worker, she was murdered by a client), and the bittersweet goodbye she conveys to the ballroom audience. The lyrics for the song suggest melancholy and joy, but toward one individual whereas Candy's performance is publicly celebratory and melancholic adhering to Snell's argument that lip sync performances do not compete with the original song, rather they are able to enlarge, subvert, and celebrate the song (2020:

69). Furthermore, these performances function, like the classical musical number, as a way of communicating the "internal states and desires" of the character (Snell 2020: 70), relating to Feuer's claim that songs exist in a more expressive realm.

Widow Von Du versus Jan

I want to end with a more recent LSFYL that is competent more than spectacular, but still closely aligns with the arguments I have presented in this chapter. In season 12, episode 8 contestants were tasked with creating a beauty and wellness product and delivering an infomercial for the product. While Jan was criticized for her lack of modulations in her delivery, the review for Widow Von Du was that she was joyless and flat, leading Widow to breakdown in tears on the runway. After the final critique, RuPaul asked all the Queens to nominate someone to go home and they all agreed it should be Widow. Within this judging, Crystal Methyd commented that she has known Widow for years and that commercial did not represent her. Guest judge Chaka Khan implored Widow that this is a bad review, but she shows great promise, and this low period could be the "making of" her. Therefore, within the narrative of the episode, Widow is at her lowest point, needing to prove her worth to the judges.

Immediately before the music begins, the episode cuts to an interview with Widow where she states, "I am not going the fuck home," prepping the home audience for the ferocious performance to follow. Widow begins the lip sync to "This Is My Night" by Chaka Khan by spinning on the stage and immediately mouthing the words to the song. Widow's facial expression is strong and determined while Jan's lacks the same dramatic effect, especially while she attempts to reduce her unwieldy dress. As compared to Jan, Widow is more stationary on the stage, but she also uses her body to articulate some of the lyrics, like "time to wake up" and "gonna let this magic shine." Halfway through the performance, there is a voice-over from contestant Jackie Cox who states: "Widow is really selling her words and the emotion of the song. I think Chaka Khan's soul has now entered Widow and is coming alive on the stage." Widow embodies the performance by connecting to the "soul" of the song, exposing the song's original intention, but also illustrating Widow's own frustration with her place in the competition (Figure 17.1). There is a dual focus in this performance through the audience following the two different performances. Just after this comment, Jan cartwheels into the shot and proceeds to dance around Widow. A voice-over from Jan indicates that her strategy is to utilize all her dance moves, showing the judges her desire to stay in the competition. It can be argued that there is an additional focus with Widow's performance through her deep connection

FIGURE 17.1 *Widow Von Du LSFYL in season 12, episode 8.*

to the song, something Jan is unable to demonstrate. This LSFYL is also excessive, intense, and highly animated with Widow truly displaying that "little something extra."

The LSFYL between Honey Mahogany and Vivienne Pinay in episode 4 of season 5 is an excellent counterexample. While the structure of the performance is similar to Widow Von Du versus Jan with voice-overs from both contestants included, a comment from one of the "safe" contestants, and cutaways to the judge's table, the content is altered through bored looks from the judges and Alyssa Edwards' comment that both contestants lack energy while lip syncing to "Oops . . . I Did it Again" by Britney Spears. Vivienne states during the performance that she was trying to "look the judges right in the eye and give them a reason" to keep her in the competition. This comment is illuminating, suggesting that the problem with the performance is that neither contestant theatrically embodied the song. This LSFYL did not present a dual register or a compare and contrast dynamic, nor celebrate the song or present a camp performance. The two Queens were eventually sent home because neither showed RuPaul the "fire" it takes to stay in the competition.

Conclusion

While there are archetypal examples of LSFYL, there are no steadfast rules for what constitutes a good or bad performance. However, I would argue that there is an unspoken criterion that the lip sync includes a camp embodiment and celebration of the song. When Naomi Smalls "won" the lip sync battle with Monét X Change in season 4 of *All Stars*, she did so because her performance was extravagant through facial expressions and bodily gestures (especially her bending body) (Figure 17.2), while Monét attempted a subtle interpretation of the Judy Garland performance of "Come Rain or Come Shine" that registered as bland. Although Monét's performance may have been more authentic to the way an individual would actually sing the song (Figure 17.3), her expressions were reserved, illustrating none of the gusto normally associated with Garland, limiting the ability of the audience to enjoy the performance. In other words, the lip sync displayed no emotion, no show; nothing camp took place.

Habitually, when classical musicals are discussed, they are mourned as though they only exist in the past. This can be attributed to the limited canon of MGM musicals that are frequently, consciously and unconsciously, viewed as the prime example of musical genre or, as Griffin notes, the redefining of the musical as integrated (2018: 8). This chapter emerges from a desire to open the musical canon and consider how the musical thrives in contemporary popular culture. There are specific contexts with *RuPaul's Drag Race* that complicate its relationship with the musical, most notably the musical's reliance on heterosexual coupling. Furthermore, the lip sync performance is an awkward fit within the musical genre owing to its separation from the performer's voice and body. Nevertheless, lip syncing has been, as Debbie Reynolds stated, a part of Hollywood musicals since their beginning, and this type of performance endures to this day through

FIGURE 17.2 *Naomi Smalls LSFYL in* All Stars *season 4, episode 8.*

FIGURE 17.3 *Monét X Change LSFYL in* All Stars *season 4, episode 8.*

the social media platform, TikTok. There is something freeing about the lip sync because it does not rely on vocal talent. Instead, as the LSFYL illustrates, the skill lies in conveying emotion and feeling through a highly stylized performance, liberated from physical bodies, including gender and sexuality. It is no wonder that the lip sync has found a natural home in *RuPaul's Drag Race* universe.

Notes

1 See Cohan (2000) for a discussion of dubbing in *Singin' in the Rain* and its impact on the film's demystification of the musical genre through sound and image.
2 Episodes of *Ru Paul's Drag Race* generally adhere to the following pattern: recap the last episode; a quick mini challenge for the contestants in the work room; a maxi challenge that involves planning and will be recorded and/or performed for the judges; a themed runway with judge's comments; and, finally, the lip sync for your life between the two lowest contestants. The *Snatch Game* began in season 2 as a maxi challenge modeled on the US panel game show, *The Match Game* (NBC 1962-1969; CBS 1973–9). In the *Snatch Game*, contestants impersonate celebrities taking part in a *Match Game*-style game show.
3 *Drag Race* and *Pose* are both indebted to the ground-breaking Queer documentary, *Paris Is Burning* (Jennie Livingston 1990).

References

Altman, R. (1987), *The American Film Musical*, London: BFI.
Altman, R. (2010), "From Homosexual to Heterosexual: The Musical's Two Projects," in S. Cohan (ed.), *The Sound of Musicals*, 19-29, London: BFI.
Babuscio, J. (2004), "Camp and the Gay Sensibility," in H. Benshoff and S. Griffin (eds.), *Queer Cinema: The Film Reader*, 121-36, London and New York: Routledge.
Brennan, N. and D. Gudelunas (2017), "Introduction," in N. Brennan and D. Gudelunas (eds.), *RuPaul's Drag Race and the Shifting Visibility of Drag Culture*, 1-11, Basingstoke: Palgrave Macmillan.
Brown, A. (2019), "Being and Performance in *RuPaul's Drag Race*," *Critical Quarterly*, 60 (4): 62-73.
Cohan, S. (2000), "Case Study: Interpreting *Singin' in the Rain*," in C. Gledhill and L. Williams (eds.), *Reinventing Film Studies*, 53-75, London: Arnold.
Cohan, S. (2004) "Introduction," in S. Cohan (ed.), *Hollywood Musicals: The Film Reader*, 1-15, London and New York: Routledge.
Cohan, S. (2005), *Incongruous Entertainment: Camp, Cultural Value, and the MGM Musical*, Durham and London: Duke University Press.
Cohan, S. (2010), "Introduction: How Do You Solve a Problem Like The Film Musical?" in S. Cohan (ed.), *The Sound of Musicals*, 1-6, London: BFI.
Donnelly, K. J., and B. Carroll (2018), "Introduction: Reimagining the Contemporary Musical in the Twenty-First Century," in K. J. Donnelly and B. Carroll (eds.), *The Contemporary Music Film*, 1-9, Edinburgh: Edinburgh University Press).
Dyer, R (1991), "*A Star is Born* and the Construction of Authenticity," in C. Gledhill (ed.), *Stardom: Industry of Desire*, 134-40, London: Routledge.
Dyer, R. (1992), "Entertainment and Utopia," in *Only Entertainment*, 17-34, London and New York: Routledge.
Fitzgerald, T., and L. Marquez (2020), *Legendary Children: The First Decade of RuPaul's Drag Race and the Last Century of Queer Life*, New York: Penguin Books.
Feuer, J. (1993), *The Hollywood Musical*, Second edn, Bloomington and Indianapolis: Indiana University Press.
Griffin, S. (2018), *Free and Easy: A Defining History of the American Film Musical Genre*, Hoboken and Chichester: Wiley Blackwell.
Kavka, M. (2012), *Reality TV*, Edinburgh: Edinburgh University Press.
Kessler, K. (2010), *Destabilizing the Hollywood Musical: Music, Masculinity, and Meyhem*, Baskingstoke: Palgrave Macmillan.
Snell, M. (2020), *Lipsynching*, New York and London: Bloomsbury.
Vesey, A. (2017), "'A Way to Sell Your Records': Pop Stardom and the Politics of Drag Professionalization on *RuPaul's Drag Race*," *Television & New Media*, 18 (7): 589-604.

Filmography

American Idol (2002-16; 2018), [TV program] Fox and ABC.
An American in Paris (1951), [Film] Dir. Vincente Minnelli, USA: MGM.

Bridget Jones' Diary (2001), [Film] Dir. Sharon Maguire, UK: Miramax.
Dancing With the Stars (2005-present), [TV program] ABC.
Ferris Bueller's Day Off (1986), [Film] Dir. John Hughes, USA: Paramount.
Les Misérables (2012), [Film] Dir. Tom Hopper, USA/UK: Universal.
Lip Sync Battle (2015–present), [TV program] Spike/Paramount Network.
The Match Game (1962–9; 1973–9), [TV program] NBC and CBS.
Paris is Burning (1990), [Film] Dir. Jennie Livingston, USA: Off-White Productions.
Pose (2018-present), [TV program] F/X.
Project Runway (2004–2008, 2019–present; 2009–2017), [TV program] Bravo and Lifetime.
Ru Paul's Drag Race (2009–2016; 2017–present), [TV program] LOGO and VH1.
Ru Paul's Drag Race All-Stars (All Stars) (2012–2016; 2018-present), [TV program] LOGO and VH1.
Singin' in the Rain (1952), [Film] Dir. Stanley Donen and Gene Kelly, USA: MGM.
A Star is Born (1954), [Film] Dir. George Cukor, USA: Warner Brothers.
Strictly Come Dancing (2004-present), [TV program] BBC.
Top Chef (2006-present), [TV program] Bravo.
The X Factor (2004-present), [TV program] ITV.
The X Factor (US) (2011–2013), [TV program] Fox.

CONTRIBUTORS

Marie Cadalanu's PhD thesis, "The French Film Musical in the Thirties: The Birth of a Genre?," was awarded in 2016. Her main fields of research are French cinema, the film musical and music in film. She has published work on the short film musicals of Nicolas Engel, on the film musical screenwriter Marcel Achard, on François Ozon, and on the reception of songs in films. She coedited *Connaît-on la chanson ? La chanson dans les cinéma d'Europe et d'Amérique latine depuis 1960* (2018). Recently, she has coauthored a book on the French film musical with Phil Powrie.

Sarah Culhane is a CAROLINE Marie Skłodowska-Curie Fellow in Media Studies at Maynooth University. In collaboration with Age Action Ireland her current research project, "Irish Cinema Audiences: Engaging older audiences and sustaining Ireland's cultural heritage," investigates the significance of cinemagoing and film in the everyday lives of Irish people in the 1950s. She holds a PhD in Italian studies from the University of Bristol. Her PhD research was conducted as part of the Italian Cinema Audiences project (AHRC 2013–16) and is featured in *Italian Cinema Audiences: Histories, Memories of Cinema-going in Post-war Italy* (2020).

Anthony Enns is an associate professor in English and Media Studies at Dalhousie University. His work on popular culture has appeared in such journals as *Journal of Popular Film and Television*, *Quarterly Review of Film and Video*, *Popular Culture Review*, *Science Fiction Studies*, *Screen*, and *Studies in Popular Culture* as well as the anthologies *The Scary Screen* (2010), *Comics and the City* (2010), *Oxford Handbook of Science Fiction* (2014), and *Believing in Bits* (2019).

Richard Farmer is Research Associate on the ERC-funded STUDIOTEC project at the University of Bristol, UK, and has previously taught at UCL and the University of East Anglia. He has published extensively on British cinema and popular culture and is the author of three monographs, the most recent of which, the coauthored *Transformation and Tradition in 1960s British Cinema* (2019), includes his chapter on the relationship between film and pop music in the 1960s.

Tamsin Graves is a final year PhD candidate at the University of Exeter researching the cinema of Tony Gatlif, with an emphasis on sound, voice, and discourse and the transnational nature of his films. She has been teaching university courses on film and TV since 2010 and has presented conference papers on themes including film sound, border-crossing, and space and place in diasporic cinema.

Aakshi Magazine is a writer based in Delhi. She received a PhD in Film Studies from the University of St. Andrews in 2020. Her doctoral thesis, "The 1950s Hindi Film Song: Between Transgression and Memory," is on the relationship of the film song to the contradictions of the Indian nationalist discourse.

Paul Mazey has published articles on aspects of British film music in the *Journal of British Cinema & Television* and *Revenant* journal, and a monograph *British Film Music: Musical Traditions in British Cinema, 1930s-1950s* (2020). He has taught film and television at the University of Bristol, UK.

Jenny Oyallon-Koloski is an assistant professor of Media and Cinema Studies at the University of Illinois at Urbana–Champaign. She is a Certified Movement Analyst in Laban/Bartenieff Movement Studies and is codirector of the Movement Visualization Lab. Her research on the musical genre, movement on screen, and the films of Jacques Demy is published in *Studies in French Cinema* (2014), *Post Script* (2016), *[in]Transition: The Journal of Videographic Film and Moving Image Studies* (2018), and *Screenworks* (2019).

Landon Palmer is Assistant Professor in the Department of Journalism and Creative Media at the University of Alabama. He is the author of *Rock Star/Movie Star: Power and Performance in Cinematic Rock Stardom* (2020), and his research focuses broadly on the historical relationships between stardom and media industries as they intersect via film and music.

Phil Powrie is Professor of Cinema Studies at the University of Surrey. He has published a number of books on French cinema, the last two being *Music in Contemporary French Cinema: The Crystal-Song* (2017) and *The French Film Musical* (2020), coauthored with Marie Cadalanu.

Joana Rita Ramalho is Lecturer (Teaching) in Film Studies, Comparative Literature and Portuguese at University College London. Her main research interests include the gothic in its many iterations, gender politics, intermediality, radical humor, satire, and dystopian film musicals. She has published on topics as varied as portraits in 1940s romantic-gothic films, haptic motifs and sensory contagion in terror cinema, thing theory and creepy dolls, dark cabaret, and postmillennial film musicals.

Kate Saccone is currently pursuing a graduate degree in Preservation and Presentation of the Moving Image at the University of Amsterdam. She is also the manager/editor of Columbia University's digital humanities resource the Women Film Pioneers Project (WFPP). She has published and presented on a wide variety of topics, such as the American film musical, the Nicholas Brothers, digital humanities, feminist film historiography, and silent cinema. She earned a Master of Arts in Film and Media Studies from Columbia University, where her thesis project looked at race and the classical Hollywood musical.

Eleonora Sammartino is a visiting lecturer in Film Studies at the University of Greenwich, the University of Reading, and Imperial College London. She holds a PhD from King's College London with a thesis on the relationship between gender representation and contemporary American film musicals. Besides the film musical, her research focuses on feminist media studies and popular media, and star studies. Her work has been published in *European Journal of American Studies* and *Journal of Italian Cinema and Media Studies*. She is currently coediting with Alice Guilluy a special issue of *Celebrity Studies* on Hugh Grant's stardom (2022).

Estrella Sendra is a film and screen media scholar, filmmaker, journalist, and festival organizer, currently working as Senior Teaching Fellow in Film and Screen Studies at SOAS, University of London, and as Teaching Fellow in Global Media Industries, at Winchester School of Art, University of Southampton. Since 2011, when she directed *Témoignages de l'autre côté / Testimonials from the other side* (2011), an awarded documentary film about migration, she has been developing a regional expertise in Senegal. In 2018, she completed her PhD on festivals in Senegal from SOAS. Her publications include "Displacement and the Quest for Identity in Alain Gomis' Cinema" in *Black Camera: An International Film Journal* (2018). She is Associate Editor of *Screenworks* and editorial board member of the *Journal of African Media Studies*.

Martha Shearer is Assistant Professor and Ad Astra Fellow in Film Studies at University College Dublin. She is the author of *New York City and the Hollywood Musical: Dancing in the Streets* (2016). Her work on the musical has also been published in *Screen*, *The Soundtrack*, and *The Oxford Handbook of Musical Theatre Screen Adaptations* (2019).

Sarah Street is Professor of Film at the University of Bristol, UK. Her publications on color film include *Colour Films in Britain: The Negotiation* *of Innovation, 1900-55* (2012), winner of the British Association of Film, Television and Screen Studies prize for Best Monograph, and two coedited collections (with Simon Brown and Liz Watkins), *Color and the Moving Image: History, Theory, Aesthetics, Archive* (2012) and *British Colour Cinema: Practices and Theories* (2013). Her latest book, coauthored with Joshua Yumibe, is *Chromatic Modernity: Color, Cinema, and Media of the 1920s* (2019), winner of the Katharine Singer Kovács Book Award.

Richard Wallace is an assistant professor in the Department of Film and Television Studies at the University of Warwick. His research interests include British film and television history, screen documentary and comedy. His monograph *Mockumentary Comedy: Performing Authenticity* (2018) examines parodic and satirical representations of the rock star and the politician. He has published in the *Journal of British Cinema and Television*, *Quarterly Review of Film and Video* and *Oral History*, and is currently writing a book on the contemporary music documentary and co-writing one on the history of cinema projection in the UK.

Julie Lobalzo Wright is a teaching fellow in Film and Television Studies at the University of Warwick. She is the author of *Crossover Stardom: Male Popular Music Stars in American Cinema* (2018), coeditor with Lucy Bolton of *Lasting Screen Stars: Images that Fade and Personas that Endure* (2016), and has published research on stardom and musical/music films in various edited collections and in the journals, *Celebrity Studies* and *Film/Philosophy*.

INDEX

20,000 Days on Earth 204

abjection 100–5, 108
acappella 35
"Ae Ajnabi" 151, 152
aerobics 17
Aesop's Fables 101, 103, 107
African cinema 55–67
Aida 117–18
Alibert, Henri 75–81
Alleluia! The Devil's Carnival 6, 7, 99–109
All Night Long 177
Altman, Rick 2–4, 18–19, 25, 32, 34–5, 45, 47, 55–6, 63, 74–5, 88, 160, 184, 188, 193, 200–1, 205, 207, 232–5
American Bandstand 220, 222
American Idol 30, 235
An American in Paris 235
animation 8, 172–84
Annie (TV) 220
Annie Get Your Gun (TV) 219
Appiah, Kwame 60
Aristocats, The 173, 177–84
Armstrong, Louis 175, 179, 181, 184
art cinema 154
Astaire, Fred 20–1, 87–8, 129–30, 135–6, 138–9
audio dissolve 7, 45, 48, 88, 205
audio-spectacle 126
Au pays du soleil 76–7, 79–80
aural filmmaking 55–67
Auslander, Philip 199–200, 224

Baby Driver 2
backstage musical 74, 104, 194–5, 200, 203
ballet 22–5, 174, 204

ballet d'action 21
ballroom dancing 23, 25
Band Wagon, The 20, 21, 138
BDSM 104
"Beat It" (music video) 18
Beatles, The 46, 183, 189, 191–6, 237
Beatles Come to Town, The 189, 191–5
Bee Gees, The 189
Bee Gees, The 16, 20–1, 189
Berkeley, Busby 36, 78, 108
Berkeleyesque 36, 108
Berlant, Lauren 51
Bharatanatyam 21
Billboard chart 16, 17, 18, 31
Birth of Jazz 174
blackface 174
Bogart, Humphrey 159
Bohemian Rhapsody 1
Bollywood 59, 100, 144–54
Bombay 145, 147–9, 153, 154
Botting, Fred 100
Bouquin, Baptiste 62
Bousman, Darren Lynn 99–100, 103, 106–8
Brah, Avtar 89, 94
breakdancing 17–19, 22–5, 33
Breakin' 15–25
bricolage 48, 87, 135–8
Bridget Jones' Diary 237
Brief Encounter 159, 163–6
Burlesque 43

Cabin in the Sky 28
Calvert, Phyllis 160
camp 162, 222, 230–6, 239–40
canon, the 2–3, 5, 7, 56, 62, 67, 140, 141, 177, 240

Capri   116, 120
Carroll, Beth   2, 6, 30, 231
Car Wash   3
Casablanca   159, 163–4, 169
Catch Us If You Can   189
Cavell, Stanley   165
Charisse, Cyd   20–1
Charles, RuPaul   234, 236–9
Charlie Is My Darling   189
Chicago   220
choir film   6, 28–38
Chopin, Frédéric   160–1, 166
Chopra, Yash   144, 154
Cinderella (TV)   219
cinéma méridional   74
civil rights movement, the   32
classical Hollywood   2, 7, 15, 90, 125, 140, 200, 203, 230–2, 235, 236
code-switching   120–3, 126, 127
Coen brothers   6
Cohan, Steven   19, 28, 30, 44, 55, 100, 108, 230, 232–6, 241
colonialism   56, 62, 65
community   6, 8, 20, 28–38, 42, 45, 46, 50, 51, 63, 74–83, 88, 90, 92, 102, 105, 182, 211, 226
Connection, The   177
Connolly, N. D. B.   43–4
Conrich, Ian   2, 5, 99, 117
Conway, Kelley   74
Cook, Pam   159
Corrigan, Timothy   50, 52
cosmopolitanism   60, 62
Cotten, Joseph   164
Cover Girl   136
Creed, Barbara   100–2, 105
Creekmur, Corey   2, 50
Crothers, Scatman   178, 179

dance   6, 15–25, 33, 41–3, 64, 66–7, 76, 78, 87–95, 105, 119, 129–41, 148–53, 210, 238
danceploitation   15–25
Dangerous Moonlight   162, 166–7
Dargis, Manohla   41
"Dave Clark Five, The"   189, 192–3, 195
decolonization   7, 56, 59, 62, 67

Deleyto, Celestino   5, 9
Demy, Jacques   2, 5, 65
Depeche Mode   8, 200–12
Depeche Mode: 101   199–212
diaspora   58–61, 89, 92, 94–5
Dil Se..   144–54
Dilwale Dulhania Le Jaayenge   146
Diop, Mag Maguette   55, 58
Diop, Mati   58, 60
Dirty Dancing   3, 16, 18, 42
Disney   28, 29, 37, 172–84
Disney, Walt   173, 183
documentary   8, 58, 78–9, 86, 177, 188, 195, 199–212
Donnelly, K. J.   2, 6, 30, 200, 231
Dont Look Back   200
Down Argentine Way   131, 133–4
drag   47, 50, 230–41
dual focus   3, 46, 206–11, 231–3, 238
dual register   19, 232, 236, 239
Duchess of Idaho   139
Dumbo   174
Dyer, Richard   3, 32, 42, 47, 51, 89–90, 116–17, 119, 124, 126, 139, 196, 201, 206, 208, 211, 234–6

entertainment   8, 34, 43, 45, 63, 89–90, 138–9, 173, 183, 195, 201, 203, 211, 221, 231
erotic dance   23
"Ev'rybody Wants to Be a Cat"   178–81
exile   62–3, 88, 91, 95–6

fairytale musical   74
Fast & Furious series   6
Felix the Cat   174
female complaint, the   51
feminism   34–5, 37, 99–109
Ferris Bueller's Day Off   237
Feuer, Jane   2, 3, 8, 28, 31, 33, 41–2, 45–6, 48, 50–1, 62, 87–8, 90, 135, 138, 141, 149, 166, 194–5, 201, 203, 206, 209, 221, 235–6, 238
film noir   4
Flashdance   15–25
folk art   34, 48, 50, 135, 221
folk musical   5, 32, 33, 63, 74–5, 83

INDEX

Fontaine, Joan 164–6
Four Hits and a Mister 189
Fritz the Cat 174

Gangsters du château d'If, Les 76, 78, 81
Garcia, Desirée 5, 23, 33, 75
Garland, Judy 21, 62, 235, 236, 240
Gatlif, Tony 7, 86–97
Gaye, Dyana 55–67
Gaye, Naïma 61, 62–3
Generation 2000 58, 60
generic boundaries 6, 25, 41–54
genre anxiety 2
genre theory 4, 8
giallo 4
Gieure, René 80
Gimme Shelter 189, 203
"Gimme That Old Time Religion" 175
Glee 29–31, 34, 37, 100, 219–20
Goldberg, Whoopi 29
Gold Diggers of 1933 47
Golden Globes 1
Gomis, Alain 58, 60
Gonks Go Beat 187
gospel 31–3, 175
Gotham, Kevin Fox 42–3
gothic musical 7, 99–109
Grease/Grease: Live 220–2, 224
Great American Broadcast, The 131, 135, 136
Great Escape, The 189
Great Migration, the 31–2
Griffin, Sean 2, 16, 18, 23, 24, 28, 30, 134, 240
griot 59, 63, 65
Guétary, Georges 74, 79, 81, 83, 235
Gulzar 144–5, 147, 151, 154
Guns at Batasi 189
gymnastics 17, 23
Gypsy (TV) 220

Hairspray/Hairspray Live! 220, 222–5
Hall, Stuart 220–1
"Hamma Hamma" 147, 149, 150, 153

Hard Day's Night, A 46, 189, 191–3, 195
Harris, Phil 178–9, 181, 182–3
Hello, Dolly! 184
Help! 189
Herzog, Amy 5, 19
heteroglossia 86–97
high concept 4
High School Musical films 28, 30, 219
hip hop 17, 23, 140
Homecoming 203
Honey 43
horror 99–101, 168
Houseboat 7, 115–27
Housemaid, The 160, 167–70
Hum Aapke Hain Koun! 146
Hunter, Holly 159

Il est charmant 78
I'll Do Anything 28
impossibility 5, 45, 48
Indignados 87, 93
integrated musical 2, 20, 28, 129, 140, 200
internal audiences 33, 45–6, 49, 90, 149
Isle of Pingo Pongo, The 174
It Started in Napes 7, 115–27
iTunes 31

Jackson, Janet 33
Jackson, Michael 17
James, David 4, 46, 199
jazz 8, 90–1, 172–84, 189
jazz dance 17, 22–5
Jazz on a Summer's Day 177
Jean, Gloria 131
Jesus Christ Superstar Live in Concert 224–5
Johnny Leyton Touch, The 189
Johnson, Celia 159
Jungle Book, The 173, 178–9, 181–4
Jungle Jazz 174

Kelly, Gene 87, 129–30, 135–6, 138–41, 235
Kessler, Kelly 2, 17, 183, 219, 236

Kim, Kyung Hyun   167
Klein, Amanda Ann   3, 5, 16, 38, 43, 49
Kohlke, Marie-Luise   100, 103–4, 107
Kramer, Lawrence   163, 166, 167
Krazy Kat: A Jazz Pantomine   174
Kristeva, Julia   100, 101

Lady Be Good   138
Laing, Heather   88, 93–5, 162, 167
Latcho Drom   86–7, 93
Lawrence, Amy   126
Led Zeppelin: The Song Remains the Same   204
Les Misérables   4, 230
Let it Be   195
Letter from an Unknown Woman   166
Lion King, The   28
Lip Sync Battle   230
lip synching   8, 148, 230–41
Live It Up   188
Lockwood, Margaret   161, 165
Lollobrigida, Gina   116, 117
Loren, Sophia   7, 115–27
"Love Is a Battlefield" (music video)   18
Love Story   163, 165

McCarthy, Todd   17
McDaniel, Hattie   131
Madonna   236
Madonna of the Seven Moons   160–2, 169
Magic Mike   7, 41–52
Magic Mike XXL   7, 41–52
Make Mine Music   175
male gaze   100, 105, 108, 125
"Mamãe Eu Quero"   129–41
Man Called Adam, A   177
Manfred Mann   190
Mangano, Silvana   117
"Maniac" (music video)   17, 22
"Man That Got Away, The"   235
marginal generic text   6
marginal musical   4, 6, 7, 50, 106–7, 177
Mariano, Luis   74, 79–81, 83
Marseille   7, 73–84

Marshall, Bill   5, 6
masculinity   24, 50, 52, 136, 162
mash-ups   33, 34
Mason, James   162, 235
Meet Me in St Louis   21
melodrama   4, 159–70
MGM   135, 236, 240
Miami   41–9
Midler, Bette   29
minstrels   23, 174
Miranda, Carmen   133, 134
Moine, Raphaelle   2, 56
monstrous feminine   100
Monterery Pop   200, 207
Monteyne, Kimberly   17, 23, 25
Motown   31–2
MTV   17, 18, 23, 30
Mueller, John   20
Mukherjee, Hrishikesh   144
Murphy, Ryan   30, 220

Naficy, Hamid   86, 91–3, 95–7
Naples   115–17, 120, 127, 164
Naremore, James   4
Neale, Steve   25
Neapolitan Carousel   116
Negra, Diane   36, 44
neighborhood musical   42, 75
neoliberalism   6, 28–38, 42–3, 47, 51
New Music Seminar   17–18
Newsies   18, 29
newsreel   190–6
Nicholas, Fayard   130–1, 133–6, 138, 139, 141
Nicholas, Harold   7, 129–41
Night Has Eyes, The   162, 167
nostalgia   7, 8, 73, 75, 81, 83, 91–2, 96, 217–18, 220, 221
Nutcracker, The   161

One + One/Sympathy for the Devil   189, 195
opera/operetta   73–84, 117–18
orality   55–67
Orchestra Wives   131

Pagnol, Marcel   74, 76
Panama Hattie   138
Pane, amore, e… series   116–17

Paris Blues 177
Pathe 188–95
Pennebaker, D. A. 200, 206–8, 210
Performance 187
performance space 6, 42–3, 52, 91, 97, 135, 201, 210
Peter Pan (TV)/*Peter Pan Live!* 218, 220
Piano, The 159
piano playing 8, 159–70
Piano Teacher, The 160
Pie, Pie Blackbird 130
Pink Panther, The series 174
Pirate, The 138
Pitch Perfect triology 29, 30, 34–8
Place of One's Own, A 161, 162
Place to Go, A 187
podcasts 2
Ponti, Carlo 118, 120
pop music 8, 19, 31, 34, 66, 187–96, 199, 236
popular feminism 34–7
Popular Front 79
pornography 4
Pose 237
postfeminism 35–6
Pretty Things, The 189
Prima, Louis 117, 181
Privilege 187
Project Runway 231
Pullen, Kirsten 115
punk rock 99, 100, 101

race 5, 24, 42, 87, 89, 129–41, 236
Rachmaninov, Sergei 159, 164–6
Rahman, A. R. 145, 146–7, 149, 152
Raimu 73, 76
Ratnam, Mani 8, 144–54
Ray, Satyajit 146
Ready, Steady, Go 192
Reagan, Ronald 32
real estate 7, 41–52
reality television 30, 34, 37, 231–2, 235
Reckless Age 130–7, 140
regionality 7, 8, 73–6, 83, 115–16, 119, 122, 144–6
Rent: Live 225–7
Repo! The Genetic Opera 99

Reynolds, Debbie 230, 240
Rhythm 'n Greens 189
Richard, Cliff 187, 196
Rio Bravo 5
road movie, the 50–1, 52
Robin Hood 179
Robinson, Bill 131, 141
rockumentary 4, 201–2, 206
Rocky Horror Picture Show, The 99
Roja 145, 147–9, 154
"Rolling Stones Gather Moss" 189, 191, 193, 195
romantic comedy 1, 5
Roma people 86, 88, 89, 96
Rossi, Tino 74, 79–80, 83
Roy, Bimal 144, 154
Royal Wedding 20
Rubin, Martin 18, 25, 45, 104
"Rukkumani Rukkumani" 147–9
RuPaul's Drag Race/All Stars 8, 230–41

Saint-Louis Blues/Un transport en commun 7, 55–67
Saturday Night Fever 15–25
Saw films 99
"Scales and Arpeggios" 178–9
scopophilia 108
Sellars, Peter 118
Sembène, Ousmane 59
Senegalese cinema 7, 55–67
September Affair 163–7, 169
"September Song" 164–6
Seventh Veil, The 165
sexsation 100, 104–5, 108
Shapiro, Helen 191
Shohat, Ella 7, 87, 90, 92, 93, 178
show musical 24, 29, 37, 47
Shumway, David 91–2, 97
Singin' in the Rain 61, 230
Sister Act/Sister Act 2 28–40
Six-Five Special 192
Small, Pauline 116, 118, 122
Smash 219, 220
Sobchack, Vivian 50
social media 30, 218, 223–6, 231, 241
soul music 32
Sound of Music Live!, The 220

soundtrack album   16, 30, 37, 220
spirituals   31
Staiger, Janet   3
Stallone, Sylvester   16
Stam, Robert   7, 87, 90, 92, 93, 178
"Satrangi Re"   151–3
Star is Born, A (1954)   235
Star is Born, A (2018)   1, 2
Staying Alive   16
Steele, Tommy   188, 196
Step Up Revolution   43
Stilwell, Robyn   5–6, 94, 219
Stop Making Sense   207
Stormy Weather   131
Strasbourg   88, 93, 96
Strickly Come Dancing/Dancing with the Stars   30, 231
stripping   46–7
subculture   75, 225
subprime mortgage crisis   44, 48
Summer Holiday   187
sung-through musical   4, 65
supradiegetic space   19–20, 22
Swing   7, 86–97
synergy   15–25, 29, 30

Tamil cinema   145, 146
Tangos   91
Tarantino, Quentin   6
Tasker, Yvonne   44, 159–60
Taubin, Amy   41
Tchaikovsky, Pyotr Ilyich   161
television   2, 6, 8, 18, 29, 30, 192–3, 199–200, 217–27, 231, 232
Telotte, J. P.   42
Thackway, Melissa   58–61
Thank Your Lucky Stars   192
This is Spinal Tap   3, 211
"Thriller" (music video)   17–18
Tincknell, Estella   2, 5, 117
Tin Pan Alley Cats   175
Titin des Martigues   77–8, 81
Todd, Ann   165
Too Late Blues   177
Toot, Whistle, Plunk and Boom   178–9
Top Chef   231
Top Gun   31

Top of the Pops   192
Travolta, John   16
trente glorieuses   75
Trois de la Canebière   79–83
Tsai Ming-liang   2
Tudor, Andrew   4–5

Umbrellas of Cherbourg. The   4
Un de la Canebière   75–83
Upturned Glass, The   162
utopianism   8, 28–37, 51, 76, 81, 83, 90, 91, 199, 204, 206, 208, 210–11, 222, 234

Variety   1, 2, 16–18, 20
Vengo   87
visual album   2, 9
voice   59, 67, 87, 92, 93, 118, 120–1, 124, 126, 130, 140, 149, 152, 162, 179, 181, 201, 204, 206, 234–40

Walbrook, Anton   162
Waller, Fats   175
Warner, Kristen   51
web series   2, 9
Wells, Paul   174, 177
Western, the   4, 5, 7
West Side Story   61, 177
While I Live   163
White, Armond   41
Wife for Souleymane, A   60
Williams, Alan   4
Williams, Esther   5
Wilson, Dooley   159
Wiz Live!, The   220
Woodstock   3, 203, 209–10

X Factor, The   231

Yellow Submarine   183
Young Girls of Rochefort, The   65
Young Ones, The   187
You're My Everything   138
Zdunich, Terrance   99, 101, 106, 107, 108
Ziggy Stardust and the Spiders from Mars   200
Zoot Cat, The   174